WALTER BENJAMIN AND ANTONIO GRAMSCI

This book marks a missed encounter between two of the most influential Marxist thinkers of our age, Walter Benjamin and Antonio Gramsci, studied here for the first time side by side.

Benjamin and Gramsci were contemporaries, whose births and deaths took place within a few years of each other in Western Europe in the first half of the twentieth century. Two Marxists sui generis, they radically changed Marxism's themes and vocabulary, profoundly influencing the most significant analyses and debates. At a time in which Marxism was considered to be outdated and in crisis, both Gramsci's and Benjamin's thoughts provided resources for its renewal: particularly in postcolonial studies for Gramsci and in new media studies for Benjamin. Both were victims of fascism, on the threshold of the catastrophe of the Second World War. These two philosophers' posthumous fortune depended on the transmission of their thought, which was first entrusted to friends and comrades, and then to entire generations of scholars from a wide range of disciplines.

Editors, Dario Gentili, Elettra Stimilli, and Gabriele Guerra explore with leading voices on Benjamin and Gramsci the most relevant and topical issues today. The book gives an indispensable new perspective in Marxism for students and researchers alike.

Dario Gentili is Professor of Moral Philosophy at the Department of Philosophy, Communication and Performing Arts at Roma Tre University. He is co-director of the Master "Environmental Humanities – Studi dell'Ambiente e del Territorio". He co-directs the editorial series "MaterialiIT", published by the Italian publishing house Quodlibet. He is co-founder of the Italian Walter Benjamin Association and a member of its Board of Directors. Among his publications: *Il tempo della storia. Le tesi "Sul concetto di storia" di Walter Benjamin* (2002; 2019); *Topografie politiche. Spazio urbano, cittadinanza, confini in Walter Benjamin e Jacques Derrida* (2009); *Italian Theory. Dall'operaismo alla biopolitica* (2012); *Crisi come arte di governo* (2018; 2022), translated into German, English, and Spanish.

Elettra Stimilli is Professor of Theoretical Philosophy at the Department of Philosophy at the Sapienza University of Rome. She directs the editorial series "Filosofia e Politica" and "MaterialiIT" by the Italian publishing house Quodlibet. She is part of the scientific committee of the Bloomsbury book series "Political Theologies" and of the Editorial Board of the Journal *Political Theology*. She is also co-founder of the Italian Walter Benjamin Association and a member of its Board of Directors. Among her publications: *The Debt of the Living*, New York: Suny Press 2017; *Debt and Guilt*, London: Bloomsbury 2018; *Jacob Taubes. Sovranità e tempo messianico* (2004), Macerata: Quodlibet 2019; *Filosofia dei mezzi. Per una nuova politica dei corpi*, Vicenza: Neri Pozza 2023.

Gabriele Guerra is Professor of German Literature at the Department of European, American and Intercultural Studies at the Sapienza University of Rome. His main research interests are German Jewry in the literature and thought of the first half of the twentieth century, the Konservative Revolution and Ernst Jünger, the historical avant-garde, and the connection between aesthetics and religion and between theology and politics in German Literature and Culture. He is the President of the Italian Walter Benjamin Association. Main Publications: *Judentum zwischen Anarchie und Theokratie. Eine religionspolitische Diskussion am Beispiel der Begegnung zwischen Walter Benjamin und Gershom Scholem*, Bielefeld 2006; *La forza della forma. Ernst Jünger dal 1918 al 1945*, Rome 2007; *Spirito e storia. Saggi sull'ebraismo tedesco 1918–1933*, Rome 2012; *L'acrobata d'avanguardia. Hugo Ball tra dada e mistica*, Rome 2020.

Marx and Marxisms: New Horizons

Edited by Marcello Musto

The peer-reviewed series *Marx and Marxisms: New Horizons* (edited by Marcello Musto, with Francesca Antonini as Assistant Editors) comprises rigorous scholarly books, accessible to general readers, that offer innovative and critical works in the field of Marx studies and Marxisms. The series publishes monographs, edited collections, and anthologies, by both prestigious and emerging international experts, in the fields of political theory, history of political thought, sociology, political philosophy, and heterodox economics. The books in this series provide original investigations within the Marxist tradition, push the boundaries of accepted interpretations and existing literatures, bring different concepts and thinkers into new relationships, and inspire significant conversations for today. They come from a wide range of academic disciplines, subject matters, political perspectives, cultural backgrounds, and geographical areas, producing an eclectic and informative collection that appeals to a diverse and international audience.

The Making of a Marxist Philosopher
A Memoir
Sean Sayers

Walter Benjamin and Antonio Gramsci
A Missed Encounter
Edited by Dario Gentili, Elettra Stimilli, and Gabriele Guerra

For more information about this series, please visit: www.routledge.com/Marx-and-Marxisms/book-series/MM

WALTER BENJAMIN AND ANTONIO GRAMSCI

A Missed Encounter

Edited by Dario Gentili, Elettra Stimilli, and Gabriele Guerra

Routledge
Taylor & Francis Group

NEW YORK AND LONDON

Designed cover image: Fototeca Storica Nazionale/ARCHIVIO GBB

First published 2025
by Routledge
605 Third Avenue, New York, NY 10158

and by Routledge
4 Park Square, Milton Park, Abingdon, Oxon, OX14 4RN

Routledge is an imprint of the Taylor & Francis Group, an informa business

Library of Congress Cataloging-in-Publication Data
Names: Gentili, Dario, editor. | Stimilli, Elettra, editor. | Guerra, Gabriele, editor.
Title: A missed encounter : Walter Benjamin and Antonio Gramsci / edited by Dario Gentili, Elettra Stimilli, Gabriele Guerra.
Description: New York, NY : Routledge, 2024. | Series: Marx and Marxisms | Includes bibliographical references and index.
Identifiers: LCCN 2024016666 (print) | LCCN 2024016667 (ebook) | ISBN 9781032599717 (hardback) | ISBN 9781032599700 (paperback) | ISBN 9781003457039 (ebook)
Subjects: LCSH: Benjamin, Walter, 1892–1940. | Gramsci, Antonio, 1891–1937. | Philosophy, Marxist. | Communism and philosophy.
Classification: LCC B809.8 .M567 2024 (print) | LCC B809.8 (ebook) | DDC 335.4092/2—dc23/eng/20240702
LC record available at https://lccn.loc.gov/2024016666
LC ebook record available at https://lccn.loc.gov/2024016667

ISBN: 978-1-032-59971-7 (hbk)
ISBN: 978-1-032-59970-0 (pbk)
ISBN: 978-1-003-45703-9 (ebk)

DOI: 10.4324/9781003457039

Typeset in Times New Roman
by Apex CoVantage, LLC

CONTENTS

CONTRIBUTORS

Daniele Balicco is Researcher in Theory of Literature at the Roma Tre University. His research field includes critical theory (aesthetics, psychoanalysis, and Marxism) and its intersection with literature and modern art.

Vittoria Borsò is Emeritus Professor of Spanish, French, and Italian Philology at the Heinrich Heine University Düsseldorf. Her current main research areas are transculturality, biopolitics, visual culture and transmediality, topology and literary topographies, memory and mediality, forms and aesthetics of life (in connection with life sciences), materiality and production, and an interdisciplinary project sponsored by the German Research Foundation/Deutsche Forschungsgemeinschaft [DFG].

Frank Engster wrote his PhD thesis on the subject of time, money, and measure and was subsequently a junior fellow at the Post-Wachstumskolleg (Degrow-College) in Jena. He works for several political institutions and foundations and is active in political groups in Berlin. His areas of interest lie in the different readings of Marx's critique of the political economy and especially in money as a technic and its connection with measurement, quantification, time, and (natural) science.

Michele Filippini is an assistant professor in the University of Bologna and is on the board of the International Gramsci Society. His research interests include the history of Marxism, the birth of Sociology in the nineteenth and twentieth centuries, and forms of political legitimation and political power.

Marco Gatto is Assistant Professor of Literary Criticism and Literary Theory at University of Calabria. He is a scholar of Marxist Literary Theory and the History of Intellectuals, with a focus on Gramsci and the Italian Marxist tradition.

Sami Khatib is an interim professor at the Karlsruhe University of Arts and Design (HfG) and a founding member of the Beirut Institute for Critical Analysis and Research (BICAR).

Marina Montanelli is a research fellow in Aesthetics at the University of Florence, where she is also a member of the Research Unit "PTS: Aesthetic Practices, Anthropological Transformations, Contemporary Scenarios". She is a member of the Board of Directors of the Italian Walter Benjamin Association. She has also written articles in Italian, Spanish, English, and German on the new feminist wave.

Wolfgang Müller-Funk is a literary scholar, cultural philosopher, essayist, and lyricist. He is currently Professor of Cultural Studies at the Department of European and Comparative Literature and Language Studies (University of Vienna) and research coordinator of his faculty. His research interests include cultural theory, narratology, Central European Studies and Austrian literature, romanticism, and avant-garde and essay studies.

Marcello Mustè is Associate Professor of Theoretical Philosophy at Sapienza University of Rome, Italy. He is a member of the Scientific Council of the "Gramsci Foundation". His recent studies are addressed to the philosophy of Italian Marxism and in particular to the work of Antonio Gramsci.

Massimo Palma is Professor of Political Philosophy at Suor Orsola Benincasa University in Naples. He is managing editor of the journal "Philosophy and Public Issues", LUISS-Unisob, Rome-Naples, and co-founder of the Italian Walter Benjamin Association and a member of its Board of Directors.

Francesco Raparelli is a philosopher and activist. He has a research grant at the University of Salerno and teaches Social Philosophy as an adjunct professor at Roma Tre University.

Massimiliano Tomba is Chair and Professor in the Department of History of Consciousness at the University of California, Santa Cruz. His work focuses on time and temporalities, Marxism, critical theory (especially the first generation of the Frankfurt School), and modern and contemporary political thought. He has written on Hegel, Kant, Marx, Walter Benjamin, the French Revolution, fascism, historical revisionism, Italian workerism, new social movements, and the impact of the last financial crisis on democracies in Europe and the United States, among others. His works have been translated into Chinese, French, English, German, Italian, Polish, Portuguese, Rumanian, Spanish, and Turkish.

Birgit Wagner is Emeritus Professor of Romance Studies at the University of Vienna, a member of the Editorial Board of "International Gramsci Journal" (IGJ), and a corresponding member of the Austrian Academy of Sciences. She is the author of numerous articles on Gramsci and Benjamin, as well as the author/editor of many books/articles on Italian and French literature and cinema and on Translation Studies.

INTRODUCTION

Dario Gentili, Elettra Stimilli, and Gabriele Guerra

Walter Benjamin and Antonio Gramsci were contemporaries: their births and deaths occurring within a few years of each other. They both lived through the first half of the twentieth century, one of the most intense and dramatic eras of European history. Two Marxists *sui generis*, they radically changed the themes and lexicon of Marxism, heavily influencing its most important analyses and debates. Whenever Marxism was deemed to be in crisis or out of date, Gramsci's and Benjamin's thought was used as a resource for its renewal, moving it into new fields: for example, Gramsci's thought in postcolonial studies and Benjamin's in new media studies, both in cultural studies. Their posthumous success depended on the transmission of their thought, first by their friends and associates, then by entire generations of scholars from a wide range of disciplines, to the point that their citations crossed the confines of academic culture and, along with images of their faces, even entered pop culture.

While they have both enjoyed posthumous transversal popularity, there has been little exploration of whether the themes, concepts, problems, and analyses of their thought were in fact similar or only comparable. Although there is a long tradition of both Benjaminian and Gramscian studies, a comparative study is a complete novelty, from both a critical and a methodological point of view. Those rare studies that have attempted to compare them focus on a few particular aspects of their thought.[1] This book aims to be the first to engage in a comparison of Gramsci's and Benjamin's thought in a general sense, albeit articulated on the basis of those aspects that are most relevant and topical today. This comparison is possible because they often begin from the same questions.

Both Benjamin and Gramsci were marginalised in their lifetimes from the dominant cultures of their respective countries, a marginalisation that their

DOI: 10.4324/9781003457039-1

historical-political and personal situations ended up reinforcing in their later years: the former in exile in Paris following the advent of Nazism in Germany and subject to precarity not only in his work but also in his life, and the latter held in prison by the fascist regime. They both died as victims of fascisms, on the threshold of the catastrophic Second World War. In some ways, their similar conditions towards the end of their lives ended up bringing their thoughts closer together than their respective origins might have suggested (Benjamin's family belonged to the German-Jewish upper middle class; Gramsci was born to a poor family in a small town in inland Sardinia). Perhaps it was their marginality, although experienced in different ways, that first led them to set off on their own paths, giving their thought an originality with respect to their own time and context, something which was only understood and appreciated later. Sometimes they drew on similar cultural and philosophical sources, without, however, ever forgetting the so-called popular culture, which was neglected by bourgeois thought, and in which emerge those new forms of life that capitalism first lures in and then betrays. Both of them, on the basis of an analysis of the political-social and artistic-cultural realities of their time, tried to lay out the tendencies that would revolutionise the conditions of their era and generate a new social and political form of life. Both ascribed a directly political value to their work, including their literature and their writings on culture and art, considering intellectual work to be a political activity. They both analysed the social and political forms, as well as the capitalist modes of production, of the time – including mass society, populism, liberalism, and Fordism – not only as objects of critique but also in order to glimpse an alternative within them, the emergence of a revolutionary political subjectivity capable of giving a new form of life to the human.

Many of the questions they posed remain open today; not only did some of their insights anticipate what was to come but they continue to contribute to the interpretation, critique, and transformation of our society, economy, and way of life. Their capacity for producing thought and conceptual tools in times of crisis is still crucial for conceiving of possible alternatives precisely where none seems to exist.

This book is divided into four parts: *Philosophy of History and Historical Materialism*; *Revolution, Counter-Revolution, and Passive Revolution*; *Capitalist Modes of Production and Production of Subjectivity*; and *Translation and Criticism, Avant-Garde and Popular Culture*. Each part aims to identify the most significant and topical points of comparison between Benjamin and Gramsci, bringing out not only their convergences, but also, and no less importantly, their differences.

A relationship with history is one of the themes that most unite Gramsci's and Benjamin's thought. In their own ways, they each reflect on temporality, questioning the Newtonian concept of space-time and the temporal "linearity" that arranges the past, present, and future as discrete, separate, and successive moments. Hence, the importance for both Benjamin and Gramsci of the conception of history, a fundamental aspect of "Western Marxism" to which both lend elements of real originality (Engster). The relationship between philosophy and history, theory, and praxis is crucial to both, and heavily influences their analyses of philosophies of history and historicism. In some respects, their respective conceptions of history could even be said to be opposed to one another (Müller-Funk). In fact, while Benjamin strongly criticises historicism in his thesis *On the Concept of History*, Gramsci, in the *Prison Notebooks*, never stops conceiving of the philosophy of *praxis*, that is, Marxism, as "absolute historicism". However, although they use the category of "historicism" in often antithetical ways, the question of temporality remains prevalent in both, leading them to conceive of a multiplicity of historical times, which allows historical materialism to intervene in the political struggle. They also both criticise the socialism of the Second International, which had taken up the weapons of the class enemy, namely positivism and machinism, as instruments for naturalisation of history (Raparelli).

Among Gramsci's categories, "passive revolution" is one of the most commonly used and discussed, due to its topicality. It is called on to interpret and analyse a political phase uninterrupted since the end of the 1970s, especially in the West: revolutionary praxis is increasingly considered outdated and most mobilisations and demands put forward by social movements are gradually losing their force of radical transformation, at best being redefined within the dominant hegemony, which feeds on them for its renewal and continuation. It is no coincidence that this hegemonic phase coincides with the rise of neoliberalism. Gramsci took the category of "passive revolution" from Vincenzo Cuoco's *Historical Essay on the Neapolitan Revolution of 1799* and then "tested" it against various historical, political, social, and economic events: from the Italian Risorgimento, to the counter-revolution that followed the nineteenth-century revolutionary uprisings in France, to Fordism, and to fascism (Mustè). We can infer from this that Gramsci understood this category as having a broad hermeneutic range, which included and deepened his other fundamental categories, such as "hegemony" and the "war of position".

Benjamin's thought had certain affinities with the dynamics of passive revolution. He also focused on the counter-revolutionary phase in France, which in *The Arcades Project* and in the figure of Charles Baudelaire is used to refer to the historical "conjuncture" at the advent of fascism in Europe at the time (Gentili). Furthermore, he has an "anthropogenetic" interpretation of Fordism, thus not limited only to a capitalist mode of production, and a conception of historical temporality that in the thesis *On the Concept of History* sees progress as "homogeneous, empty time" capable of neutralising the intermittency of the *Jetztzeit* produced by the struggle of the oppressed classes (Filippini). In today's world, in which revolution has lost its grip on history, it is perhaps necessary to transform passive revolution itself, guiding it from below, thereby contesting the hegemony of the ruling classes (Borsò).

The book highlights their common, albeit different, analysis of capitalist modes of production that, contrary to the Marxist approaches most in vogue at the time, did not focus in the classical sense only on "labour" as opposed to capital, but involved the production of subjectivity. Both Benjamin and Gramsci were interested in investigating the anthropological transformation that sees the decline of the old "individual" and the rise of a new "type of human", a new "machinism" that also includes intellectual labour and new forms of technique. This anthropological transformation reflects the disintegration of the distinction between public and private, in opposition to all useless forms of bourgeois nostalgia (Tomba). It is thus no surprise that the "sexual question", which Gramsci focuses on as the central problem of the Fordist mode of production, also emerges in Benjamin with the prostitute as a prophetic figure of the further development of the capitalist forms of production, which, today, in the process defined as the "feminisation of labour", has become the general condition of post-Fordist production (Stimilli). They also share an interest in George Sorel's non-fascist use of myth in order to redefine a new relationship between individuals and the masses (Palma), in which the "subalterns" – such as Davide Lazzaretti as described by Gramsci or the rag picker of Baudelaire's poetry in Benjamin – are the protagonists of a new "living philology" rather than simply being marginalised by the history of the victors (Wagner).

Beginning from these premises and typologies, we can also begin to understand the specific work of Benjamin and Gramsci in the field of literary criticism and their interpretations of different artistic practices, which are the focus of the last section. The first text analyses their relationship to their national literatures, in Gramsci's application of the concept of the "national-popular" and in Benjamin's particular interpretation of the critic's work, where he investigates the contribution of certain categories to both the production of texts and their intended audience, thus re-articulating the old popular-elitist relationship along the interpretive lines of a rigorous *materialist* critique (Gatto). The second text in this section traces the specifically linguistic interpretations of the two thinkers, from the sociolinguistic analysis of Esperanto in Gramsci to the virtuosic interpretation of "pure language" in Benjamin, thus tracing in both a "communicability" of language that goes well beyond its function as a communicative tool, becoming rather a critical instrument for the interpretation of the capitalist world in the forms of the linguistic history of class struggle (Khatib). The third text analyses their parallel critical interpretations of futurism. The latter's avant-garde practice of a radical rupture with the bourgeois world undeniably fascinated both of them; however, they reinterpreted its aestheticisation of politics as the politicisation of art, thus turning it from a sounding board for totalitarianism into a means for critically intervening in reality (Balicco). And the last text examines the Gramscian interpretation of folklore and the Benjaminian interpretation of kitsch, identifying deep and fertile theoretical duplicities within each of them. While in Gramsci the deep ambivalence of the concept of folklore – between the cultural manifestation of a political and social subjugation and the practice of resistance to this subjugation – gives rise to a kind of dialectic of Enlightenment that advocates an *enhanced humanism,* Benjamin's reflections on kitsch and its dual character as both a useful function for the rising bourgeoisie and an implicit critical power present an equally enhanced Enlightenment that can help to redefine the human (Montanelli).

In short, in retracing the various phases in the thought of Walter Benjamin and Antonio Gramsci, this volume intends not only to offer a way of reinterpreting many of their theoretical positions, to detect their commonalities and more or less convergent intentions, but also, and, in some sense, above all, to use this unprecedented comparison to reactivate categories and tools of critical thought for which there is now urgent need.

Acknowledgements

The editors would like to thank the Istituto Italiano di Studi Germanici (IISG) in Rome, the headquarters of the Associazione Italiana Walter Benjamin (AWB), which supported a conference dedicated to Benjamin and Gramsci held in the premises of the IISG on 25, 26, and 27 November 2021, the papers from which are published here.

Note

1 To our knowledge, the only comparison between Benjamin and Gramsci – that preceded and provided contributions for this book – can be found in the Special Issue: Birgit Wagner and Ingo Pohn-Lauggas, eds., "Gramsci und Benjamin – Passagen/ Gramsci and Benjamin – Bridges", *International Gramsci Journal* 3, no. 4 (2020), https://ro.uow.edu.au/gramsci/vol3/iss4/. In texts dedicated specifically to Benjamin or to Gramsci, comparisons are rare, aside from a few exceptions, for example, Renate Holub, "Towards a Global Space of Democratic Rights: On Benjamin, Gramsci, and Polanyi", in *Walter Benjamin and the Aesthetics of Change*, ed. Anca M. Pusca (London: Palgrave Macmillan, 2010). Also, Fredric Jameson, who studied both Benjamin and Gramsci, only sporadically mentioned some commonalities, without developing them; see Fredric Jameson, *Benjamin Files* (London and New York: Verso, 2020).

Bibliography

Holub, Renate. "Towards a Global Space of Democratic Rights: On Benjamin, Gramsci, and Polanyi". In *Walter Benjamin and the Aesthetics of Change*, edited by Anca M. Pusca, 10–54. London: Palgrave Macmillan, 2010.
Jameson, Fredric. *Benjamin Files*. London and New York: Verso, 2020.
Wagner, Birgit, and Pohn-Lauggas, Ingo, eds. "Gramsci und Benjamin – Passagen/Gramsci and Benjamin – Bridges". *International Gramsci Journal* 3, no. 4 (2020). https://ro.uow.edu.au/gramsci/vol3/iss4/.

Translated by Clara Pope

PART 1

Philosophy of History and Historical Materialism

1

BENJAMIN'S BREAK WITH NEWTONIAN TIME AND THE INTRODUCTION OF RELATIVIST SPACE-TIME INTO CRITIQUE

Frank Engster

> The social revolution of the nineteenth century cannot draw
> its poetry from the past, but only from the future.
>
> Marx[1]

> The past carries with it a secret index
> by which it is referred to redemption
> ... There is a secret agreement between past generations and the present one.
>
> Benjamin[2]

> The tradition of all the dead generations
> weighs like a nightmare
> on the brain of the living.
>
> Marx[3]

> It is the tiger's leap (*Tigersprung*)
> into the past.
>
> Benjamin[4]

> Let the dead bury their dead and mourn them.
>
> Marx[5]

The question taken up here is the most radical question with which Benjamin struggled: how to overcome capitalist society? The thesis that follows is that Benjamin became a unique figure in a tradition who posed this question precisely because of his intervention *into* this tradition. His intervention brought a radical rupture into the traditional understanding of revolution – and with this rupture,

DOI: 10.4324/9781003457039-3

he advanced a new understanding of "tradition" itself.[6] Both a break and a new understanding were possible because Benjamin broke with nothing less than *time*, that is, with the classical concept of chronological Newtonian time and historical progress. This break simultaneously builds a bridge between "classical" or "traditional" Marxism and a post-structuralist and even post-Marxist critique, or in a broader sense, "postmodern theory".

Benjamin broke with the chronological and linear understanding of time and history by introducing Einstein's *space-time*. In the field of critique of capitalism, he made a *relativist* use of time, or better, of space-time, and as such also broke with the Newtonian understanding of time and space dominating and even driving classical Marxism.[7] Yet in a sense, Benjamin also "fell out of time", insofar as the status of his critique remains unclear. He combined philosophy and literature, aesthetics and politics, and Marx and religion – a strange constellation for a unique figure (and at once everybody's darling). However, as hard it may be to summarise Benjamin's widespread, colourful, and opaque oeuvre, his relativist use of space-time is striking and thoroughgoing. We find it in his critique of historicism and social democracy, in his use of pictures and images and in his conception of the "trick" of turning wish images into dialectical images, in his concepts of the past, *Jetzt-Zeit* and *Geistesgegenwärtigkeit*, of the messianic and the divine, of aura, magic, and phantasmagoria, of myth and law, of language, archive, remembrance and memory, cult and debt, storytelling and tradition, in his short fragment *Capitalism as Religion* as well as in his *Passage-Work*, in his reference to the entanglement between childhood and spatial experience, in his passion for fragments, details, monuments, and ruins, but also in his interest in the technique of photography, recording, translation, and reproducibility, and of course in his critique of the linear concept of progress and the homogeneous concept of time, as well as in his technique of montage and constellation.[8]

Even though no introduction to the actual physical dimension of space-time can be given here, what follows aims to open up, with Benjamin, what the relativist concept of space-time, transferred into social relations, means in comparison to the Newtonian concept of time. However, even if physics is always a kind of pilot science for other sciences, social critique included, its modes of knowledge and practices are in turn determined by the social form of capitalism, and what the experiment is to physics, the great "experiment" of radical critique is for the critique of capitalism: revolution.

The first step therefore will be to demonstrate how time and revolution were conceptualised in classical Marxism, which presumed classical Newtonian time. This conception was already contested by an inner Marxist (self-)critique which introduced a subjective and at once temporal factor. The four most representative and striking of these factors came from Luxemburg, Lenin, Gramsci, and Lukács. But it was only Benjamin who actually broke with classical Marxism by showing that a revolution *in* time aims for a revolution *of* time itself, and that the revolution must be anticipated by this new understanding and new use of time, or better of space-time. Subsequent to these three steps, two different but quite complementary uses of space-time will be examined, that of Ernst Bloch and Theodor W. Adorno.

1.1 The Chronological Time of Classical Marxism and Its Openings

The assumption or even the expectation of classical Marxism – the (mass) organisations and parties of the socialist (labour) movement and the Second International – was that the capitalist society will progress by itself towards its own overcoming, namely through its contradiction between labour and capital and between productive forces and relations of capitalist production, whether this overcoming occurs through crisis or by progressive development, whether gradually or by revolution. However, although these contradictions in a quasi-objective and determinist manner point to their own overcoming, both theoretical critique and revolutionary politics have to identify themselves with the standpoint of a *practical* overcoming by a revolutionary subject: the working class. Even in classical Marxism, there was no social and historical necessity without the necessity to actively take part and become practical for social and historical progress, emancipation, and revolution.

But regardless of this need for revolutionary engagement, in classical Marxism, especially in its concept of historical materialism and its understanding of nature and objectivity, time and space remained the objective and unsurpassable conditions for dealing with the contradictions of society and their historical development. It is upon this that world history struggles, as it were, on a natural world stage; and not only is this arena built by a homogeneous time and space but social practice, and even revolutionary, also has to act in a chronologically linear and causal manner.

Meanwhile, already before Benjamin, a kind of self-critique intervened in this determinism and objectivism within Marxism. Yet this critique only led to the threshold of the rupture which Benjamin still had to make, since the critique still attempted to retain the classical Marxist concept of revolution and its revolutionary subject. Moreover, the critique was constructed to *fix a problem* contained in the classical concept of homogeneous time and space, rather than overcome it, namely that contrary to initial expectations, there was seemingly no immanent necessity in capitalist society which led to revolutionary consciousness and praxis. To solve this problem, critique sought a *subjective factor*. Although this subjective factor was conceptualised in various directions, there are four striking versions which cover the range of possibilities for solving the problem, coming from possibly the most influential revolutionaries of the time: Lenin, Luxemburg, Gramsci, and Lukács.

1.1.1 Lenin, the Technique of the Political and the Kairos

Already Lenin emphasised what probably remains the main problem in Marxist politics up to today. He stated that the proletariat "spontaneously" produces "only trade-unionist consciousness",[9] that is, a reformist rather than revolutionary consciousness. Thus, revolutionary progress does *not* by necessity derive from capitalist contradictions, and it will automatically lead neither to revolutionary class consciousness nor to a revolutionary organisation. On the contrary, according to Lenin, without an "external addition", the consciousness of the working class remains "trapped" within capitalist conditions and within immediate and reformist economic class interests.

This addition which must come from without is the notorious *party*. For Lenin, the party must substitute what is absent in capitalist objectivity: the party must stand in for the *lack* of progress towards a revolutionary situation and a respective consciousness and praxis. In short, the party must *replace* the determinism that classical Marxism expected from social and historical progress, and act *in its stead.*

As a replacement for determinism, Lenin conceived of a party of a "new type". A "new type" means a party that must literally sustain the consciousness of the working class, accelerating and guiding it as a *vanguard* which leads consciousness out of immediacy and beyond its reformist and economist immanence. But the party also must prepare for the pivotal moment of a decisive situation: the party is a means for the political *technique of the Kairos*, for the opportunity of seizing economic and political power at the opportune moment and in the right situation.

1.1.2 Luxemburg and the Non-Linearity of Self-Organisation

The complementary pole to Lenin was marked by Rosa Luxemburg. Luxemburg too criticised the objectivism and historical determinism of the Marxism of her time, and she too saw the necessity to organise and accelerate revolutionary consciousness. But in contrast to Lenin, the subjective factor does not come from the outside in the form of a vanguard party of professional revolutionaries. Luxemburg rather emphasised that revolutionary development must come from the *inside*, from inner learning processes, self-organisation, and from the spontaneity of the masses. This focus on self-organisation forced Luxemburg to also deal with the inner contradictions of the political situation of her time. She sought a way in between fainthearted Social Democracy and authoritarian Bolshevism, wanting the class to adjust to a sustained but chronological non-linear development between progress and regression, victory and defeat, social reform and revolution, interruptions and leaps, organisation and spontaneism, and masses and leadership.

1.1.3   *Gramsci's Supplements*

Logically situated between Lenin's vanguard party and Luxemburg's processes of self-organisation, it was Gramsci who introduced into the contradiction of labour and capital and into class struggle the subjective factor in the most proper sense of the term; or better said, he introduced a whole *series* of factors, all of which had a particular and forceful subjective determination. They can all be condensed as *supplements*. To name only the most important or prominent of these supplements: the subalterns and civil society, common sense, education and pedagogy, language and the intellectuals, culture and a philosophy of praxis. All supplements can be seen as practices and even *techniques* to gain civil, cultural, and political hegemony in the course of the "wars of position" and "cultural struggles" with all its manoeuvres, alliances, tactics, united fronts, etc. They are also supplements insofar they don't come directly from the so-called economic and material basis but from its superstructure. While in classical Marxism the superstructure was mechanically derived from an economic and material basis, Gramsci probed the entire superstructure as a supplement to the contradiction of labour and capital and class struggle. This attention to the superstructure became a common feature of Western Marxism and Critical Theory. Yet there is another feature that distinguishes Gramsci: long before operaism, he was interested in *compositions*, and while operaism focused on technical, political, and social compositions, Gramsci addressed the *temporal* composition of a present into which the past extends, but which can also foresee its own future and make strategical use for a different future.

1.1.4   *Lukács' Existentialism*

In Georg Lukács, we find not only a fourth version of the subjective factor but also a final and conclusive one, as the subjective factor receives an "existentialist" turn.[10] In his famous essay on the concept of reification from his epochal *History and Class Consciousness*, Lukács confronts Lenin and Luxemburg's critique of social and historical objectivism, but summersaults their subjective factors in an attempt at finding a kind of immediate identification between objectivism and subjectivity.

It is this identification that provides a kind of short circuit to the "existentialist" position. This existentialist seems to be, at first sight, simply the existence of the worker in capitalist society, as his existence, according to Lukács, is "alienated" and "reified" by the form of capitalist mediation, namely, the notorious *commodity-form*. "He [the worker] is therefore forced into becoming the object of the process by which he is turned into a commodity and reduced to a mere quantity. But this very fact forces him to surpass the immediacy of his condition".[11]

However, the crucial point is that in capitalism, not only *labour* and its results – the objects and the social objectivity produced – become commodified but for the first time in history *labour-power itself*, hence the subject of this production of objectivity becomes a reified and alienated commodity – and here, according to Lukács, the position of the proletariat differs radically, or better, existentially, from the bourgeoisie's class position and epistemological perspective. While the bourgeois standpoint reflects on labour, and with it the essence of society and the practical production of its objectivity, only from an external and contemplative standpoint and takes objectivity as it is immediately given, the dramatic and existential insight for the proletariat is that under capitalism their own labour power, that is, their own subjectivity, practice, and life, becomes an object and a commodity for capital. Such self-acknowledgement is existentialist since it can no longer remain external to labour and social objectivity, as in the case of the bourgeois standpoint, which remains merely epistemological and without practice, philosophical at best. The standpoint of the proletariat requires a leap into a practical self-conquest beyond mere contemplative reflection, similar to the leap which characterises existentialism since Kierkegaard.

Lukács' conception is a climax and at once a turning point in critique "after Marx" – "after" in both a logical and a chronological sense – since the revolution becomes possible at *any* time; at "any time" insofar as it is independent of empirical and objectively necessary social conditions as well as of the historical development and ripeness of the situation. Lukács' revolutionary leap jumps, as it were, over all of the *objectively* necessary conditions upon which classical Marxism insisted, while it is also relieved from the different *subjective* factors that have been added to this objectivity. In a word, revolution becomes *timelessly* possible. It is a purely logical moment, the decisive act of self-reflection and self-identification which turns the proletariat into a self-appropriation, one transformed into the praxis of self-realisation in a new, communist society.

Lukács situated this idea within the formula of the "identical subject-object of history". Here, not only does the subject identify itself with the objectivity it creates but this identification also unifies theory and practice, necessity and freedom, logic and history, in *one* – in the praxis of material production and social mediation, in short, the *essence* of social being. With his existentialist formula, Lukács already places the proletariat directly into a quasi-divine position, and he indeed later criticised himself for that conception as "messianic zeal". Nevertheless, this messianic fervour only bounded the proletariat back to the Hegelian supra-individual Spirit, not to the divine, and so it was left to Benjamin to cross the threshold and follow through with the divine and the messianic.

But before examining Benjamin's definitive break with chronological time, a look at the use of time in classical Marxism and of the temporal status of the various factors mentioned might be helpful. The takeaway of Benjamin's break is only revealed when we follow the *temporality* of first the objectivism of classical Marxism and then the *temporality* of the subjective factors.[12]

Classical Marxism expected that the *economic* contradictions must come *politically* to consciousness by an automatic progress with objective, inner necessity, and that this progress will turn the working class, through quasi-causal necessity, into a revolutionary subject which will overcome capitalist society. All four of the subjective factors, in contrast, were a reaction to the displacement of that determinist expectation, and all four introduced with the subjective factor a *temporal* factor. Something must stand in to execute social progress and an incomplete logical and historical necessity, not yet ripe without an addition. The subjective factors are not only such an addition but the proper *techniques* for intervening into social objectivity and into society's conditions by calculating with its time and progress. The factors are set in an empty void of social objectivity and its conditions, which at the same time stands for the openness of history and is operative as indeterminacy and freedom.

With the vanguard party, Lenin introduced a hyper-political moment and at once a pure technical lever into chronological time to accelerate revolutionary consciousness and practice, in preparation for the right social situation and historical constellation; Luxemburg calculated with the non-linearity of self-organisation and spontaneity; Gramsci introduced various supplements that accorded with different social situations, compositions, and temporalities to shift and transform power relations; finally, with the identical subject-object, Lukács addressed a pure logical and as such timeless act of self-knowledge that becomes an existentialist leap into a kind of self-realisation of productive power – as if the proletariat could calculate, like a supra-individual Spirit, with the time and space of society by identifying itself (in advance) with the social reality it produces and mediates.

However, precisely because these factors have this temporal status, they could all only play out in *classical Newtonian* conceptions of time, in chronological-linear time and progress. This was the situation in which Benjamin intervened and executed a break. However, we will see that after the break the decisive elements reappear, but transformed into space-time: Lenin's reckoning with favourable political constellations, Luxemburg's self-organisation, Lukács' existential leap, and Gramsci's temporal composition.

1.2 Benjamin's Break With Chronological Time

Lukács was the last prophet of revolutionary subjectivity: he announced with the proletariat a straightforwardly divine subject that could create the same social objectivity through which it wants to enter. However, the last prophet is, in the religious order, not definitive and final with the ultimate message. He is only in the chronological order of time the one closest to us, and it was Benjamin who retroactively made Lukács into this last prophet – not because Benjamin after Lukács no longer had a revolution to proclaim, but because he broke with this chronological order of time itself by introducing relativist space-time into critique. (Lukács will thus remain the last prophet only in and with the old chronological Newtonian time.) This introduction equals the revolutionisation of Newtonian time by Einstein's relativist space-time, and what Benjamin did was a kind of socialisation of that space-time. "Socialisation" does not here mean that he had designed a new communist society of the future. Rather, he introduced the concept of space-time to find a new understanding of how to revolutionise the existing *present* of society.

In short, with space-time, Benjamin revolutionised the concept of revolution itself. For this, Benjamin sought an exit from two capitalist dimensions of time: from the *quantified abstract time* of the capitalist economy, especially dominant by quantifying labour-time and the social relation of things, as well as an exit from *homogenous and continuous historical time*, a chronological and linear time altogether similar to the cyclical time of empty repetition. Thus it can be said that this historical time is a *function* or derivative of that abstract social time dominant in the capitalist economy.

In Benjamin's *On the Concept of History*, revolution is neither the outcome of social progress and a seizure of economic and political means,[13] as in classical Marxism, nor is revolution an existentialist leap, as in Lukács. It is a suspension of time *as such*. While Lukács led the revolution to the timeless point of an existentialist leap that was *logically* possible at any moment in capitalism, the revolution for Benjamin now ought to, first of all, *suspend* time (which, as with Lukács, can occur at any time). Here Benjamin revolutionises chronological time negatively, that is, by interrupting the continuity of time, withdrawing from homogenous capitalist time, and disinvesting from historical time.[14]

This suspension of time is supposed to be a political or even revolutionary act of the working class, just like in classical Marxism and in Lukács, namely a kind of general strike. But the proletariat receives its power not because it is the social productive force per se, it receives it by the "secret agreement between past generations and the present one".[15] For Benjamin, this power comes from a past that is incomplete and thereby persists: it is about the return of a history of oppression which is itself suppressed, as it were, and it is as if this unredeemed past has a gravitational force that warps and curves space-time, forcing social and emancipatory progress to return to its unfinished past rather than move straight forward towards the completion of history. This curving of the present by its past, although only a "weak" messianic power,[16] must conquer with *divine* violence in order to suspend time.

Revolution, the Marxian "locomotives of history", no longer ultimately leads to a communist future. Revolution equals only "the human race grabbing for the emergency brake".[17] Thus the suspension of time shall not fulfil a progress of history through a communist revolution, but shall "only" interrupt the course of a disastrous history – so that another time may occur, or rather that time itself may be different.

Consequently, in Benjamin's conception, the revolution first and foremost *actualises the past*. This actualisation does not mean, like in classical Marxism, that it fulfils the mission of a working class which, developed under capitalist conditions, becomes ripe to finally gain its fully self-presence in a communist future. The past actualised refers to the unredeemed victims and missed opportunities in history, the *Kairos* and different futures that could have happened, but are lost in time. Just as in Lukács, the revolution is timeless and at any point possible, but not because the moment of self-identification of the proletariat as the social essence and productive power of society and history is, at least logically, possible at any moment. Rather, the revolution is timelessly possible because it should have already happened, and insofar it remains present – not as a lost opportunity, but that the present *is* the present because of these missed and lost chances of its own past.

The past becomes actualised, but also recognisable, in *Jetzt-Zeit* or the "here and now time". This motif is maybe the most striking socialisation of space-time Benjamin accomplished in the field of radical critique, together with the gravitation of a past that curves society's present, and the *Jetzt-Zeit* could be construed as the moment in which this curving collapses and the whole past becomes present. The past becomes present – in one stroke – like an image: if space-time and its curving by the past is somehow productive for the present, then its products are, in the broadest as well as in the literal sense, *images*. Benjamin reads images as products of collective wishes, and in these images, society's space-time becomes reified, just as social labour is reified in commodities, yet without the notion that the social essence could be reflected in the sense of Lukács' conception of reification, where in the self-consciousness of the commodity labour-power, both social labour time and historical time recognise themselves and collapse in a divine self-transparency. While in Lukács the productive power and social essence embodied in the working class, if it gains self-consciousness, becomes the moment of a leap into revolutionary praxis and eventually into practical communist self-realisation, in Benjamin, the truth of society's history and past cannot become fully present in an image. Truth is only in its details: with Benjamin, it is not the devil that resides in the details, but the messianic.[18] This truth is expressed by constellating these details in such a way that, on the one hand, reference is made to the lack of realisation of wishes and hopes and, on the other hand, their realisation is demanded through their dialectical transformation into practice and wishful images become what Benjamin calls "dialectical images". So what is actually brought into a constellation are past and present: the present is charged by its past, but with a kind of dangerous emptiness through which *Jetzt-Zeit* is supposed to activate social practice. To interpret means to decipher and actualise the constellations presented in the details of an image, rather than find a coherent system or logic therein. The reading of an image, in which the dialectic is held at a standstill, but also charged, is, in contrast to a linear and chronological reading of a text, non-linear, and this non-linearity corresponds to Benjamin's concern with a non-evolutionary and non-deterministic use of time, progress, and history. Images and pictures present and literally show what relativist space-time is about: space and time, which appear to be separable and distinct in the world view of classical Newtonian physics, are entangled.

Not only details but fragments also play an important role in how society's space-time presents itself. For Benjamin, the truth has a "time kernel", a *Zeitkern*. Yet the truth of this time kernel is rather fragmented. It is a time shard or, as he puts it in the "Passage-Work", "a crystal" which freezes and mirrors, but also contorts the dynamic of past events; crystallised events in fact do give insight into historical constellations, but only as if in a hall of mirrors.[19]

With images, despite their fragmented and constellated character, the weak messianic power can nevertheless be brought to bear: the weak power is here *bound*. Society's history and social relations are bound in the constellations of the details and fragments, as if they were *monads*. The messianic power bound in these monads is nothing less than historical truth, which can only be released *destructively*, like the energy bound to the atomic nucleus – only by destroying and shattering. It must be released or even redeemed by shattering the positivism of a historicism that treats historical facts as if they were dead matter. To release this power bound in historical "facts" with regard to social functions is analogous to the shattering of the atomic nucleus in physics, which releases the power of mass (its "truth") according to Einstein's formula on the convertibility and transformability of mass into energy: $E = mc^2$.

1.3   The Use of Space-Time in Adorno and Bloch

As with every true revolution or "event" in the strong Badiouian sense, truth comes afterwards: by the causes and effects a revolution *temporalises*, and as Benjamin's use of space-time paradoxically revolutionised the classical understanding of time itself, here all the more truth must come afterwards, by the new use of time made by radical critique. Further, this truth presented itself in a new development of critique that began after Benjamin by Western Marxism and Critical Theory.

Just as it was possible to demonstrate the temporal status of the subjective factors with four striking examples, so too for the use of space-time in Western Marxism and Critical Theory it is possible to highlight its dimensions with notable representatives, and since time has three dimensions, we can assign each of these dimensions to one representative and his concept.

The dimension of time as the past is already covered with Benjamin's intervention into linear-chronological time and historical progress. Ernst Bloch's use of space-time is complementary. Instead of the actualisation of an unsettled, unavenged past, an anticipated future should become present, yet one, just like in Benjamin, that seeks to change the present. In order to keep communism alive as mankind's daydream, Bloch relied on the materialism of "desire", "concrete utopia", and the "principle of hope".[20] He also thereby relies on the power of the untimely, or of anachronism in the sense found in the work of Jacques Rancière and Patrick Eiden-Offe. But in contrast to Benjamin, Bloch reaches ahead and relies not on an unaccomplished *past*, but on an anticipated *future past*, an anticipation that is capable of changing the present by a kind of non-simultaneity or non-synchronism, a "simultaneity of the untimely", as he puts it.

Theodor W. Adorno finally marked for relativist space-time, just as Lukács did for the subjective factor, a kind of end point in terms of temporality. Adorno, although influenced by both Lukács and Benjamin, found a position of its own, and his critique can be located between Benjamin and Bloch, hence between past and future, indexing at once an end point insofar as he saw the present blocked and standing still. The contradictions of society in "late capitalism" (Adorno), instead of pushing society towards progress and emancipation, experience a reconciliation that is as immanent as it is coerced, leading to, as Marcuse would term it for *man*, a "one-dimensional" closure. As a result, the present, and time in general, are blocked. Moreover, Adorno, especially in his *Negative Dialectics*, radicalises Benjamin's critique of progress: Adorno was concerned neither with revolutionary development nor with its absence, but with the "dialectic of enlightenment", namely, that progress in science and technology and in the development of the productive forces promoted by it turn into their opposite, into mass ideology and regression, resentment, destruction, and even extermination.

Thus Adorno also transferred capitalist contradictions and their development away from a Newtonian world view of space and time, and he too socialised space-time. But with this transition, Adorno, unlike Lenin, Luxemburg, Lukács, and Gramsci, was not concerned with the temporal technique of a subjective factor, nor was he, like Benjamin and Bloch, concerned with how to invoke the past or the future to chance the present. He was rather concerned with the dialectic that leads to a *closure* of the present and, even worse, that turns progress into regression and social destruction. According to Adorno, the closure and this fateful turn occur through three registers of *identification*: identification via conceptual thinking, identification via the exchange principle, and identification through scientific-technical reason. It is because of these three forms of identification – and the hidden connection between them – that capitalist contradictions become hermetically closed in a forced reconciliation, and that any historical progress in economy, science, and technology corresponds to regression for individual and social emancipation. With regard to space-time in late capitalism, through these techniques of identification, Adorno finds its closure in the immanence of a false totality, and consequently makes an ordered retreat and holds society's space-time open by referring to the "non-identical". The non-identical stands as a placeholder for that which cannot be completely mastered and subordinated to identity: use value and nature, misery and suffering, the preponderance of the object on the one hand and individual autonomy on the other, but also, not least, a totally different society.

Thus Adorno marks a kind of zero point between Benjamin's actualisation of the past and Bloch's anticipation of the future. This point registers at once also an end point for the use of space-time in Critical Theory and Western Marxism, just as Lukács marked an end point for all the subjective-temporal factors still embedded in classical Marxism's use of Newtonian time. Tellingly, both marked this end point by the technique of identification, but in a complementary way. While Lukács' identification of the subject-object mediation through the self-consciousness of the commodity labour-power pointed to a way out, as an existentialist leap out of capitalist contradictions, Adorno saw in identification a closure of social contradictions and referred only to what resists the principle of identity. Whereas Lukács gave speculation on a kind of self-identification of the productive force of society and history, Adorno was criticising such a hypostasis of identification as blocking society's time and space. And whereas in Lukács' conception the proletariat, by its self-identification, should reflexively make use of its own social essence and potentiality to literally *reckon*, like a god, with its own praxis and at once society's time and space, Adorno saw by the techniques of identification the hubris of a presumptuous, haughty calculation that turns into a fatalistic doom. Rather, reflection should emerge in a reserved, individual, and (self-)critical manner.

1.4   The Current Situation: Quantum Physics and Post-Marxism

After classical Marxism and the subjective factors have been assigned to the classical Newtonian conception of space and time, and after Benjamin, Bloch and Adorno had integrated the introduction of space-time into social critique, the next step would be to correlate the critique of current post-structuralism and post-Marxism to the paradoxes, effects, and entanglements of quantum physics.

Among the possible starting points could be Lacan's structuralist use of Saussure and Freud, Althusser's "structural causality", Deleuze and Guattari's concept of "virtuality" and "actualisation", and Derrida's temporalisation of meaning by the materialism of scripture. Similar to quantum physics, post-structuralist and post-Marxist concepts revolve around entanglements, paradoxes, and uncertainties, while operating with the non-representable and inaccessible: an inoperative "différance" (Derrida), an inoperative "other" (Levinas), an inoperative "community" (Nancy), etc. This applies in particular to the classic entities or identities: subject and object exist only decentred, barred and split, broken, fluent and fuzzy, divided and scattered, multiple, uncertain, unavailable, perverse, queer, hybrid, etc.

Despite their differences, these later critiques have in common the search for concepts adequate to the quandary that subjects cannot identify and represent themselves, nor each other, nor their objects with any real stability. Common in all these conceptions is also that they don't lead to a common understanding of social time and social space – social time and space seem to be, just as in quantum physics, blurred, uncertain, entangled, fragmented, non-homogenous, hybrid, etc., and like subject and object, they too have to be "deconstructed" to reveal their precariousness.

It has been demonstrated that space and time are by no means neutral, innocent categories, neither for social critique nor for the natural sciences, and that there seems to be a hidden inner relation between social critique and natural science. If the concepts of space and time, and thus their respective concept of *materialism*, have an analogous or homologous status and history in both social critique and natural science, the question arises as to what this analogy refers to. My thesis would be that it refers to our capitalist form of socialisation, which constitutes both a physical *and* a social space-time relation and seems to build a first *and* a second nature. Thus, a further step in this investigation would be to demonstrate that first, external nature and second, purely social nature overlap in what Marx called an "economy of time".[21] If we want to understand the analogous or homologous status of space-time in nature and in capitalist society, we have to understand the technique of quantification and measurement that take place in both the natural sciences and the capitalist economy[22] – a task that social critique has not yet been able to accomplish.

Notes

1 Karl Marx, "The Eighteenth Brumaire of Louis Bonaparte", in *Marx Engels Collected Works* (London: Lawrence & Wishart, 2010), vol. 11, 106.
2 Walter Benjamin, "On the Concept of History", in *Selected Writings, Vol. 4: 1938–1940*, ed. Howard Eiland and Michael W. Jennings (Cambridge, MA: Belknap/Harvard University Press, 2003), 389f.
3 Marx, "The Eighteenth Brumaire of Louis Bonaparte", 103.
4 Benjamin, "On the Concept of History", Thesis XIV.
5 Karl Marx, "Letter From Marx to Arnold Ruge", in *Marx Engels Collected Works*, digital ed. (London: Lawrence & Wishart), vol. 3, 134.
6 On Benjamin's non-conservative use of tradition, see Sami Khatib, "Where the Past Was, There History Shall Be: Benjamin, Marx, and the 'Tradition of the Oppressed'", *Anthropology & Materialism*, Special Issue, 1 (2017): 1–22.
7 According to Peter Fenves, Benjamin was informed by Einstein's specific relativity theory and his new conception of time and space, but it was not before 1914/1915 that it explicitly appeared in his terminology; see Peter Fenves, *The Messianic Reduction: Walter Benjamin and the Shape of Time* (Stanford: Stanford University Press, 2010).

Benjamin introduces *The Work of Art in the Age of Mechanical Reproduction* from 1935 with a striking quote from Paul Valéry: "For the last twenty years neither matter nor space nor time has been what it was from time immemorial."

8 Benjamin was informed and impressed by modern natural science, like, for example, Marx, Engels, or Bebel, but searched, like Brecht, explicitly for a different technical and social use. In general, his work is characterised by the fact that the penetration of the second industrial revolution into everyday life becomes legible; see Kyung-Ho Cha, ed., *Aura und Experiment. Naturwissenschaft und Technik bei Walter Benjamin* (Wien: Turia und Kant, 2017).

9 Vladimir I. Lenin, "What Is to Be Done?", in *Lenin's Selected Works* (Moscow: Progress Publishers, 1970).

10 Frank Engster, "Lukács's Idea of Communism and Its Blind Spot: Money", in *Confronting Reification: Revitalizing Georg Lukács's Thought in Late Capitalism*, ed. Gregory R. Smulewicz-Zucker. Studies in Critical Social Sciences (Leiden: Brill, 2020), vol. 166, 203–223.

11 Georg Lukács, *History and Class Consciousness: Studies in Marxist Dialectics* (Cambridge, MA: Merlin Press, 1971), 166.

12 At least implicitly, Laclau and Mouffe have addressed these temporal dimensions; Ernesto Laclau and Chantal Mouffe Chantal, *Hegemony and Socialist Strategy: Towards a Radical Democratic Politics* (London and New York: Verso, 1995).

13 "There is nothing which has corrupted the German working-class so much as the opinion that they were swimming with the tide." Benjamin, "On the Concept of History", Thesis XI.

14 Michael J. Thate, "Messianic Time and Monetary Value", *Religions* 7, no. 9 (2016): 112, 1–18.

15 Benjamin, "On the Concept of History", Thesis II.

16 Benjamin, "On the Concept of History", Thesis II.

17 Benjamin, "On the Concept of History", 402.

18 Benjamin, "On the Concept of History", Thesis XI.

19 Benjamin elaborates this in convolute N of Walter Benjamin, *The Arcades Project* (Cambridge, MA: The Belknap Press, 1999).

20 Ernst Bloch, *The Spirit of Utopia* (Stanford: Stanford University Press, 2000); Ernst Bloch, *The Principle of Hope* (Cambridge: MIT Press, 1995).

21 Frank Engster, *Das Geld als Maß, mittel und Methode. Das Rechnen mit der Identität der Zeit* (Berlin: Neofelis, 2014).

22 Frank Engster, "Measure, Machine, Money", *Capital & Class* 44, no. 2 (June 2020): 261–272; Frank Engster, "The Place of Capitalist Self-Critique", *Identities* 19, no. 1–2 (2022): 8–26.

Bibliography

Benjamin, Walter. *The Arcades Project*. Cambridge, MA: The Belknap Press, 1999.

Benjamin, Walter. "On the Concept of History". In *Selected Writings*, edited by Howard Eiland, and Michael W. Jennings, translated by Harry Zohn, vol. 4, 1938–1940. Cambridge, MA: Belknap/Harvard University Press, 2003.

Bloch, Ernst. *The Principle of Hope*. Cambridge: MIT Press, 1995.

Bloch, Ernst. *The Spirit of Utopia*. Stanford: Stanford University Press, 2000.

Cha, Kyung-Ho, ed. *Aura und Experiment: Naturwissenschaft und Technik bei Walter Benjamin*. Wien: Turia und Kant, 2017.

Engster, Frank. *Das Geld als Maß, mittel und Methode. Das Rechnen mit der Identität der Zeit*. Berlin: Neofelis, 2014.

Engster, Frank. "Lukács's Idea of Communism and Its Blind Spot: Money". In *Confronting Reification: Revitalizing Georg Lukács's Thought in Late Capitalism*, edited by Gregory R. Smulewicz-Zucker. Studies in Critical Social Sciences, vol. 166, 203–223. Leiden: Brill, 2020.

Engster, Frank. "Measure, Machine, Money". *Capital & Class* 44, no. 2 (June 2020): 261–272.

Engster, Frank. "The Place of Capitalist Self-Critique". *Identities* 19, no. 1–2 (2022): 8–26.

Khatib, Sami. "Where the Past Was, There History Shall Be: Benjamin, Marx, and the 'Tradition of the Oppressed'". *Anthropology & Materialism*. Special Issue, 1 (2017): 1–22.

Laclau, Ernesto, and Mouffe, Chantal. *Hegemony and Socialist Strategy: Towards a Radical Democratic Politics*. London and New York: Verso, 1995.

Lenin, Vladimir I. "What Is to Be Done?". In *Lenin's Selected Works*. Moscow: Progress Publishers, 1970.

Lukács, Georg. *History and Class Consciousness: Studies in Marxist Dialectics*. Cambridge, MA: Merlin Press, 1971.

Marx, Karl. "The Eighteenth Brumaire of Louis Bonaparte". In *Marx Engels Collected Works*, vol. 11, 99–197. London: Lawrence & Wishart, 2010.

Marx, Karl. "Letter from Marx to Arnold Ruge". In *Marx Engels Collected Works*, vol. 3, 133–145. London: Lawrence & Wishart, 2010.

Thate, Michael J. "Messianic Time and Monetary Value". *Religions* 7, no. 9 (2016): 1–18, 112.

2

BETWEEN DETERMINISM, FREEDOM, AND MESSIANISM

Gramsci and Benjamin on History

Wolfgang Müller-Funk

History as a "dialectical relationship of subject and object in the historical process" is, as the title of Lukác's famous book *History and Class Consciousness* reveals, a central category of Marxist thought.[1] Moreover, history is not a collection of events and facts, but always their narrative arrangement.[2] The assumption of a radical historicity has many facets and aspects in the case of the tradition of thought founded by Marx. They are based on the idea that history is heading towards a goal and that human conditions and thus also man as a species are constantly changing. In a way, as Lukács has pointed out, human being is a product and producer of itself.

Referring to Engels and Kautsky, the concept of Marxism in the last quarter of the nineteenth century according to which history is leading to its self-destruction as a result of socio-economic conditions, the development of the "productive forces" (technology and science) and the crisis of capitalism open the window to a classless society without exploitation and private property, as it were, is continuously damaged and irreversibly shaken in the short twentieth century.

The crisis of deterministic socio-biological models of evolution has an internal and an external reason. Modern technology showed its terrible and destructive side for the first time in World War I.[3] It makes it possible to increase the collective mass murder of people (including the civilian population), especially the civilian population, to an unprecedented extent. At least as irritating and disturbing is the fact of the political failure of the workers' movement in the 1920s and 1930s, which surprisingly few theoreticians in the context of Marxism have faced. Trotsky, Gramsci, and some "right-wing" opponents within the German KPD (August Thalheimer and Heinrich Brandler) or the *Partito Comunista Italiano* are exceptions. The often-repressed question they pose together is: How

DOI: 10.4324/9781003457039-4

was it possible that the radical economic crisis of the interwar period did not lead to socialist transformation but caused a chain of defeats of the Marxist parties, which ultimately enormously facilitated the rise of totalitarian forces (National Socialism, Fascism, military dictatorships, Stalinism)?

There is an external political and an internal theoretical aspect that we want to focus on. It provokes a discomfort with the mechanistic conceptions of overly optimistic pre-war Marxism with its assumption of historical, quasi-scientific laws that determine the linearly conceived course of history. This is a heritage from the Age of Enlightenment from Condorcet to Comte. In this picture of history, the role of man is reduced to that of the enforcer of lawful developments. This is in unmistakable contradiction to the idea of a revolution that can be understood as a free act of history.

There is an obvious connection between the theoretical and practical aspects, as the deterministic conceptions of history of socialists and communists have clearly led to the fact that, for example, the most powerful workers' movement in Europe, that in Germany, capitulated to National Socialism without any fight and resistance. It had already been overrun in Italy by the movement of the ex-socialist Mussolini. Historical determinism has clearly fostered a wait-and-see policy that assumed that the new political movements from the right would blow themselves up, which would then create room for a left-wing takeover. According to Gramsci, this is a "conception that belongs to everyday understanding and is associated with the passivity of the great mass of the people".[4] And elsewhere Gramsci refers dryly to the "wisdom of the Zulus": "Better to advance and die than to step on the spot and die".[5]

Related to this is what the author of the *Prison Notebooks* understands as the "fetishization" of collective organisms such as parties, state, and trade unions. Fetishism consists in attributing a magical power to these organisms: "The individual expects the organism to act, even if he does not do anything himself, and does not reflect that precisely because his attitude is very widespread, the organism is necessarily inoperative".[6] In extension of this argument, it could be said that the use of the term "progress" in the discourse of pre-war socialism also carried such a fetishist character.

Following Labriola and in contradiction to Croce, Gramsci's attempt to reformulate Marx's theory as a philosophy of practice is essentially based on the *Theses ad Feuerbach*. According to Gramsci, they ultimately postulate an "identity of history and philosophy",[7] which, in contrast to Croce's liberal Hegelianism, is supplemented by the unity of history and politics. The philosophy of practice is not simply a philosophy of history or a philosophy of politics, but rather history and politics in their case form integral components of such a philosophy of practice, which, in contrast to classical deterministic concepts, neutralises freedom, but refers to the process of action and thus does not limit it to theory. Gramsci quotes Marx: Feuerbach "therefore considers in the essence of Christianity only theoretical behaviour to be genuine and human, while practice is only grasped and fixed 'in its dirty Jewish manifestation'". It is evident that Gramsci, like Marx, uses the formula of the "dirty Jewish manifestation" exclusively critically and ironically in connection with anti-Semitic stereotypes. It is also used in his discussion of Croce's philosophy to make it clear that a certain type of idealism juxtaposes pure thinking with impure selfish acts.[8]

Gramsci sharpens his conceptions of history not at least in the critic of Croce and his political and philosophical companion Adriano Tilgher and his writings *Saggi di etica e di filosofia del diritto* and *Storia e Antistoria* (*Quaderni critici*, 1928). There is a whole series of commentaries on both works in the letters, which, as is so often the case in Gramsci, fluctuate between approval and critical thoughtfulness. Gramsci sees Tilgher's merits above all in the fact that he "emphatically represents the doctrine of freedom and the 'being-should'" and gives space to the personality in history again. Where there is no "freedom of choice", there are, according to Tilgher, only mere nature rules.[9]

It is revealing how Gramsci understands the two oppositional terms. For him, Gentile, who understands history as the history of the state, is a representative of "history", while he puts Croce's ethical-political conception of history close to "anti-history". As we will see, the author of the *Prison Notebooks* repeatedly makes attempts to synthetically bridge the opposite pair of history–anti-history, so to speak, thus also the oppositions of gradual and progressive development, of a progression in "leaps", and reform and revolution, of necessary and arbitrary, of collective and individual.[10] Both concepts are reciprocally opposed as antitheses, which the author would like to subject to the process of synthesis, not least with the help of the concept of a "passive revolution".[11] He sees the concept of anti-history as an important moment in a necessary critique of historicism and determinism, but at the same time he criticises the Nietzsche-trained "to fashionable titanism, to a taste for wishful thinking".[12]

The question of the opposition between history and anti-history is accompanied by that of the predictability of historical events. Understood as a determined continuum, there is the possibility of historical foresight and predictability, which would be the rational moment of history. Anti-history, on the other hand, is its sheer opposite, but at the same time the element that surprisingly interrupts history. It represents the collapse of the rationally unpredictable, which interrupts history as a predictable event and questions and counteracts it.

In another commentary, the understanding of synthesis is shifted. This obviously has to do with the fact that "the dialectical process in real history crumbles apart into countless partial moments". In the dialectics of preservation and renewal "cannot be determined a priori", "what is preserved in the dialectical process"; rather, "it will emerge from the process itself".[13] With critical reference to Croce, Gramsci criticises an idea of history as a sporting arrangement and as a "conception of mechanical causalism".[14]

To understand the historical development as a sporting game, with a referee and loyally respectable, predetermined norms, is a form of history-by-plan, in which the ideology is not based on the political "content" but on the form and method of the struggle.[15] For Gramsci, the "search for constant, regular uniform lines" is linked to a "childlike and naïve need to finally solve the practical problem of the predictability of historical events".[16]

In summary, it can be said that Gramsci takes cautious steps to the development of his conception of history within the framework of a philosophy of practice and proves to be a virtuoso of synthesis who objects to the Marxist Vulgate of the pre-war concept. His philosophy of practice is, here similar to the case of Lukács or Korsch, conceptualised as a return to Marx. At the same time, however, the author works on the idealistic thought of Croce's, Tilgher's, or Gentile's, similarly to how Marx worked his way through his contemporary opponents, Gramsci does this far less polemically than he does and also largely avoids the juxtaposition of "bourgeois" and Marxist positions. He would like to shift the Marxist idea of "historical mission" in the direction of Kant's "concept of teleology".[17] He criticises the narrowing of the concept of freedom in liberal thought, but leaves no doubt that freedom is central to a philosophy of practice: "What is new about our idea of history is that, for the first time, the people of the 19th century act in the knowledge that history is the history of human freedom. It is this that guarantees the unity of philosophy, history and politics".[18]

If we take the dual pair of concepts of history and anti-history as a methodical tool for determining Benjamin's philosophy of history and its most salient features, then one will not be able to avoid assigning it to anti-history. Benjamin hardly knows any compromise and synthesis in his reckoning with historicism and vulgar materialism (Darwin-Marxism) of the late nineteenth century – these are also Gramsci's antipodes and rubbing trees. After all, the task of both thinkers is similar, namely, to develop a materialistic conception of history in the light of the historical experiences of the catastrophes of the early twentieth century, which is contemporary and theoretically consistent. From a text-type point of view, there could hardly be a greater contrast than between Gramsci and Benjamin. Gramsci is characterised by a concentrated argumentation that seeks to bring something to the point, while Benjamin operates at a central point with poetic means – compaction, displacement, parable, tableau, paradox, and irony – and thus often generates ambiguity.

In sections XI and XIII, the author of *Über den Begriff der Geschichte* (1940), Benjamin, denounces like Gramsci the economist conception of history of social democracy before World War I. It had corrupted the working class by the idea that it was swimming in the "stream" of history and that economic development would lead by itself to the new society.[19] According to Benjamin, progress as understood by social democracy had three aspects: increase in "skills and knowledge", "infinite perfection", and inexorability. This conception of progress, which Gramsci also questions and relativises, albeit far less radically, for example, when he weighs moments such as progress, reaction, and renaissance against each other is based on the "idea" of a "homogeneous and empty time".[20]

Historicism is also committed to such a purely quantitative concept of time, as Heidegger critically described it in *Being and Time*. He operates with linearity and causality. Historicism proceeds from the permanence and immutability of the past. The underlying concept of empathy is based on the fact that the historian, who relives a bygone epoch, should forget the "later course" (Fustel de Coulanges).

Benjamin's renewed historical materialism opposes these two defining historical concepts of his time. Following Derrida's method, the term revision is to be understood here in a double sense of the word, as revocation and rejection, but also as a reunion and as a "consideration". Such a reformulation of historical materialism includes:

1. The idea that history is a construction and reconstruction.
2. A revision of the linear concept of time.
3. A revision of materialism in which the theological figure of salvation and messianism comes into play.
4. A revision of the historical movement in which the view of the past replaces that of the future.

These anti-historical revisions, in the sense of Gramsci, are linked together implicitly rather than explicitly in the text, which is evident in the first erratic section on the chess machine. This opening of the theoretical combination game in the text is erratic because it contains moments of irony and ambiguity. So, the ingenious dwarf, who hides in the automaton and who is equated with historical materialism, operates as a manipulator – this does not make the comparison particularly flattering. But it could be that his mechanical deceptions are more like the traditional understanding of "historical materialism", which the text does not put in quotation marks without ulterior motive and of which it is ironically said that it should always win.[21] But this "doll" can only do that, as it is said in a rhetorically sophisticated turn, when it takes theology into its service.

What is meant by this becomes clearer in the next text module, which shifts the image of happiness from the future to the past (thesis 4) and relates the missed happiness or the missed to salvation. Between the living and the dead, there is therefore a kind of pact, an "appointment". In this way, history is transformed into a secularised event of redemption: "Then, like every gender that was before us, we are given a *weak* messianic force."[22] At this point runs the fault line between the old and the new historical materialism. Benjamin says it not without hesitation: "Hatred and the will to sacrifice . . . are nourished by the image of the downtrodden ancestors, not by the ideal of the liberated grandchildren".[23] The most famous piece of Benjamin's writing on history turns this statement highly paradoxically, as the new angel is driven into the future, but he turns his back on it and looks spellbound into the past with his astonished and frightened face.[24]

Benjamin's messianic materialism takes its origin from the respective energy of the present time, a time of crisis and the state of emergency. From this situation, the past flashes and lights up briefly, as it were. From the present – at one point Benjamin even praises fashion – the past is invoked.[25] Benjamin thus questions the (seemingly) objectivity of a causal and linear time. It is replaced by the "tiger jump into the past". If the *Angelus Novus* in the essayistic Medallion IX is pushed into the future by the storm (passive revolution), then in text piece XIV an active "jump under the open sky of history" takes place – and thus the "revolution".[26]

In Benjamin's case, the materialism of history formulated in this way mutates into its construction from the point of view of the respective present – that would be, as it were, the cultural-scientific-narrative aspect of Benjamin's post-Marxist philosophy of history: history is the result of a narrative that always starts from the present (thesis 1).

In addition, Benjamin may argue that Marx also saw the proletariat as a redemptive subject, that one's own situation of exploitation and oppression can only be changed by abolishing exploitation and oppression in the first place. Of course, unlike Gramsci, this model also leads to the narrowing of history, philosophy, and politics – but in Benjamin's case it leads to a messianic and mystical theology, which is also evident in the text's understanding of time.

The revision of the concept of time (thesis 2) has three aspects that are linked to each other. It dissolves the seemingly equal triad of past, present, and future through the primacy of a timeless present (lightning, moment). Associated with this is the idea of a standstill that breaks through and interrupts time – that would be the structurally mystical element of Benjamin's philosophy of history. Third, salvation, which in the sense of Jewish tradition is never certain whether it will ever take place, aims not only at the abolition of exploitation and oppression but also at the end of history: "only the redeemed humanity has its past become quotable in each of its moments. Each of their lived moments becomes a *citation à l'ordre du jour* – which day is the youngest".[27]

Gramsci's and Benjamin's historical-philosophical concepts and considerations have grown out of the theoretical and political-practical crisis of traditional Marxism. They are unthinkable without its criticism, on which both are widely in agreement. Although their concepts are incompatible, they do not cancel each other out, but they cannot be reconciled by any daring synthesis.

Gramsci's reflections, which are heading towards the restitution of Marxism as a practical philosophy, may not go far enough, because they seek to avoid the pathetic, anti-historical break with classical Marxism, while Benjamin's anti-historical sacralisation of history and historical materialism, regardless of literary brilliance, goes far too far. It is theoretically and politically compatible with the memory discourses of our day, which no longer revolve only around the Shoah but also around the victims of colonialism and its aftermath. Speaking against Benjamin's messianic perspective, one can be said that the hope for the messianic power of the oppressed and marginalised has historically been an illusion. Gramsci's concept has the decisive advantage that it remains relevant in terms of political acting.

Notes

1 Georg (György) Lukács, *Geschichte und Klassenbewußtsein. Studien über marxistische Dialektik* (Neuwied and Berlin: Luchterhand, 1970), 58–93.
2 Wolfgang Müller-Funk, *Die Kultur und ihre Narrative* (Wien and New York: Springer, 2008²).
3 Walter Benjamin, "Der Erzähler", in *Ausgewählte Schriften* (Frankfurt am Main: Surhkamp, 1974), vol. 1, 385–410.
4 Antonio Gramsci, *Quaderni del carcere* (Torino: Einaudi, 1975), Q. 15 § 13, 1770. [Translations by the author].
5 Gramsci, *Quaderni*, 1769 [Q 15 §12].
6 Gramsci, *Quaderni*, 1769–1770 [Q15 §13].
7 Gramsci, *Quaderni*, 1241 [Q 10 II, §2].
8 Gramsci, *Quaderni*, 977 [Q 8 §61].
9 Gramsci, *Quaderni*, 395 [Q 3 § 135].
10 Gramsci, *Quaderni*, 1063 [Q 8, §203].
11 Gramsci, *Quaderni*, 1324 [Q 10, II §41/XIV].
12 Gramsci, *Quaderni*, 1267 [Q 10, II, §28/X].
13 See Gramsci, *Quaderni* [Q 10, I, § 6].
14 Gramsci, *Quaderni*, 1404 [Q 11, § 15].
15 Gramsci, *Quaderni*, 1327 [Q 10, II, §41/XVI].
16 Gramsci, *Quaderni*, 1404 [Q 11, § 15].
17 Gramsci, *Quaderni*, 1426 [Q 11, § 23].
18 Gramsci, *Quaderni*, 1007 [Q 8, § 112].
19 Walter Benjamin, "Über den Begriff der Geschichte", *Gesammelte Schriften 1.2*, ed. Rolf Tiedemann and Hermann Schweppenhäuser (Frankfurt am Main: Suhrkamp, 1991), 699.
20 Benjamin, "Über den Begriff der Geschichte", 701.
21 Benjamin, "Über den Begriff der Geschichte", 693.
22 Benjamin, "Über den Begriff der Geschichte", 694.
23 Benjamin, "Über den Begriff der Geschichte", 700.
24 Benjamin, "Über den Begriff der Geschichte", 697–698.
25 Benjamin, "Über den Begriff der Geschichte", 701.
26 Benjamin, "Über den Begriff der Geschichte", 701.
27 Benjamin, "Über den Begriff der Geschichte", 694.

Bibliography

Benjamin, Walter. *Gesammelte Schriften*, edited by Rolf Tiedemann, and Hermann Schweppenhäuser. Frankfurt am Main: Suhrkamp, 1991.
Gramsci, Antonio. *Quaderni del carcere*, edited by Valentino Gerratana. Torino: Einaudi, 1975.
Lukács, Georg (György). *Geschichte und Klassenbewußtsein. Studien über marxistische Dialektik*. Neuwied and Berlin: Luchterhand, 1970.
Müller-Funk, Wolfgang. *Die Kultur und ihre Narrative*. Wien and New York: Springer, 2008.

3

HISTORICAL MATERIALISM AND PHILOSOPHY OF PRAXIS

Walter Benjamin and Antonio Gramsci Critics of Socialism

Francesco Raparelli

The two men were undoubtedly linked by "misfortune", in the sense that another victim of adversity of the time, Simone Weil, gave the term. In different ways, they both died at the hands of fascism. Walter Benjamin after almost a decade on the run, Antonio Gramsci after almost a decade in prison. The latter, of course, paid for his political activism, while the former, whose brother was a militant communist and died in a Nazi prison camp, paid for his status as a Jewish intellectual and Marxist. However heretical we may think him, Benjamin was a Marxist – at least from the mid-1920s onwards; better still, a Leninist. Contrary to the claims of recent times, when it is fashionable to portray him as a liberal, Gramsci was an absolutely unrepentant Leninist.

They were both victims of misfortune, Leninists, targets of European fascism. What else holds these two extraordinary (and moving) figures of twentieth-century Europe together? If we shift our gaze from their lives to their thought, the matter becomes more complicated. There are, of course, plenty of studies that have correctly and elegantly captured a significant coincidence of their ideas on the subject of translation. So much so that, both Benjamin and Gramsci have gained a renewed global prominence in the field of Cultural and Postcolonial studies.[1] And even the most casual reader cannot fail to notice how both took very seriously the problem of "superstructures", and more generally of language, culture, and ideologies. In his theses "On the Concept of History", however, Benjamin declares war on historicism, whereas in his *Notebooks* Gramsci never ceases to regard the philosophy of praxis, that is, Marxism, as "absolute historicism". A difference that is of no small consequence if, as we shall attempt to do in the following pages, we wish to consider both as critics

DOI: 10.4324/9781003457039-5

of socialism. For the former, historicism and German social democracy coincide; for the latter, socialism – Italian socialism, as well as "real" socialism in Russia – lacks historicism.

My conviction is that both, while using the word "historicism" in (sometimes) antithetical terms, share very similar thoughts on the problem of temporality, more specifically on the multiplicity of historical times. In doing so, they push socialism into a corner and innovate historical materialism (Section 3.1). And it is precisely the latter innovation that has made them decisive authors for "the study of race and ethnicity",[2] and fertile inspiration for postcolonial critique. Their polemic with socialism, however, is not limited to offering useful theoretical tools in the present; it also brings into play a network of practical concepts capable of enlightening the social and political struggle in an era like ours, marked by war and other catastrophes – economic, climatic, and medical – not too dissimilar to those that swept through the lives of Benjamin and Gramsci. Thinkers *in* and *of defeat*, both innovate Leninism through a somewhat unconventional use of György Lukács, the former, and Machiavelli's *The Prince*, the latter (Section 3.2). And again, though they are by no means nostalgic for the old world (Benjamin was impressed by the Soviet cinema and Gramsci by the Fordist factory), they both, quite coincidentally, engaged in a critique of technology (Section 3.3). If historical materialism is the decisive weapon of the class struggle, it is praxis that liberates the future, that realises the unfulfilled possibilities of past struggles, and that lays the roots of antagonistic prediction (Section 3.4). Both pessimists, because hostile to the positivist optimism of the various socialisms, Benjamin and Gramsci maintain only one optimism: the optimism of proletarian organisation, on the assumption that it owes much to cultural hegemony, to the conflict in the field of "complex superstructures" (Section 3.5).

3.1   Retroaction

It is widely known that Engels, in a letter to Joseph Bloch in 1890, already offered an eminent clarification of historical materialism, notably in comparison with what Marx had written in the 1859 preface to *A Contribution to the Critique of Political Economy*. Engels makes important clarifications regarding the controversial relationship between the economic base and legal and political superstructures, stating that the economic base is decisive only "in the last instance"; the superstructures, and the struggles that take place within them, have a reciprocal relationship with the economic base. In the course of the twentieth century, the letter in question has been a source of original forms of Marxism and their dialogue with postcolonial criticism. If this has happened, we owe it first of all to the breach Benjamin and Gramsci opened.

The former writes in a preparatory note for the *Passagen-Werk*, a project that was never completed and whose preparatory materials were partly incorporated into the *Theses*:

> Historical materialism aspires to neither a homogeneous nor a continuous exposition of history. From the fact that the superstructure reacts upon the base, it follows that a homogeneous history, say, of economics exists as little as a homogeneous history of literature or of jurisprudence.[3]

On several occasions, and in particular in the following passage, the latter has stated:

> it is not true that the philosophy of praxis 'detaches' the structure from the superstructures when, rather, it conceives their development as intimately connected and necessarily interrelated and reciprocal.[4]

Benjamin is clarifying the role of the historical materialist, developing the critique of "empty, homogeneous time", that is, the time of the historicism of Fustel de Coulanges and Lepold von Ranke (and their disciples), certainly not of Marx. Gramsci is instead rejecting the critique of Marxism put forward by Benedetto Croce. Contrary to what the latter argued, the economic base is not a "hidden god", an essence that manifests itself in the semblance of political conflicts and regulatory frameworks. Rather, it is the rifts that permeate the "complex superstructures" that create tensions in the economic base to the point of changing it.

For Benjamin, the critique of "empty, homogeneous time" means a critique of historicism or of the "positivist conception of history", meaning by the latter the ideology of time peculiar to German social democracy. Progressivism, the primacy of the future over the past, the celebration of technology and labour: these are the traits of an ideology that, according to Benjamin, "corrupted German workers", facilitating the rise of Nazism. Josef Dietzgen, one of the most highly regarded philosophers of social democratic reformism (that of Eduard Bernstein first and later of Karl Kautsky), is among the most frequent targets of the *Theses*. Having mystified the Marxian idea of "classless society" into a Kantian ideal, that is into an "infinite task" to achieve in small progressive steps, social democracy has also transformed "empty and homogeneous time" into a sort of "anteroom" in which to "wait for the emergence of the revolutionary situation with more or less equanimity".[5] Benjamin's break with social democratic historiography and praxis is radical. Returning to Jewish messianism in an original way, Benjamin ceases to think of the present as a passage, understanding it instead as a time that "takes a stand",

and that has come "to a standstill".[6] A time, that of the class struggle, which realises and redeems the *past* of the oppressed and their rebellion; a past, we should note, that only the historical materialist at the moment of danger is able to grasp, and to seize in an interactive constellation with the present struggle. It is also, however, a time that opens up to the new, making the *present* itself indeterminate and full of junctions, and the *future* something that has yet to be entirely written. The revolution, then, interrupts the train of progress and universal history, which is always that of the victors, and presents itself as an "emergency brake", as in the famous expression that appears in the preparatory materials of the *Theses*.

For Gramsci, in the maturity of his reflection on Machiavelli, in that groundbreaking workshop that is *Notebook 13*, it is a question of completely rethinking historical materialism against economistic fatalism and extremist adventurism. In Gramsci's definition of economism, we cannot fail to grasp something very similar to waiting in the anteroom of "empty and homogeneous time", which for Benjamin typifies the praxis of German social democracy. The economism that Gramsci tears to pieces erases political praxis, it obliterates struggle, with its necessarily aleatory, occasional, contradictory characteristics. Voluntarism, on the other hand, cannot come to terms with what endures or changes more slowly, namely the economic base, social groupings.

In Gramsci, "real" Socialism and/or democratic Socialism both undoubtedly rhyme with mechanism. Mechanistic and deterministic is the social universe and its evolutions as defined by Bukharin in his *Popular Manual* (*Historical Materialism. A System of Sociology*), and which Gramsci incessantly criticises from 1930 onwards. Equally a child of mechanism is the notion of "empty and homogeneous time", the polemical target – as we have just seen – of Benjamin and his *Theses*. If German, and European, historicism generally affirms with Dilthey (1883), the distinction between the "natural sciences" and the sciences of the "spirit", the acceptation Benjamin attacks is the one that, with Ranke, seeks to seize history "the way it really was";[7] the one that, with a merely contemplative attitude, does not mean to judge but to grasp the eternal truth of past events, inevitably understood according to an "empty and homogeneous time" – which is indeed the time of classical mechanics. Gramsci's historicism confirms what Eugenio Garin (1984) correctly affirmed, that is, that historicism is a manifold and diverse cultural and philosophical phenomenon, with the most disparate political uses. It is not the Gramscian acceptation of historicism that Benjamin rejects, but the one that is considered positivist and anti-dialectical, and that runs from Ranke to Dilthey.[8]

Retroaction and the radical critique of mechanism/determinism mean blowing up the concept of "universal history". This is explicitly true of Benjamin, but also of Gramsci. Both think of history in plural and "zigzagging" terms,[9] dense with anachronisms and sudden accelerations. As Gramsci makes clear, it is the personality of the men of the masses themselves that is composed in the most bizarre way:

> it contains Stone Age elements and principles of a more advanced science, prejudices from all past phases of history at the local level and intuitions of a future philosophy which will be that of a human race united the world over.[10]

And so, for Gramsci as much as for Benjamin, Esperanto, a universalism incapable of grasping the rifts, the discontinuities, and the coexistence of irreducible historical times and forms of life, is to be condemned.[11]

3.2   Lenin With Lukács, Lenin With Machiavelli

Lenin, as we said at the beginning, is a crucial influence on both Benjamin and Gramsci. But the former approaches him through frantic and somewhat chaotic study, and of course through his romance with Asja Lācis;[12] the latter as a militant revolutionary communist, from the bold experience of the workers' councils in Turin to his dramatic imprisonment by the fascist regime. Despite this not insignificant difference, and despite the fact that Benjamin very rarely mentions Lenin, the rupture of 1917 and the early phase of the Soviet revolution are central to the thinking of both. All the more so because they both see the events of 1917 in the light of the defeat of the revolutions in Italy and Germany, of the rise of fascism, of the tragic authoritarian and criminal turn that Stalin imposed on the Soviet experiment.

Why Lenin? Because it was Lenin – together with Rosa Luxemburg, it should never be forgotten – who fought against the cultural and political degeneration of the parties of the Second International.[13] Cultural degeneration: the uncritical acceptance of scientific positivism and historicism, mechanism and fatalism, and in many cases – as in Germany and Austria – of neo-Kantianism. Political degeneration: the opposition to or paralysis of the class struggle in the name of reformist gradualism, but above all the rape of proletarian internationalism by supporting the catastrophe of the nationalistic Great War. It was Lenin who, through an original dialectical approach, fought against the mechanistic materialism, revisionism, and opportunism of the social democratic and socialist parties and of their theoretical sources. Significantly, it was Lenin – and again Rosa Luxemburg – who inspired the works *History and Class Consciousness* (1923) by György Lukács and *Marxism and Philosophy* (1923) by Karl Korsch, which paved the way for the so-called "Western Marxism" and were decisive for Benjamin. Gramsci, who knew Lukács and Korsch indirectly, instead had a direct association with Lenin, Moscow, and the Third International. A brilliant and creative scholar, the author of the *Notebooks*, but also and *above all* a communist leader; a role he certainly did not abandon when, forced by imprisonment, he dedicated himself to studies "*für ewig*".

As we know, among the heterogeneous inspirations of Benjamin's *Theses*, a prominent place is held by both Nietzsche, with the second of his *Untimely Meditations* (1874), and *History and Class Consciousness*. Without going down a well-trodden path,[14] it is worth dwelling on the distinctive traits of historical materialism as alternative to vulgar materialism, which Lukács presents in his essay on the "Changing Function of Historical Materialism".[15] On crisis as both a temporary collapse of capitalist rule and as a revolutionary *chance*, on the intimate connection between capitalist accumulation and violence. According to Lukács, the capitalist crisis, that only the historical materialism of the proletariat in struggle can properly know, "always signifies a point of – relative – suspension of the immanent laws of capitalist evolution".[16] This means that no linear, nor always and everywhere "organic" development of capitalism exists. If the crisis, in the absence of a workers' offensive can make it possible "to force production back *once again* into the path laid down by capitalism",[17] there is also a "necessary contingency" – that is, a possibility that the proletariat grasps as necessary to capitalistic development itself – to ensure that the socialisation of productive forces can manifest itself as a communist alternative. We can hardly fail to notice the proximity to the problems that Benjamin raises both in his essay on Eduard Fuchs and in the *Theses*. The same proximity we notice if we consider the relationship between violence and the economy. Lukács firmly believed that the Marxism of the Second International had been rendered vulgar by a flawed approach to thinking and writing history. A nefarious political consequence? Removing violence as one of the inherent and necessary instruments to achieve a radical transformation of the existing system. For both Lukács and Benjamin, historical materialism means recognising the intimate connection between capitalism and violence and, conversely, promoting the necessarily destructive, not merely constructive, nature of revolutionary praxis.

In his short essay on Lenin, which Benjamin was also familiar with, Lukács argues that the Bolshevik genius was the only figure who effectively recognised the topicality of revolution as an essential characteristic of his era, as a tendency guiding the struggle, autonomy, and leadership of the working class. This went against the idea of an orderly development in stages of Russian society and its transformations – from tsarism to liberal and bourgeois democracy to socialism. "If the basic character of the times is revolutionary, an acutely revolutionary situation can break out at any moment"[18]: Lukács writes in his *Lenin*. "In reality, there is not a moment that would not carry with it its revolutionary chance- provided only that it is defined in a specific way, namely as the chance for a completely new resolution of a completely new problem",[19] Benjamin writes in the *Theses*. It would be wrong to gloss over the messianic flavour of this work, but it would be equally wrong to omit their direct reference to Lukács, and indirect reference to Lenin. It was Lenin who effectively broke with the socialist mechanism (of the Second International) opening history to diversion, to the unexpected. In spite of the Stalinist catastrophe, a catastrophe that Benjamin, unlike Lukács, never ceased to condemn – suffering the ridicule of his friend Bertolt Brecht because of it.

In Gramsci, and in the *Prison Notebooks* in particular, Lenin is associated with two crucial concepts: "hegemony" and "translation". Though the latter is an issue both Gramsci and Benjamin addressed, it is worth shining a light on the former. Not only because it again calls into question the relationship between structure and superstructure but also because it offers Gramsci the opportunity to innovate Leninism through an original reading of Machiavelli. In this way, ethics and aesthetics, culture in general and historical research, become the locus of politicisation and, therefore, of a radicalisation of the class struggle. Among other things, Gramsci uses the notion of hegemony to redirect the critique of economism from the "theory of historiography" to "the practice of politics".[20]

Best to clear up any misunderstandings: for Gramsci, hegemony is not a means of doing away with Leninism, or of abandoning revolution, organised violence, and the seizure of power. This version began circulating in Italy with Palmiro Togliatti and "the Italian way to socialism".[21] Already in his political writings, before his imprisonment, Gramsci derived the concept of hegemony from Lenin and (his) Bolshevism. In particular, the term appeared in March 1924 with the resumption of the publication *Ordine Nuovo* and with an explicit reference to Lenin's well-known essay commenting on the 1905 revolution, *Two Tactics of Social Democracy in the Democratic Revolution*. Gramsci makes use of the term to productively process the defeat of the workers' councils and of the "Red Biennium" of 1919–1920. In fact, as early as 1926, the "Southern Italian question" was identified as crucial to overcoming the isolation of the workers. The "Hegemony of the proletariat", the workers' ability to gain "the consent of the broad peasant masses", is therefore "social basis of the proletarian dictatorship and the workers' State". In line with the reading offered by Christine Buci-Glucksmann,[22] it is worth highlighting Gramsci's convergence with Lenin, and in particular with Lenin who, at the 10th Congress of the Communist Party, specified and expanded "the dialectic between hegemony and the dictatorship of the proletariat".[23] A problem already present in Gramsci's 1924 text on Lenin, in which he introduces the notion of the dictatorship of the proletariat – through its conscious vanguard, the party – understood as "expansive", as opposed to the repressive variety proper to the bourgeoisie, and more specifically to fascism.

But it is through his rereading of Machiavelli and *The Prince* (the modern proletarian political party), that Gramsci feels he is interpreting Lenin's indications accurately: a ruthless critique of economism and the primacy of praxis; a concrete analysis of the situation and the ability to grasp, and act upon, power relations effectively; the transition from "war of manoeuvre" to "war of position"; the conflict over "prestige"; the relationship between leadership and domination, and leadership and consensus. Going to "the effectual truth of the matter",[24] in the sense of Machiavelli's realism, means for Gramsci being able to consider the possibility of communism in the West after the failures in Italy and Germany that followed the events of 1917 in Russia, after the triumph of the various fascisms. This means reckoning with the capitalist crisis in a new way, understanding the temporal multiplicity that marks it, distinguishing the organic from the conjunctural and occasional aspects of the struggle that permeates, and deepens, the crisis. The analysis of the concrete situation, of the concrete relations of power, is in this sense a "political-historical" analysis, the recovery of that historical materialism which has no place for mechanistic fatalism, in which "fortune" plays a role that is no longer ancillary and subordinate to organic, relatively permanent phenomena. Lenin and Machiavelli were again his way, both direct and indirect, of distancing himself from Bukharin, as well as from Stalin, from real socialism, and from the kind of socialism that had put aside the problem of the revolution and the proletarian state.

3.3   On Technology

Socialist progressivism places confidence in technology at the heart of its optimism. Encouraging the development of technology is always a driving force for positive transformation and therefore for the progressive advancement of social conquests. Benjamin and Gramsci, in various ways, promptly oppose this thesis. One that unites the socialist positivism of the Second International and the Soviet dogmatism of Bukharin, for example, both incapable of critically addressing the entirely new problems posed by the construction of the class-less society. Both are equally convinced that there can be no communist society without modifying the superstructures, the forms of sensibility and culture, and that there can be no technology without social relations, specific modes of production, domination, and political direction. In other words, there can be no technology for the benefit of the proletariat without a politically proletarian use of technology itself.

In particular, Benjamin has two positions on technology, both of which are highly original. The first is expressed in *The Work of Art in the Age of Its Technological Reproducibility* (1936):

> [I]f the natural use of productive forces is impeded by the property system, then the increase in technological means, in speed, in sources of energy will press toward an unnatural use. This is found in war, and the destruction caused by war furnishes proof that society was not mature enough to make technology its organ, that technology was not sufficiently developed to master the elemental forces of society. The most horrifying features of imperialist war are determined by the discrepancy between the enormous means of production and their inadequate use in the process of production.[25]

The second followed shortly after in his essay on Eduard Fuchs:

> Technology, however, is obviously not a purely scientific development. It is at the same time a historical one. As such, it forces an examination of the attempted positivistic and undialectical separation between the natural sciences and the humanities. The questions that humanity brings to nature are in part conditioned by the level of production. This is the point at which positivism fails. In the development of technology, it was able to see only the progress of natural science, not the concomitant retrogression of society. Positivism overlooked the fact that this development was decisively conditioned by capitalism.[26]

The first statement, still extremely relevant today, clearly illustrates the relationship between ungoverned, non-organic technology and imperialist war. The reference to the organic dimension, always crucial in Gramsci, becomes equally and unexpectedly crucial in Benjamin. When there is an increase in technological means in the absence of a proletarian political direction, we have an authentic "uprising on the part of technology", Benjamin writes, *which demands repayment in 'human material' for the natural material society has denied it.*[27] The second assertion, which is taken up again in the *Theses on the Philosophy of History*, in open polemic with German social democracy and Dietzgen in particular, thus becomes intelligible: without the breakdown of bourgeois social relations, the development of technology comes with the regression of society. Once again we find a radical critique of progressivism; and more than that, the definition of a multiple, multidirectional historical time.

Gramsci, on the other hand, attacks the socialist economist Achille Loria, and again Bukharin, whom he considers not too far removed from the former: both mystify historical materialism, replacing the totality of social relations of production with the mere technical instrument. As Gramsci writes in his *Notebooks*:

> In reality the philosophy of praxis does not study a machine in order to know about and to establish the atomic structure of its materials or the physical, chemical and mechanical. properties of its natural components (which is the business of the exact sciences and of technology) but only in so far as it is a moment of the material forces of production, is an object of property of particular social forces, and expresses a social relation which in turn corresponds to a particular historical period. . . . The ensemble of the material forces of production is at the same time a crystallisation of all past history and the basis of present and future history: it is both a document and an active and actual propulsive force.[28]

Here too he seeks to contrast socialist degeneration, which falls under the spell of the inexorable forces of scientific innovation without realising that they can contribute to increased exploitation, to a cultural impoverishment of society and its destruction by war. But the uncritical glorification of technology in socialist rhetoric goes hand in hand with the celebration of the exact sciences: Gramsci's polemic is sharply directed at this crux too. The philosophy of praxis as absolute historicism means that there can be no science without social relations, without their radical historicity. Gramsci goes further, challenging, from a more conventionalist than idealist perspective,[29] the objectivity of the real world, as understood by both positivism and the various socialisms. On the one hand, and in the light of his original reading of Marx's *Theses on Feuerbach*, Gramsci does away with the rigid distinction between subject and object, clarifying that there can be no knowledge of the world without a practical, and therefore a social and historical, transformation of the world. On the other hand, through the example of the notions of "East" and "West", he insists on the socio-historical, conventional, and linguistic character of scientific knowledge.[30] The convention in question, like language and its practices, does not exclude reality; rather, it reformulates the concept of matter, extending its scope and modifying its substance. Like in Lenin's critical study of the *Science of Logic*,[31] Gramsci insists on the ontological creativity of praxis.

3.4 Prophecy and Prediction

As clarified earlier, Benjamin views the present dialectically, that is, no longer as passage, but as time in equilibrium, a time that has "come to a standstill". In a preliminary note to the *Theses*, he further specifies:

> it defines precisely that present in which history is written each time. This present, strange as it may seem, is the subject of a prophecy. However, this prophecy does not announce something to come. It only allows us to know what the bell has tolled. And the politician knows better than anyone else how much, to say this, one needs to be a prophet. . . . The same can be said of history. The historian is a prophet facing backward. He discerns his own time in the medium of past calamities. But certainly, then, for him it all ends with the placidness of storytelling.[32]

The same theme, with some additions, recurs in a later note:

> The seer's gaze is kindled by the rapidly receding past. That is to say, the prophet has turned away from the future: he perceives the contours of the future in the fading light of the past as it sinks before him into the night of times. This prophetic relation to the future necessarily informs the attitude of the historian as Marx describes it, an attitude determined by actual social circumstances. Should criticism and prophecy be the categories that come together in the "redemption" of the past?[33]

First of all, we should clarify that for Benjamin *dialectics* and *critique* coincide. Better still, dialectics is also and above all the corrosive, destructive moment of theory, especially in historical research, but of course in praxis too. More precisely, historical materialism exists because revolutionary praxis in action exists. In the act of revolutionary praxis, time comes to a standstill, and in the present the image of past struggles flashes up, the struggles of the oppressed which, on the one hand, were defeated, but which, on the other, left unrealised possibilities to be realised in the present. The present of praxis is then the object of prophecy, because the seer, like the historian, turns his back on the future. Contrary to what is commonly believed, the rubble that accumulates in the past and with which the materialist historian works does not paralyse the conflict. It is true, however, that in this way "politics attains primacy over history".[34] "The Messiah truncates history"[35] in the same way as the class struggle. The suspension of *chronos* makes possible for praxis the invention of the new, which is not simply the result of a historical, teleological, or mechanistic development. The past, as Benjamin understands it, is a *discontinuum* extracted with constructive force, in the present critical moment, from the mere course of history. Following the Jewish prescription, the prophet does not question the future, but by recalling the past frees the future from the spell of determinism.

For Gramsci, too, politics takes precedence over history. More precisely, for him, historical-critical analysis is a weapon of praxis. The theme of prophecy is absent from Gramsci's work, but the concept of prediction stands out in various ways. As with Benjamin, the view of the future comes into conflict with the written history, necessary in its evolution, of mechanistic materialism. So much so, in fact, that, after addressing the subject several times before his arrest, he writes in the *Notebooks*:

> In reality one can "scientifically" foresee only the struggle, but not the concrete moments of the struggle, which cannot but be the results of opposing forces in continuous movement, which are never reducible to fixed quantities since within them quantity is continually becoming quality.[36]

Here we find the Hegelian dialectic – as Lenin read it. First of all, there is no prediction, in the sense of the natural sciences, in the class struggle or, more generally, in politics. Secondly, the political struggle is constantly marked by discontinuity, by opportunity, by fortune. In close analogy to the principles of thermodynamics, Gramsci often speaks of an "unstable equilibrium". Thirdly, history does not follow a linear evolution, instead there are leaps, sudden and unpredictable transitions from quantity to quality, or from necessity to freedom. Lenin again, undoubtedly, but also an original way of looking at the epistemological contribution of David Ricardo. In several notes, and also attempting an in-depth epistolary discussion with Piero Sraffa (via Tatiana Schucht), Gramsci insists that Ricardo introduced the notion of the "law of tendency" before Marx: against determinism and naturalism, the free position of certain conditions can, on the one hand, encourage consequences that are largely foreseen and, on the other, facilitate a new "automatism", which Gramsci calls "rationality". To those who claim that Marx and historical materialism are merely a philosophy of history, a Darwinian philosophy in the epistemological canon, Gramsci replies that Ricardo, with the method of "supposing that", made possible the elaboration of an original notion of "regularity", thus favouring the Marxian critique of political economy as a renewed and anti-idealistic philosophy of immanence, another name for the philosophy of praxis.[37]

3.5 "Organising Pessimism"

Gramsci's motto "pessimism of the intelligence, optimism of the will"[38] is well known and has become almost a cliché. Perhaps less clichéd, but equally well known, is Benjamin's formula in his text on the Surrealists,[39] "to organise pessimism". It would be foolish not to acknowledge the theoretical depth of both maxims, but this does not diminish the fact that both Gramsci and Benjamin wrote after the defeat of revolution in the West and with fascisms on the rampage – the former, in particular, in fascist captivity. The facts, if anything, make the claims even more radical and clear the field of any possible revisionist or anarchist use of them.

The two passages from Gramsci are particularly relevant even to the times we live in:

On the contrary, it is necessary to direct one's attention violently towards the present as it is, if one wishes to transform it. Pessimism of the intelligence, optimism of the will.[40]

And, in a subsequent notebook:

Every collapse brings with it intellectual and moral disorder. We need to create sober, patient people, who do not despair in the face of the worst horror and who do not become excited about every little thing. Pessimism of the intellect, optimism of the will.[41]

The first exhortation is undoubtedly Machiavellian. Only "the effectual truth of the thing", not things as they ought to be, are useful for political praxis. Putting an end to idle dreams, coming to terms with the real, which is harsh and tragic, consequently organising the fight. The second exhortation, on the other hand, sets out the style of the revolutionary militant: sobriety in the face of the "worst horror", no excitement over trivialities. Will needs to be understood in the sense

of the party, of the "modern prince". It is not to be confused with ideological voluntarism, incapable of becoming rooted in society, in its extremism and devotion
to the event. Will and organisation, must be thought of together, despite the difficulties and despite the historical period. Only organisation can tackle the crisis,
keep uncertainty at bay, and seize the opportunity.

In his short masterpiece on the Surrealists, Benjamin also insists on organisation of pessimism. The latter to be contrasted with the optimism of socialist
poetry, with the progressivism that dreams of sources where future generations
will be angelic and free. Benjamin expresses radical distrust in progress, hence
the urgency of communist organisation. Benjamin writes:

> For to organize pessimism means nothing other than to expel moral meta-
> phor from politics and to discover in political action a sphere reserved one
> hundred percent for images. This image sphere, however, can no longer be
> measured out by contemplation. If it is the double task of the revolutionary
> intelligentsia to overthrow the intellectual predominance of the bourgeoisie
> and to make contact with the proletarian masses, the intelligentsia has failed
> almost entirely in the second part of this task because it can no longer be per-
> formed contemplatively.[42]

A little further down, defining the imaginative space as "bodily", a product of
the dialectical destruction of individual interiority and of the "well-meaning"
bourgeois "intelligentsia", the criticism is directed against Bukharin's materialism, a constant polemical target in Gramsci's pages too. And matching Gramsci's
is the hatred of contemplation, the style that renders revolutionary intellectuals
incapable of contact with the masses. In the essay on Fuchs, almost a decade
later, he writes:

> Yet without confidence no class could, in the long run, hope to enter the politi-
> cal sphere with any kind of success. But it makes a difference whether this
> optimism directs itself towards the active strength of the class, or whether it
> centres on the conditions under which the class operates. Social Democracy
> leaned toward the latter, questionable, kind of optimism.[43]

Again in opposition to social democracy, and in words very similar to those of
the *Notebooks*, Benjamin argues that the only possible optimism is organisation,
the constant and creative organisation of the class struggle, despite the catastrophe of the present.

From different positions, but with the same focus on the decisive confrontation that takes place in the imagination, in language, in "complex superstructures", the thought of Benjamin and Gramsci has reached its full relevance at this
very moment. Weapons of thought against fascism, but also against socialism. In

the pursuit of a communist transformation to defeat the rampant capitalist catastrophe of war and economic, social, and environmental disaster.

Notes

1 See Stuart Hall, "Race, Articulation and Societies Structured in Dominance", in *Sociological Theories: Race and Colonialism* (Paris: UNESCO Publishing, 1980), 16–56 and "Gramsci's Relevance for the Study of Race and Ethnicity", *Journal of Communications Inquiry* 10, no. 2 (1986): 5–27; Gayatri Chakravorty Spivak, "Can the Subaltern Speak?", in *Marxism and the Interpretation of Culture*, ed. Cary Nelson e Lawrence Grossberg (Basingstoke: Macmillan, 1988), 271–313; Dipesh Chakrabarty, *Provincializing Europe: Postcolonial Thought and Historical Difference* (Princeton, NJ: Princeton University Press, 2000).
2 See Stuart Hall, "Gramsci's Relevance for the Study of Race and Ethnicity", *Journal of Communications Inquiry* 10, no. 2 (1986): 5–27.
3 Walter Benjamin, *The Arcades Project (1927–1940)*, ed. Howard Eiland and Kevin McLaughlin (Cambridge, MA and London: The Belknap Press of Harvard University Press, 2002), 470.
4 Antonio Gramsci, *The Gramsci Reader: Selected Writings 1926–1935*, ed. David Forgacs (New York: New York University Press, 2000), 193.
5 Walter Benjamin, "On the Concept of History", in *Selected Writings: Volume 4, 1938–1940*, ed. Howard Eiland and Michael W. Jennings (Cambridge, MA and London: The Belknap Press of Harvard University Press, 2006), 402.
6 Benjamin, "On the Concept of History", 396.
7 Benjamin, *The Arcades Project*, 463, 863.
8 See Walter Benjamin, "Eduard Fuchs, Collector and Historian", in *Selected Writings: Volume 3, 1935–1938*, ed. Howard Eiland and Michael W. Jennings (Cambridge, MA and London: The Belknap Press of Harvard University Press, 2006 [1937]), 260–302.
9 See Hans Magnus Enzensberger, *Zickzack* (Frankfurt am Main: Suhrkamp Verlag, 1997).
10 Gramsci, *The Gramsci Reader*, 326.
11 See Daniel Bensaïd, *Marx l'intempestif* (Paris: Fayard, 1995).
12 See Howard Eiland and Michael W. Jennings, *Walter Benjamin: A Critical Life* (Cambridge, MA and London: The Belknap Press of Harvard University Press, 2014).
13 See Antonio Negri, *Trentatré lezioni su Lenin* (Roma: manifestolibri, 2023 [1974]).
14 See Dario Gentili, *Il tempo della storia. Le tesi Sul concetto di storia di Walter Benjamin* (Macerata: Quodlibet, 2019 [2002]).
15 György Lukács, *History and Class Consciousness*, ed. Rodney Livingstone (Cambridge, MA: The MIT Press, 1971 [1923]), 223–255.
16 Lukács, *History and Class Consciousness*, 243.
17 Lukács, *History and Class Consciousness*, 243.
18 György Lukács, *Lenin: A Study on the Unity of His Thought* (London: Verso, 2009 [1924]), 31–32.
19 Benjamin, "On the Concept of History", 402.
20 Gramsci, *The Gramsci Reader*, 215–216.
21 See Paolo Capuzzo and Sandro Mezzadra, "Provincializing the Italian Readings of Gramsci", in *The Postcolonial Gramsci*, ed. Neelam Srivastava and Bairik Bhattacharya (London and New York: Routledge, 2012), 34–54.
22 See Christine Buci-Glucksmann, *Gramsci e lo Stato. Per una teoria materialista della filosofia* (Roma: Editori Riuniti, 1976).
23 Christine Buci-Glucksmann, *Gramsci e lo Stato*, 216.

24 Niccolò Machiavelli, *The Prince*, ed. Peter Bondanella (Oxford: Oxford University Press, 2005), 53.
25 Walter Benjamin, "The Work of Art in the Age of Its Technological Reproducibility", in *Selected Writings: Volume 4, 1938–1940*, ed. Howard Eiland and Michael W. Jennings (Cambridge, MA and London: The Belknap Press of Harvard University Press, 2006 [1936]), 270.
26 Benjamin, "Eduard Fuchs", 266.
27 Benjamin, "On the Concept of History", 270.
28 Antonio Gramsci, *Selections from the Prison Notebooks*, ed. Quintin Hoare and Geoffrey Nowell Smith (London: ElecBook, 1999), 837.
29 Nicola Badaloni, "Gramsci: la filosofia della prassi come previsione", in *Storia del marxismo* (Torino: Einaudi, 1981), vol. 3, 251–340.
30 Gramsci, *Selections from the Prison Notebooks*, 809–811.
31 Vladimir Ilyich Lenin, *Philosophical Notebooks*, Marxist Internet Archiv. Public Domain. Accessed March 23, 2024, www.marxists.org/archive/lenin/works/cw/volume38.htm
32 Walter Benjamin, *Über den Begriff der Geschichte* (Berlin: Suhrkamp Verlag, 2010 [1940]), 112.
33 Benjamin, "On the Concept of History", 407.
34 Benjamin, *The Arcades Project*, 388–389.
35 Benjamin, *Über den Begriff der Geschichte*, 131.
36 Gramsci, *Selections From the Prison Notebooks*, 796.
37 Gramsci, *Selections From the Prison Notebooks*, 755–761.
38 Gramsci attributed the motto to Romain Rolland in an article written as early as 1920, while Benjamin adopted the expression "organising pessimism" from the surrealist Pierre Naville. Unquestionably, however, it was Gramsci and Benjamin who gave fame to the two maxims.
39 Walter Benjamin, "Surrealism", in *Selected Writings, Volume 2, Part 1, 1927–1930*, ed. Howard Eiland and Michael W. Jennings (Cambridge, MA and London: The Belknap Press of Harvard University Press, 2005 [1929]), 207–221.
40 Gramsci, *Selections From the Prison Notebooks*, 395.
41 Antonio Gramsci, *Quaderni del carcere*, ed. Valentino Gerratana (Torino: Einaudi, 1977).
42 Benjamin, "Surrealism", 217.
43 Benjamin, "Eduard Fuchs", 273–274.

Bibliography

Badaloni, Nicola. "Gramsci: la filosofia della prassi come previsione". In *Storia del marxismo*, vol. 3, 251–340. Torino: Einaudi, 1981.
Benjamin, Walter. *The Arcades Project (1927–1940)*, edited by Howard Eiland, and Kevin McLaughlin. Cambridge, MA and London: The Belknap Press of Harvard University Press, 2002.
Benjamin, Walter. "Surrealism (1929)". In *Selected Writings: Volume 2, Part 1, 1927–1930*, edited by Howard Eiland, and Michael W. Jennings, 207–221. Cambridge, MA and London: The Belknap Press of Harvard University Press, 2005.
Benjamin, Walter. "Eduard Fuchs, Collector and Historian". In *Selected Writings: Volume 3, 1935–1938*, edited by Howard Eiland, and Michael W. Jennings, 260–302. Cambridge, MA and London: The Belknap Press of Harvard University Press, 2006.
Benjamin, Walter. "On the Concept of History". In *Selected Writings: Volume 4, 1938–1940*, edited by Howard Eiland, and Michael W. Jennings, 389–400. Cambridge, MA and London: The Belknap Press of Harvard University Press, 2006.

Benjamin, Walter. "The Work of Art in the Age of Its Technological Reproducibility". In *Selected Writings: Volume 4, 1938–1940*, edited by Howard Eiland, and Michael W. Jennings, 258–283. Cambridge, MA and London: The Belknap Press of Harvard University Press, 2006.

Benjamin, Walter. *Über den Begriff der Geschichte*. Berlin: Suhrkamp Verlag, 2010.

Bensaïd, Daniel. *Marx l'intempestif*. Paris: Fayard, 1995.

Buci-Glucksmann, Christine. *Gramsci e lo Stato. Per una teoria materialista della filosofia*. Roma: Editori Riuniti, 1976.

Capuzzo, Paolo, and Mezzadra, Sandro. "Provincializing the Italian Readings of Gramsci". In *The Postcolonial Gramsci*, edited by Neelam Srivastava, and Bairik Bhattacharya, 34–54. London and New York: Routledge, 2012.

Chakrabarty, Dipesh. *Provincializing Europe: Postcolonial Thought and Historical Difference*. Princeton, NJ: Princeton University Press, 2000.

Dilthey, Wilhelm. *Einleitung in die Geisteswissenschaften*. Leipzig: Verlag von Duncker & Humblot, 1883.

Eiland, Howard, and Jennings, Michael W. *Walter Benjamin: A Critical Life*. Cambridge, MA and London: The Belknap Press of Harvard University Press, 2014.

Enzensberger, Hans Magnus. *Zickzack*. Frankfurt am Main: Suhrkamp Verlag, 1997.

Garin, Eugenio. "Storicismo". In *Enciclopedia del Novecento*. Roma: Istituto dell'Enciclopedia Italiana, 1984.

Gentili, Dario. *Il tempo della storia. Le tesi Sul concetto di storia di Walter Benjamin*. Macerata: Quodlibet, 2019.

Gramsci, Antonio. *Quaderni del carcere*, edited by Valentino Gerratana. Torino: Einaudi, 1977.

Gramsci, Antonio. *Selections from the Prison Notebooks*, edited by Quintin Hoare, and Geoffrey Nowell Smith. London: ElecBook, 1999.

Gramsci, Antonio. *The Gramsci Reader: Selected Writings 1926–1935*, edited by David Forgacs. New York: New York University Press, 2000.

Hall, Stuart. "Race, Articulation and Societies Structured in Dominance". In *Sociological Theories: Race and Colonialism*, 16–56. Paris: UNESCO Publishing, 1980.

Hall, Stuart. "Gramsci's Relevance for the Study of Race and Ethnicity". *Journal of Communications Inquiry* 10, no. 2 (1986): 5–27.

Korsch, Karl. *Marxismus und Philosophie*. Leipzig: C.L. Hirschfield, 1923.

Lenin, Vladimir Ilyich. *Philosophical Notebooks*. Marxist Internet Archiv. Public Domain. Accessed March 23, 2024, www.marxists.org/archive/lenin/works/cw/volume38.htm.

Lenin, Vladimir Ilyich. *Two Tactics of Social-Democracy in the Democratic Revolution*. Lenin Internet Archiv. Public Domain. Accessed March 23, 2024, www.marxists.org/archive/lenin/works/1905/tactics/.

Lukács, György. *History and Class Consciousness*, edited by Rodney Livingstone. Cambridge, MA: The MIT Press, 1971.

Lukács, György. *Lenin: A Study on the Unity of His Thought*. London: Verso, 2009.

Machiavelli, Niccolò. *The Prince*, edited by Peter Bondanella. Oxford: Oxford University Press, 2005.

Montanelli, Marina, and Palma, Massimo, eds. *Tecniche di esposizione. Walter Benjamin e la riproduzione tecnica dell'opera d'arte*. Macerata: Quodlibet, 2016.

Negri, Antonio. *Trentatré lezioni su Lenin*. Roma: manifestolibri, 2023.

Spivak, Gayatri Chakravorty. "Can the Subaltern Speak?". In *Marxism and the Interpretation of Culture*, edited by Cary Nelson e Lawrence Grossberg, 271–313. Basingstoke: Macmillan, 1988.

PART 2

Revolution, Counter-Revolution, and Passive Revolution

4

PRESENT, PRESENCE, PASSIVE REVOLUTION

Gramsci and Benjamin

Vittoria Borsò

4.1 The Present in and of Crisis

> If the ruling class has lost consensus, that is, if it no longer "leads" but only "rules" – it possesses sheer coercive power – this actually means that the great masses have become detached from traditional ideologies, they no longer believe what they previously used to believe, etc. The crisis consists precisely in the fact that the old is dying and the new cannot be born: in this interregnum, morbid phenomena of the most varied kind come to pass.[1]
>
> The Copernican revolution in historical perception is as follows. Formerly, it was thought that a fixed point had been found in "what has been" and one saw the present engaged in tentatively concentrating the forces of knowledge on this ground. Now this relation is to be overturned, and what has been is to become the dialectical reversal – the flash of awakened consciousness.[2]

I intend here to bring focus to the spatio-temporal configuration of the present, investigating the extent to which it is linked to the phenomenon Gramsci describes as "passive revolution", a concept developed from the diagnosis of a great crisis involving the disintegration of national apparatuses, which sees social groups detach themselves from the State. A crisis, then, of authority and the State, a conflict between nationalities or economic individualism and a planned economy we would describe today as global. In the passage cited, Gramsci refers directly to the crisis in Italy and Europe for which politics is unable to offer any remedy. This crisis identified by Gramsci is one of Old Europe's decadence combined with the advent of fascism and national socialism, a source of international disintegration of the old without any hope that a new might be born. The temporality of the crisis has a latent threat of "morbid" phenomena, in which Gramsci presages fascism and a new war.[3]

DOI: 10.4324/9781003457039-7

Gramsci's scepticism refers to the present as a particular historic moment. But it remains to be seen whether, in the research of practical tools of transformation carried out in his *Notebooks* within the context of passive revolution, the analysis of the present takes on a particular relevance. The two quotes that introduce my reflections refer to different dimensions. Gramsci is well aware of the political situation, viewed by Benjamin with the same profound scepticism. It is, however, faith in any potential mutations of material praxis that unites them. But while Gramsci's hopes in his *Prison Notebooks* are focused on new social practices that find one of their clearest expressions in his analysis of Fordism in America, Benjamin instead considers those operations linked to cultural or aesthetic praxis. The actors Gramsci refers to are the workers, whereas Benjamin's reference is to the intellectuals. He emphasises the political importance of "reawakening" in the present, where the present becomes the space of the dialectical image that makes it possible to "wake up" and abandon the myths of history. In this dimension, and that of historical materialism, we once again find harmony between and a significant moment for both thinkers, who have left their mark throughout twentieth-century political philosophy and cultural studies.

The apprehension about the great political and economic crisis of the 1930s is, for both, the driving force behind the creation of a "new" political philosophy of history. It is therefore worthwhile to delve into the potentialities of the present of this crisis throughout the various phases of Gramsci's thought, starting with his *Notebook 22* (1922) on Americanism and Fordism. Such potentialities are, in my opinion, visible if we consider crisis not as a situation or political dispositif in the ways it validates power but as a spatio-temporal configuration of a mode of existence in which temporality is the field of the possible, understood as unforeseen. In this configuration, the present becomes particularly dense and sensitive, and the materiality and singularity of the experienceable can give rise to historical ruptures and bifurcations, to moments of possible new beginnings even if these have not been borne out in consolidated discourse, according to the interpretation Foucault provides of Nietzsche's genealogy.[4]

Throughout this chapter, I will consider the missing dialogue between Gramsci and Benjamin, whose points of agreement shed light on crucial moments in the analysis of historical temporality.

4.2 Revolution and Passive Revolution: Gramsci

While Benjamin does not deal head-on with the formation of the political and the emergence of a collective revolutionary body, Gramsci is explicit when it comes to the relationship between social condition and the political formation of class, between the structural localisation of the productive and social pyramid and the construction of a political project with hegemonic and counter-hegemonic capability. But rather counter-hegemonic in the sense of a movement, passive revolution, which initially indicates a special path for Italian politics and that of other European states in the absence of a Jacobean moment, he refers here to the possible formation of a collective will that, even without movements of struggle, is capable of transforming the vulnerability of subaltern classes towards or against the material and psychological initiatives for co-option employed by the dominant classes. Passive revolution is a transformation that comes about thanks to a social vector rather than a political or class movement providing leaders and a potentially organised and self-instituting autonomy of worker classes. Contrary to the permanent revolution of Marx and Engels, which Gramsci views as discontinuous continuity, as a movement of overcoming and actualisation, of transformation and conservation,[5] the oxymoron of passive revolution, half-way between noun and adjective, indicates the danger of passive revolutions, in which, despite change being brought by the working or subaltern classes, the hegemonic validation remains in the hands of the ruling classes, historically the bourgeoisie, which has the task of assimilating and carrying out "from on high" those innovations that the workers' movement had introduced to world history. We know full well that in Europe, at the beginning of the twentieth century, this task was not carried out, leading to the outbreak of two world wars. So, not only is transformation possible in passive revolutions but so is conservation. Despite this, the importance of passive revolution, which evolves in Gramsci's thought alongside the development of his reflections and the events he pinpoints, is yet to be seen. Not only on a historical level (as a transformation that leads to a modern alternative) but in particular in the scrutiny of structures on a macro-social level where it is necessary to insist on the existing contingency on micro levels. Here we see a particular consensus with Benjamin's historical materialism.

In the most diverse versions, or rather, contexts, in which Gramsci elaborates on this concept between 1930 and 1935, the contradictions of modernisation[6] and the temporality of crisis are notable constants. It is the present that potentially opens history up to alternatives time and again. As with all of the key categories in *Notebooks*, passive revolution also has a double nature because it represents both a paradigm of historical comprehension and a tool of practical transformation. Passive revolution can refer to a change of era and comes about as an alternative to revolution as a movement of war, examples of which are the French and Russian revolutions. It is an alternative that is, potentially, the result of a modernity that is different from that centring the power and global dominion of capitalism because it emerges in subaltern classes through transformations in customs, lifestyles, materiality, and technology. It does not need the emancipatory movement of ideologies. All it requires (though this is not nothing) is the materiality of praxis, of practical materials that eliminate the dualism between subject and object, founding other relations and establishing new ontologies.

The emergence and actualisation of latent potentialities in the present of crisis that are not visible in a macro model of political action require space, actors, and practical materials in order to develop living, historically tangible forms of a passive revolution that does not relapse into a conservation of the old. Gramsci makes this clear in his comments on permanent revolution in his preface to Marx in 1850.[7] In this sense, for Gramsci, we can and must revisit the past and even the Unification of Italy as a possible locus of "molecular changes".[8] It is these kinds of transformations through which the potential for a passive revolution might emerge as the singular and common praxis of a present understood as an intermediate yet continuous state of instituting praxis.[9]

4.3 Fordism/Americanism, or the Productivity of Material Modes of Existence

The potential of passive revolution can be seen in the notebook on Americanism and Fordism. The geopolitical and geo-cultural insight shown by Gramsci is exceptional. Starting with a material analysis of Fordism, he pinpoints within Americanism the global hegemony that ensures its continuation. The scientific rationalisation promoted by Taylor and perfected in the 1930s by Henry Ford overtakes the entire American society to the point of becoming a typically American way of life. Gramsci puts into focus the "passage from the old economic individualism to the planned economy".[10] With his critical reading of Marx's work on political economy, in which Gramsci recognises in the organisation of work the emergence and productivity of the worker's "free time" through the passage to a rationalisation of production, he brings into focus the forms of resistance of the working class (and, in part, of the dominant classes). It is the resistance "of the 'subaltern' forces, which have to be 'manipulated' and rationalised".[11] Gramsci then extends this analysis of Fordism to the comparison between less developed and more advanced societies, asking whether the corporatism of the fascist Italian state might become a form of Taylorism, in which the parasitic strata in Italy and Europe – the "pensioners of economic history"[12] – lead to particularly brutal forms of Fordism, particularly in the de-professionalisation of the manual worker in favour of the automatic function of the machine, the affirmation of the mass production worker alongside the decline of the artisanal worker, and the radicalisation of Taylorism through Ford, who introduces the capillary control not only of work but of the workers' consciences and private lives. In *Notebooks*, Gramsci returns many times over to the difficulties of introducing new forms of economy such as Fordism to Italy and other countries that use "backwards capitalism" in a productive way, analysing with precision the structure of the economy, industry, and the market in relation to the mass of workers found in factories and on agricultural estates. With almost visionary precision, he describes the deepening of geopolitical and social asymmetries that accompany the cult of profit even in twenty-first-century neo-liberalism.[13]

In terms of Fordism in America, Gramsci highlights the internal contradiction of the capitalist process that reduces the worker to "trained gorilla", with control over their private lives exerted by the big industrialists, transforming the economic administration of the factory into the widespread surveillance of culture and politics, but does not criticise innovation or rationalisation. Effectively, the contradiction between disciplining and the production of free time and new lifestyles can be the fulcrum of an antagonism capable of giving rise to transformations that act on a psycho-physical level. Furthermore, precisely because of these internal contradictions, because of the hegemony in which it results, Fordism can foment a different sensibility, a new mentality, and a different kind of common sense. The ideological structure of Fordism, despite having as its goal the maintaining, defending, and developing of the theoretical and ideological front in society, involves all kinds of material forms of public life: newspapers, magazines, libraries, schools, the press, clubs, and so on. From the subaltern classes comes a material praxis with the potential for liberation.[14] The objective of domesticating the worker could well be destined to fail, as every material activity potentially contributes to intellectual developments. Therefore, to the list of internal contradictions inherent in capitalism, we can add those within the social field that deepen its organic crisis.

In this analysis of Fordism, we find ourselves faced with the possibly indeterminate nature of the present moment. Moreover, resistance to the rationalisation of workers is also formed in sections of the dominant forces. This is how Gramsci's text on Fordism and Americanism begins: "the 'subaltern' forces, which have to be 'manipulated' and rationalised to serve new ends, naturally put up a resistance. But resistance is also offered by certain sectors of the dominant forces, or at least by forces which are allied to those which are dominant".[15]

Let's just consider the comparison between the new and old continents in the reflections on Fordism and Americanism that, with the thesis of the political burden of European history, allows us to reflect upon where they agree with Benjamin's historical diagnosis. With an insight that is just as pertinent today, Gramsci observes that the contradictions of Fordism, which in America lead to a transformation of forms of life, manifest themselves in the old continent with "the old, anachronistic, demographic social structure of Europe".[16] As such, the introduction of Fordism to Europe finds " 'intellectual' and 'moral' resistance, and takes place in particularly brutal and insidious forms, and by means of the most extreme coercion".[17] What follows is the famous diagnosis of the European inability to open itself up to modern forms of production and market circulation: "To put it crudely, Europe would like to have a full barrel and a drunken wife, to have all the benefits which Fordism brings to its competitive power while retaining its army of parasites who, by consuming vast sums of surplus value, aggravate initial costs and reduce competitive power on the international market".[18]

America was not weighed down by this historical burden. Quite the opposite. Americanism consists of hinging one's entire life on production. Europe, on the other hand, has too many mediators, a truly historical burden. Using this, Gramsci begins on a theme that Benjamin goes on to develop, comparing the old and the new world on both the plane of space and that of time. If we now move on to Benjamin, it is to consider two moments in which we can see commonalities with Gramsci: historical comparativism or praxis of the present, and the need to analyse the materiality of the praxis not only on a social macro level but on the micro level of singularity, perceptions, and sensations in material situations.

4.4   Benjamin and the Critique of Revolution: "Destructive Character" and the Space of the Present as a Crossroads

The following comparison with Benjamin refers to his method of considering history, confronting historicism with historical materialism. In Benjamin's 1937 essay *Eduard Fuchs, Collector and Historian*, we can already find the constellation of theses that will be evolved in the 1940 *On the Concept of History*: "Cultural history presents its contents by means of contrast. Yet for the historical materialist this contrast is illusory and is conjured up by false consciousness".[19] From this foundation, Benjamin will claim in the seventh thesis *on the Concept of History*: "There is no document of culture which is not at the same time a document of barbarism. No cultural history has yet done justice to this fundamental state of affairs, and it can hardly hope to do so".[20] In perfect harmony with Gramsci, Benjamin identifies the problem with the traditional, idealistic ideology of the history of culture, which considers artefacts without placing them in relation with the process of production that has produced or received them. Furthermore, given the idealisation of the concept of culture, "cultural history lacks the destructive element which authenticates both dialectical thought and the experience of the dialectical thinker".[21] The distance Benjamin expresses towards the concept of militant revolution adopted by the left can be seen in his 1929 critique of Surrealism's political compromise. Instead, he prefers revolt that abstains from binding the dynamic of destroying the old structures to a revolutionary politics. It is in his lucid 1931 fragment *The Destructive Character* that Benjamin, in his character study à la Theophrastus and La Bruyère, drafts the concept of "destructive character" as a way of opening up new paths without specific political purpose.

We are focusing on this concept because, although it is aimed at intellectuals[22] rather than at the "new" worker's praxis of life, it shows an affinity with the production of the present as a possible space of mutation and transformation, a space that can correspond to the productive dimension of passive revolution.

For Benjamin, the destructive character has a praxis that always stays "fresh and young". It is a praxis against the "étui-man", a praxis that aimed at creating not a solitary genius but a person who moves in and among the crowd, who provokes and experiences *shock*, enamoured of being intentionally misunderstood and who has only one "watchword: make room; only one activity: clearing away. His need for fresh air and open space is stronger than any hatred".[23] The destructive character razes structures in order to produce "empty" spaces and possible paths, without fixing any actions or positions (without wars of position, as Gramsci would say). In this fragment, in which the syntax highlights movement, original- ity, and pleasure, the messianic nature of the present as *Jetzt-Zeit*, as an image of the past and hope for future redemption, is muted. Here, more than anything else, Benjamin sees the space of the present as an empty space, open to various paths. In this fragment, the motifs that refer to crisis are brought together in a *Denkbild*. For Benjamin, the destructive character represents an *engagement* for the politics of change, the possible turning point, crisis[24]: "The destructive character sees nothing permanent. . . . Because he sees ways everywhere, he always positions himself at crossroads. No moment can know what the next will bring".[25] The present is this moment without pre-established actions or aims, it is a moment of potentiality. The end of the fragment clarifies the temporality of the praxis of the destructive character: the tension between past and future produces present as an opening to a *Schwell*e, a threshold, understood as a crossroads of paths and potential for change, as potentialities of passage without end or aim, as an open- ing without passing to the other side.[26] This is the modality that corresponds to the historical being, Benjamin points out, whose fundamental sentiment is their pessimism towards the passing of things, while the relationship between past and future implies a present whose most productive modality consists in the avail- ability to bear in mind the fact that everything could go wrong: "The destruc- tive character has the consciousness of historical man, whose deepest emotion is an insuperable mistrust of the course of things and a readiness at all times to recognize that everything can go wrong. Therefore, the destructive character is reliability itself".[27]

Unlike Gramsci, who has a greater belief in possible changes, Benjamin's pessimism is undoubtedly an echo of the dark political situation during which he writes. However, from 1930 to 1931 generally and particularly in this fragment, pessimism is not synonymous with mistrust, but with a suspension of every structure and critique of revolutionary aims. It is the method of production of an open present, with potential paths that in the *Passagearbeit* are labyrinths of image spaces (*Bildraum*) – a present that is moved by *shock*.[28] This method that uses *shock* to defeat the "given" without revolutions or revolutionary demands is highly significant both to the concept of history developed in *Eduard Fuchs, der Sammler, der Historiker* and condensed in *Theses*,[29] and to the theory of the avant-garde, implicit in Benjamin's writing, where *shock* is the preferred method of avant-garde movements such as Dadaism, because it transforms reality into a *Bildraum*.[30] In his 1929 essay, this critique of surrealism revolves around the political compromise with militant left, with Benjamin expressing his distance to the concept of revolution. The function of avant-garde art should instead be to "organize pessimism [meaning nothing other than] to expel moral metaphor from politics and to discover in political action a sphere reserved one hundred percent for images".[31] Benjamin defines the characteristic trait of the left-wing bourgeois position as represented by the surrealism of André Breton and "its irremediable coupling of idealistic morality with political practice".[32] The revolution for Breton represents the truth of the political dream of art. However, the dream has no truth, contrary to what is stated by Breton in his second Manifesto of 1930.[33] Benjamin, however, maintains that it must be the *Bildraum* of the material manifestation of dream that inspires political praxis, referencing the *Traité du style* with which Aragon, in 1928, detached himself from the militant role laid out in Breton's diktat. The function of such a poetic praxis is to discover a "sphere of images" within reality. The praxis consists of a "dialectical annihilation" through the *Witz*, the misunderstandings and images in movement that demolish the myth: "precisely after such dialectical annihilation – this will still be a sphere of images and, more concretely, of bodies".[34] It is therefore a praxis that needs a destructive principle, that acts to suspend the old structure in order to make way for possible social modifications, irrespective of the political mythologies that would fall into the linearity and the idealism of the history of culture.

The historical materialism Benjamin sets in motion with his writing process and the space of images in which he acts as a writing subject – the similarity with Gramsci's asymptomatic writing has been studied extensively[35] – is also the principle observed in Eduard Fuchs as a collector. Signalling the ambivalence of traditionalist historian Fuchs, Benjamin criticises both the idealised vision of revolution and the democratic tradition in nineteenth-century France, and the French Revolution's transformation into hegemony, to use Gramscian terminology.[36]

In Fuchs, who is inspired by French intellectuals, only the collector's part leads to the avant-garde of historical materialism that would change the concept of culture.[37] Instead, the historian's German inheritance has, as a consequence, a national moralism that not even psychoanalysis is capable of eliminating. And it is because of this "unconscious" moralism that Fuchs directs his criticism exclusively at the conscience of the middle classes,[38] developing a revisionist understanding of the French revolutions.[39] As a historian, Fuchs does not recognise that conscience is not decisive for historical fact but actually the form of behaving oneself caused by the position assumed within the production process. It is precisely this aspect that remains unconscious, while ideology is instead overestimated and the art used to legitimise the dominant sociopolitical situation is idealised.[40] For Benjamin also, this attitude is responsible for the missing relationship between those who hold power in economic life and those who are being exploited. It is a lacking relationship because between them "an apparatus of legal and administrative bureaucracies intervenes between the rulers of economic life and the exploited. The members of these bureaucracies no longer function as fully responsible moral subjects, and their 'sense of duty' is nothing but the unconscious expression of this deformation".[41]

In the concept of culture, in its being based on the praxis of production and material experience, key moments in the philosophy of praxis, we recognise the agreement with Gramsci that praxis lies at the basis of the theory of existing contradictions in society and, therefore, of that political theory that contrasts the art of governance as hegemony over the subaltern classes.[42] More than anything else, praxis is the expression of will by these classes to educate themselves in the art of governance. Benjamin is in agreement when it comes to the relationship between culture and economy, but with the difference that the emancipation of the so-called subaltern classes does not exist in Benjamin's thought, which tends instead towards a critique of the bourgeois society. As Benjamin states in *The Arcade Project*: "It is not the economic origins of culture that will be presented, but the expression of the economy in its culture. At issue, in other words, is the attempt to grasp an economic process as perceptible *Ur*-phenomenon, from out of which proceed all manifestations of life in the arcades (and, accordingly, in the nineteenth century)".[43] Culture is not manifested as ideology or *Überbau*, nor as tradition or Spirit, but in the historical-dialectic process, mediatised by the conditions of production. In *Eduard Fuchs, der Sammler und der Historiker*, the collector of caricatures, erotic art, and customs is viewed by Benjamin as a pioneer of this kind of historical materialism. While historicism generates an eternal image of bygone eras, historical materialism produces a unique and material experience of every past, as a genealogist of every present moment: "To bring about the consolidation of experience with history, which is original for every present, is the task of historical materialism".[44] For the subject, this difference with historicism is fundamental. While historicism acts on consciousness in the same way it does a possession, much like the power of capital on work, historical materialism opens up the subject to new experiences and works, acting, therefore, on micro levels.

The similarities here with Gramsci are significant. In *Past and Present*, Gramsci's dissensus with Benedetto Croce is directed at the historical idealism of the "State-Government", the elitist idea of culture and the inability to conceive of a civil society.[45] One of the fundamental arguments behind this dissensus is the concept of "historical dignity" which, according to Gramsci, "only the struggle and its outcome – which is not to say its immediate outcome but the outcome that manifests itself in a permanent victory – will reveal that which is rational or irrational, that which is 'worthy' of victory because it continues the past in its own way and moves beyond it".[46] The parallel between Gramsci's rejection of Croce and Benjamin's rejection of Eduard Fuchs' historicism once again demonstrates their strict adhesion to historical materialism. As a "critical phase in philosophy",[47] historical materialism reinterprets Marxism as the philosophy of praxis, human nature as a "collection of social relationships",[48] and material as "socially and historically organised for production" and belonging to "a human relationship".[49]

4.5 Materiality of the Contradictions and Temporalities of the Present

From the disenchantment with history and the reawakening from historical myths in the often-conflictual relationship between past and present, a perceptive density of the present time can emerge, dissociated from the weight of tradition and the future collateral – a present whose materiality stimulates new forms of sensibility, new praxis, an alternative mode of existence.

> *Past and present.* How the present is a *criticism* of the past, besides land because of "surpassing" it. But should the past be discarded for this reason? What should be discarded is that which the present has "intrinsically" criticized and that part of ourselves which corresponds to it. What does this mean? That we must have an exact consciousness of this real criticism and express it not only theoretically but *politically*. In other words, we must stick closer to the present, which we ourselves have helped create, while conscious of the past and its continuation (and revival).[50]

For Gramsci, adherence to the present and the transformation with regard to the past are expressed in the praxis of conflict and sociopolitical mutations in which the crisis of the past continues to modulate the present making constant criticism necessary – or, as Benjamin might say, a constant reawakening from past and present myths.

Both Gramsci and Benjamin pinpoint the emergence of the present in the most extreme point of disenchantment with the path of history. With this crisis of historical disenchantment, the present could initiate a politics that is a field of potentialities, as a way of opening up the course of history once more. It is here that the common critical attitude to orthodox Marxism manifests itself. In both, the present expresses the criticism of the cult of progress and its illusory promises.[51] For Gramsci and Benjamin, universal history is not the completion of a destiny nor an essence, but something that has become fact but that could have potentially taken a different course. It is when historical promises disappear that what Benjamin calls the catastrophe of history takes place, referring to the condition in which a "precious instant" reawakens or is born and from which everything becomes possible once more. Here, the potentiality for a different politics emerges, one that could bring about the threefold crisis of contemporary capitalism: the crisis of modern historicism, of emancipation strategies, and of critical theories.[52]

Benjamin makes the observation that disenchantment renders the present materially possible and politically productive when, fully aware of the sovereign's weakness, the conflict becomes a conflict of forces between various alternatives. He states that it is the prince's task to avoid a state of exception, and certainly not to decide on one, as the political theology of Carl Schmitt asserts. Benjamin's model is that of the Baroque sovereign,[53] characterised by their melancholy and inability to make a decision. It is a melancholy that, according to the postmodern interpretation of allegory, comes from the abyss, somewhere between signs and reality, and which a political reading would describe as a symptom of the void between symbol and power, between idea and the real. A void that makes it impossible to make a decision when faced with an extreme crisis in the state of exception and which could reopen the very foundations of politics, that is, the One's indecision entrusts the decision to the conflict of the different parts.[54] With this indecision in the present of the crisis, time is disconnected from the spatiality that segments it, making the present a mere interval between past and future.

Benjamin elaborates the phenomenology of the present more explicitly in the context of the *flaneur*. The *flâneur*'s time is slowed down, they abandon the fury of the future to immerse themselves in the perception of materiality that surrounds them without consuming it. The metaphor of the tortoise, used several times in *The Arcade Project* and in his study of Baudelaire,[55] expresses the intense becoming of the present that is produced in the labyrinths of the modern city. If Paris is representative of modernity in the nineteenth century, then that of the twentieth century is Berlin.

Here, the situation of the *flaneur* leads to the formation of new subjects, as evidenced in the essay *Die Wiederkehr des Flaneurs*, which is dedicated to Franz Hessel's book, *Spazieren in Berlin*. The socio-historical value of modern Berlin lies in the fact that those passing through have left the enjoyment of leisure behind them, a previously aristocratic pursuit that became middle class in the 1800s. The protagonists, on the other hand, are comparable to the "*Lumpensammlern*", marginalised figures who are poor, destitute werewolves that roam "in a social wilderness".[56] To use Gramsci's terminology, they are proletarian figures who invade the cities, demolishing the bourgeois predominance of the city's image. With his reference to "wild sociality", Benjamin highlights the destructive, and therefore potentially performative element of this new urban dimension. The city becomes inaccessible to reason, it is transformed into a "crime scene" – the perception of which is analysed in more depth in his 1935 essay on technical reproducibility in reference to Atget's photography, in which the streets of Paris are emptied of any human presence. In these photographs, the camera holds fleeting and mysterious images. The observer's *shock* upon seeing the scene halts any association with the known[57]: "To pry an object from its shell, to destroy its aura, is the mark of a perception whose 'sense of the universal equality of things' has increased to such a degree that it extracts it even from a unique object by means of reproduction. Thus [it] is manifested in the field of perception",[58] while the *shock* of the void makes impossible the recognition of the real. Echoing the destructive character, Benjamin describes the space using the image of an emptied apartment that does not yet have new tenants. The experience of the *shock* and the disintegration of the aura are the conditions that give weight to the sensory experience (*Erfahrung*) and, as for the collapse of the myths of history, Benjamin sees Baudelaire as a poet who "shines in the sky of the Second Empire as a 'star without atmosphere'",[59] invoking a sensitive and corporeal presence that renders the present an instant open to the advent of potentiality. With the intensity of sensitive experience, the present opens itself up to a form of emancipation that is not derived from ideological foundations but from a sensitive reawakening in the activities of the body, material praxis, and experience.

In the becoming of the present, the evenemential quality changes the rhythm of the bodily experience, generating an open field of possibility. The present is a space in which a form comes into being through material practices of relation, which require a micro-analysis of that which is experienced (Benjamin) and the materiality of the praxis (Gramsci). By revisiting Benjamin and Gramsci using this interpretation, we discover a latent ontology of becoming that can solicit a political praxis of restructuring and transforming the space of the present and of presence in every single subject.

Notes

1 Antonio Gramsci, *Prison Notebooks*, ed. Joseph A. Buttigieg (New York: Columbia University Press, 1996), vol. 2, 32–33 [Notebook 3, § 34].
2 Walter Benjamin, *The Arcades Project* (Cambridge, MA and London, UK: Harvard University Press, 1999), 388.
3 See Marcello Mustè, *Rivoluzioni passive. Il mondo tra le due guerre nei Quaderni del carcere di Gramsci* (Rome: Viella, 2022). On the difference between Marx and Gramsci in the conceptualisation of crisis, see Dario Gentili, *The Age of Precarity: Endless Crisis as an Art of Government* (London and New York: Verso, 2021).
4 See Michel Foucault, "Nietzsche, Genealogy, History", in *The Foucault Reader*, ed. Paul Rabinow (New York: Pantheon Books, 1984), 76–100.
5 See Peter D. Thomas, "Gramsci's Revolutions: Passive and Permanent", *Modern Intellectual History* 17, no. 1 (2020): 153.
6 See Antonio Gramsci, *Quaderni del carcere*, ed. Valentino Gerratana (Turin: Einaudi, 1975), vol. 2, 961 [Notebook 8, § 35].
7 In 1932 (April–May), the concept of hegemony as an overcoming of permanent revolution becomes increasingly salient with his analysis of fascism. See Antonio Gramsci, *Selections from the Prison Notebooks*, ed. Quentin Hoare and Geoffrey Nowell Smith (London: Laurence and Wishart, 1992), 175–184 [Notebook 13, § 17].

8 "One may apply to the concept of passive revolution (documenting it from the Italian Risorgimento) the interpretative criterion of molecular changes which in fact progressively modify the pre-existing composition of forces, and hence become the matrix of new changes." Gramsci, *Selections from the Prison Notebooks*, 109 [Notebook 15, § 11].

9 See Roberto Esposito, *Instituting Thought: Three Paradigms of Political Ontology* (Cambridge: Polity Press, 2021).

10 Gramsci, *Selections From the Prison Notebooks*, 279 [Notebook 22, §1].

11 Gramsci, *Selections From the Prison Notebooks*, 279.

12 Gramsci, *Selections From the Prison Notebooks*, 281 [Notebook 22, §1].

13 "In those countries that use backwards capitalism and that have an economic composition that balances large modern industry, small and medium agriculture and sharecropping, the masses of workers and peasants are not considered a market. The market for industry is considered abroad, and in those backwards countries where there is a possibility of political penetration for the creation of colonies and areas of influence. Industry, with its internal protectionism and low salaries, procures foreign markets with an authentic and permanent dumping." Gramsci, *Quaderni del carcere*, vol. 2, 799 [Notebook 6, §135].

14 "Passage from the purely economic (or egotistical-passionate) moment to the ethical-political moment, the greater elaboration of structure in the superstructure within the conscience of men. This also means the passage from 'objective to subjective' and from 'need to freedom'. The structure of external force that crushes the man, assimilating him, rendering him passive, is transformed into a means for freedom, into a tool with which to create a new ethical-political form, into an origin of new initiatives." Gramsci, *Quaderni del carcere*, vol. 2, 1244 [Notebook 10, § 6].

15 Gramsci, *Selections From the Prison Notebooks*, 279 [Notebook 22, §1].

16 Gramsci, *Selections From the Prison Notebooks*, 280.

17 Gramsci, *Selections From the Prison Notebooks*, 281.

18 Gramsci, *Selections From the Prison Notebooks*, 281.

19 Walter Benjamin, "Eduard Fuchs, Collector and Historian", *New German Critique*, no. 5 (Spring 1975), 35.

20 Benjamin, "Eduard Fuchs, Collector and Historian", 35. The seventh thesis sums up the project of historical materialism: "There is no document of civilization which is not at the same time a document of barbarism. And just as such a document is not free of barbarism, barbarism taints also the manner in which it was transmitted from one owner to another. A historical materialist therefore dissociates himself from it as far as possible. He regards it as his task to brush history against the grain." Walter Benjamin, "Theses on the Concept of History", in *Illuminations* (New York: Schocken Books, 2007), 264–265.

21 Benjamin, "Eduard Fuchs, Collector and Historian", 36.

22 Going by Benjamin's letter to Scholem on 28 October 1931, Benjamin's model here is probably banker and patron Gustav Glück, who was a member of the Berlin Communist Party and a friend of Benjamin. See also Werner Hamacher, "Das theologisch-politische Fragment", in *Benjamin-Handbuch. Leben-Werk-Wirkung*, ed. Burkhardt Lindner (Stuttgart and Weimar: Metzler, 2006), 191.

23 Walter Benjamin, "The Destructive Character", in *Reflections: Essays, Aphorisms, Autobiographical Writings*, ed. Peter Demetz (New York: Schoken Books, 2007), 301.

24 *Krisis und Kritik* is the title of a review developed with Bertolt Brecht. The first edition was due to be published with Rowohly on 15 January 1931. In his planning notes, Benjamin points out that "the review's field of work is the current crisis in all ideological fields; the task is to prove this crisis, provoke it even, using the tools of critique". Cited in Michael Opitz, "Literaturkritik", in *Benjamin-Handbuch*, ed. Burkhardt Lindner, 330 (author's translation).

25 Benjamin, "The Destructive Character", 302–303.
26 See Maria Teresa Costa, "Für ein Ethos des destruktiven Charakters im Ausgang von Walter Benjamin", in *Benjamin-Studien 2*, ed. Daniel Weidner and Sigrid Weigel (Munich: Fink, 2011), 179–194.
27 Benjamin, "The Destructive Character", 302.
28 "The heavier the blow . . . the better are his chances of picturing the destructive character." Benjamin, "The Destructive Character", 301.
29 See Dario Gentili, *Il tempo della storia. Le tesi. Sul concetto di storia di Walter Benjamin* (Macerata: Quodlibet, 2019), 82.
30 "The space within which the writing subject exists is a space of images (*Bildraum*), a place of hieroglyphic signs. These signs can only be deciphered through the conjunction of subjective past and current *shock*." Mauro Ponzi, "Walter Benjamin e il surrealismo: Teoria delle avanguardie", in *Tra simbolismo e avanguardie. Studi dedicati a Ferruccio Masini*, ed. Caterina Graziadei, Antonio Prete, Fernanda Rosso Chioso, and Vivetta Vivarelli (Rome: Editori Riuniti, 1992), 296.
31 Walter Benjamin, "Surrealism", in *Reflections: Essays, Aphorisms, Autobiographical Writings*, ed. Peter Demetz (New York: Schoken Books, 2007), 191.
32 Benjamin, "Surrealism", 186.
33 "Poetic Surrealism . . . has focused its efforts up to this point on re-establishing dialogue in its absolute truth." André Breton, *Manifestoes of Surrealism* (Ann Arbor, MI: University of Michigan Press, 1972), 43.
34 Benjamin, "Surrealism", 192.
35 See Raul Mordenti, *Quaderni del carcere di Antonio Gramsci* (Turin: Einaudi, 1996), 33. Even these "nuances" that render vague the differences between genres, such as notes and writing, remind us of the topographical dynamics of *The Arcade Project*.
36 "Fuchs remains within the democratic tradition when he attaches himself to France with a particular love. He admires France as the soil of three great revolutions, as the home of the exiles, as the source of Utopian socialism, as the fatherland of haters of tyranny such as Michelet and Quinet, and finally as the soil in which the Communards are buried." Benjamin, "Eduard Fuchs, Collector and Historian", 45.
37 Benjamin, "Eduard Fuchs, Collector and Historian", 324.
38 Benjamin, "Eduard Fuchs, Collector and Historian", 326.
39 Here we find traces of the similarity between Benjamin's critique of Fuchs' historicism and Gramsci's critique of Croce's: "It is yet to be seen whether, in its own way, Crocian historicism is not a cleverly masked form of history by design, like all reformist liberal conceptions." Gramsci, *Quaderni del carcere*, vol. 2, 1327 [Notebook 10, § 41].
40 See Benjamin, "Eduard Fuchs, Collector and Historian".
41 Benjamin, "Eduard Fuchs, Collector and Historian", 50.
42 See Gramsci, *Quaderni del carcere*, vol. 2, 1423 [Notebook 11, § 25].
43 Benjamin, *The Arcades Project*, 460.
44 Benjamin, "Eduard Fuchs, Collector and Historian", 29.
45 Gramsci, *Prison Notebooks*, vol. 3, 6–10 [Notebook 6, §10].
46 Gramsci, *Prison Notebooks*, vol. 3, 8.
47 Gramsci, *Quaderni del carcere*, vol. 2, 1069 [Notebook 8, § 211].
48 Gramsci, *Quaderni del carcere*, vol. 2, 885 [Notebook 7, § 35].
49 Gramsci, *Quaderni del carcere*, vol. 2, 1442 [Notebook 30, § 30].
50 Gramsci, *Prison Notebooks*, vol. 1, 234 [Notebook 1, § 156].
51 See Daniel Bensaïd, *Qui est le Juge? Pour en finir avec le tribunal de l'Histoire* (Paris: Fayard, 1999).
52 Bensaïd, *Qui est le Juge? Pour en finir avec le tribunal de l'Histoire*, 152.

53 "Whereas the modern concept of sovereignty amounts to a supreme executive power on the part of the prince, the baroque concept emerges from a discussion of the state of emergency, and makes it the most important function of the prince to avert this." Walter Benjamin, *Origin of German Tragic Drama* (London and New York: Verso, 2003), 65.

54 See Ernesto Laclau, *Emancipation(s)* (London and New York: Verso, 1996); on the lacking decision in Baroque drama, see Albrecht Koschorke, "Das Problem der souveränen Entscheidung im barocken Trauerspiel", in *Urteilen/Entscheiden*, ed. Cornelia Vismann and Thomas Weitin (Munich: Fink, 2006), 175–195.

55 "Around 1840 it was briefly fashionable to take turtles for a walk in the arcades. The flaneurs liked to have the turtles set the pace for them." Walter Benjamin, *Charles Baudelaire: A Lyric Poet in the Era of High Capitalism* (London and New York: Verso, 1997), 54. See Vittoria Borsò, "Baudelaire, Benjamin et la/les modernité/s", *L'année Baudelaire*, no. 8 (2004): 149–172.

56 "Here [in Berlin], and not in Paris, it is possible to understand how the *flâneur* was able to distance themselves from the philosophical stroller, taking on the likeness of the werewolf that roams a social wilderness defined by Poe in *The Man of the Crowd*." Walter Benjamin, "Die Wiederkehr des Flaneurs", in *Angelus Novus. Ausgewählte Schriften* (Frankfurt am Main: Suhrkamp, 1988), 420 (author's translation).

57 For example, "The enlargement of a snapshot does not simply render more precise what in any case was visible, though unclear: it reveals entirely new structural formations of the subject." Walter Benjamin, "The Work of Art in the Age of Mechanical Reproduction", in *Illuminations* (New York: Schocken Books, 2007), 238.

58 Benjamin, "The Work of Art in the Age of Mechanical Reproduction", 225.

59 See Benjamin, *Charles Baudelaire: A Lyric Poet in the Era of High Capitalism.*

Bibliography

Benjamin, Walter. "The Work of Art in the Age of Mechanical Reproduction". In *Illuminations*, edited by Hannah Arendt, translated by Harry Zohn, 1–26. New York: Schocken Books, 1969. Accessed January 2024, https://web.mit.edu/allanmc/www/benjamin.pdf.

Benjamin, Walter. "Eduard Fuchs, Collector and Historian". *New German Critique*, no. 5, translated by Knut Tarnowski (Spring 1975): 27–58.

Benjamin, Walter. "Eduard Fuchs, der Sammler und der Historiker". In *Angelus Novus. Ausgewählte Schriften*. Frankfurt am Main: Suhrkamp, 1988.

Benjamin, Walter. *Charles Baudelaire: A Lyric Poet in the Era of High Capitalism*, translated by Harry Zohn. London and New York: Verso, 1997.

Benjamin, Walter. *The Arcades Project*. Prepared on the Basis of the German Volume edited by Rolf Tiedemann, translated by Oward Eiland, and Kevin McLaughlin. Cambridge, MA and London: Harvard University Press, 1999.

Benjamin, Walter. *Origin of German Tragic Drama*, translated by John Osborne. London and New York: Verso, 2003.

Benjamin, Walter. "The Destructive Character". In *Reflections: Essays, Aphorisms, Autobiographical Writings*, edited by Peter Demetz, translated by Edmund Jephcott, 301–303. New York: Schoken Books, 2007.

Benjamin, Walter. "Surrealism". In *Reflections, Essays, Aphorisms, Autobiographical Writings*, edited by Peter Demetz, translated by Edmund Jephcott, 177–192. New York: Schoken Books, 2007.

Bensaïd, Daniel. *Qui est le Juge? Pour en finir avec le tribunal de l'Histoire*. Paris: Fayard, 1999.

Borsò, Vittoria. "Baudelaire, Benjamin et la/les modernité/s". *L'année Baudelaire*, no. 8 (2004): 149–172.

Breton, André. *Manifestoes of Surrealism*. Michigan: University of Michigan Press, 1972.

Costa, Maria Teresa. "Für ein Ethos des destruktiven Charakters im Ausgang von Walter Benjamin". In *Benjamin-Studien 2*, edited by Daniel Weidner, and Sigrid Weigel, 179–194. Munich: Fink, 2011.

Esposito, Roberto. *Instituting Thought: Three Paradigms of Political Ontology*. Cambridge: Polity Press, 2021.

Foucault, Michel. "Nietzsche, Genealogy, History". In *The Foucault Reader*, edited by Paul Rabinow, translated by Donald F. Bouchard, and Sherry Simon, 76–100. New York: Pantheon Books, 1984.

Gentili, Dario. *Il tempo della storia. Le tesi Sul concetto di storia di Walter Benjamin*. Macerata: Quodlibet, 2019.

Gentili, Dario. *The Age of Precarity: Endless Crisis as an Art of Government*. London and New York: Verso, 2021.

Gramsci, Antonio. *Quaderni del carcere*, edited by Valentino Gerratana. Turin: Einaudi, 1975.

Gramsci, Antonio. *Selections from the Prison Notebooks*, edited and translated by Quentin Hoare, and Geoffrey Nowell Smith. London: Laurence and Wishart, 1992.

Gramsci, Antonio. *Prison Notebooks – Volume II*, edited and translated by Joseph A. Buttigieg. New York: Columbia University Press, 1996.

Hamacher, Werner. "Das Theologisch-Politische Fragment". In *Benjamin-Handbuch: Leben-Werk-Wirkung*, edited by Burkhardt Lindner, 451–464. Stuttgart and Weimar: Metzler, 2006.

Koschorke, Albrecht. "Das Problem der souveränen Entscheidung im barocken Trauerspiel". In *Urteilen/Entscheiden*, edited by Cornelia Vismann, and Thomas Weitin, 175–195. Munich: Fink, 2006.

Laclau, Ernesto. *Emancipation(s)*. London and New York: Verso, 1996.

Mordenti, Raul. *Quaderni del carcere di Antonio Gramsci*. Turin: Einaudi, 1996.

Mustè, Marcello. *Rivoluzioni passive. Il mondo tra le due guerre nei Quaderni del carcere di Gramsci*. Rome: Viella, 2022.

Opitz, Michael. "Literaturkritik". In *Benjamin-Handbuch*, edited by Burkhardt Lindner, 311–331. Stuttgart and Weimar: Metzler, 2006.

Ponzi, Mauro. "Walter Benjamin e il surrealismo: Teoria delle avanguardie". In *Tra simbolismo e avanguardie. Studi dedicati a Ferruccio Masini*, edited by Caterina Graziadei, Antonio Prete, Fernanda Rosso Chioso, and Vivetta Vivarelli, 295–319. Rome: Editori Riuniti, 1992.

Thomas, Peter D. "Gramsci's Revolutions: Passive and Permanent". *Modern Intellectual History* 17, no. 1 (2020): 117–146.

5

ON GRAMSCIAN TEMPORALITY

Michele Filippini

"Current events" lead us to relive the past and the psychology of our predecessors.

And it helps us clarify our ideas, and forces us to transform our vocabulary.

Antonio Gramsci, 5 February 1918

5.1 The Dual Character of Gramscian Time

The *Prison Notebooks*, for the best part of their existence as a political work, have regularly been interpreted in the same way with regard to their alleged temporal structure. In fact, Western Marxism's use of Gramsci's work has been heavily conditioned by the Italian Communist Party's political use of the notebooks, at least up until the 1970s.[1] Gramsci's thoughts were classified as part of the historicist school of thought, on the basis of the presumed continuity with an Italian tradition that, starting with Francesco De Sanctis, was later developed by Antonio Labriola, and ultimately by Benedetto Croce, and is thus also considered to take in Antonio Gramsci. This historicist school of thought implied a linear, progressive conception of time, in which each historical moment could be broken down and comprehended on the basis of the relationship between its component parts.[2] In addition to the political consequences of the aforementioned classification, which was so often reiterated that it became a cliché difficult to negate, the conception of time inherent in these interpretations concealed, for a long time, the much more complex temporal structure of Gramsci's work. Interest in this topic has re-emerged in recent years,[3] the emphasis on the "multiple temporal levels" present in the *Prison Notebooks* has therefore led to the work's interpretation tending in the opposite direction, that is, towards the

DOI: 10.4324/9781003457039-8

unreserved valorisation of the temporal pluralities present in Gramsci's works, thus offering an intriguing reading of the notebooks, but possibly one that is a little too audacious.[4]

Thus, whosoever wishes to analyse the question of the structure of time in Gramsci must first acknowledge that it is not an easy thing to identify. Together with an understanding of temporality as a plural entity – as in the case of the theory of personality, of linguistic phenomena, and of considerations regarding common sense, all questions that will be shortly dealt with here – there is, in fact, a "hegemonic temporality" in the *Prison Notebooks* that overdetermines these relations and acts as a type of "temporal unifying device".[5] This is not a case *merely* of one of the many temporal layers that, within a presumed unit such as the individual or a language, carries on its battle by trying to impose its own course. In fact, this is *also* a case of the temporality of that force that, temporarily and not "naturally", prevails over others despite not managing to, or being able to, assimilate them completely. This force not only struggles to unify and conform time, as a specific mode if its own prevalence over other temporalities, but at least in part it also overdetermines the rules of this struggle. These two forms of temporality – plural temporality that always contains a struggle to prevail and singular temporality represented by the hegemonic force at the time – are constantly at play at one and the same time in Gramsci's analysis. In the case of plural temporality, the outcome of the struggle is different each time, from one case to the next; within singular temporality, the upheaval occurs at the beginning of every new epoch, when the "temporal line" changes and points in another direction.

This dual character of time inherent in the *Prison Notebooks* reflects the dynamic character of the historical blocs, of the determined market, and of the competing organic systems which Gramsci describes. The dominant bloc that "predominates and 'dictates law'",[6] in practice also dictates time. The overdetermination of this "temporal force" in relation to the plurality of conflicting times thus needs to be taken into account: the groups governing society fight their war of position with the benefit of this force that overdetermines the conflict. This plurality does not therefore occur in neutral territory, but in a context partially structured by hegemonic time, and this privileged position of the dominant bloc is merely the thing that is at stake here, that is, hegemony: and the establishment of one given time structure is a specific development of this hegemony.

In this regard, Alberto Burgio was the first to point out the difference between the Gramscian concepts of "duration" and of "constituting an epoch". Burgio identified the dual structure of historical temporality in Gramsci, which sees the continuity of duration interrupted by the intervention of an epoch-making phenomenon.[7] However, Burgio appears to situate these two temporalities in succession, on the basis of a linear model that, rather paradoxically, seems to reassemble historical development. The only possible asynchronous movement in this model is represented by the geographical differences that stagger the levels of linear temporality, producing the effect of a "contemporaneity of the non-contemporaneous", as in the case of French history compared to the histories of the other European nations fighting a battle that had already been won in France by the Revolution.[8] However, the dual structure of Gramscian time that we are trying to reconstruct here is based in the *Prison Notebooks* on the consubstantiality of these temporalities rather than on their consecutiveness, following that relationship between the permanent and the occasional, whereby the two terms are not determined a priori but are dependent upon the organic system of which they are part.[9]

Duration and epoch thus coexist as temporal courses. The former is the stage for the imminent struggle between social forces within a system of hegemonic power. The latter is the unequal background in which this struggle is played out. In regard to duration, there are no novelties at the level of overall social organisation, but only diverse forms of organisation of the system. Constituting an epoch, on the other hand, entails establishing a new civilisation, destroying the old automatisms, creating new ones, and modifying the relationship between the occasional and the permanent. However, if the event that constitutes an epoch arises only rarely, this does not mean that the temporality inscribed in an epoch is not present and does not play a decisive role in the epoch's duration. On the contrary, an epoch manifests itself in every hegemonic conflict, both in the force that at that moment governs the process and in the structure of the battlefield that, at least in part, is determined by this same force. Likewise, while it is true that duration characterises homogeneous, linear time, and any ripples in that time are relegated to the ranks of the accidental, it is also true that it is impossible to determine the precise moment at which duration becomes epoch; likewise, it is not possible to determine the moment at which the struggle at the occasional level becomes permanent struggle.[10]

There are four notes in the *Prison Notebooks* in which the concept of "constituting an epoch" emerges. These four notes refer, respectively, to four movements: (1) the idea of progress; (2) what Gramsci termed the "Dreyfus movement"; (3) Fascism; and (4) Americanism. In Gramsci's view, only the first of these constitutes an epoch, while Dreyfusism, Fascism, and Americanism do not constitute an epoch but are simply "transitory" moments within the capitalistic epoch, the idea of progress, on the other hand, is epoch-making since it marks the emergence of a new "mentality", of a new "relationship . . . between society and nature" that may be rationally interpreted, which means that "mankind as a whole is more sure of its future and can conceive 'rationally' of plans through which to govern its entire life".[11] This is, for Gramsci, a revolution in mentality comparable solely with Soviet efforts to construct a "new Man" for a new epoch-making transition.

5.2   Signs of Time: Theory of Personality, Common Sense, Language, East and West

The question of temporality innervates many Gramscian notes, for example, those that define a theory of personality.[12] The key element here is the notion of the individual as a stratified being composed of strictly individual elements together with others that are socially determined. The conflict between these two components is summed with the conflict inherent in the social elements of individuality, which reproduce in the individual those conflicts that characterise a society divided into different social classes. The individual is thus the object of different, competing temporalities that express present and past conflicts:

> it contains Stone Age elements and principles of a more advanced science, prejudices from all past phases of history at the local level and intuitions of a future philosophy which will be that of a human race united the world over.[13]

This temporal plurality is the point of departure for each individual, who experiences his own life according to the different times – just for the sake of example – of folklore and of "disenchantment" of the world,[14] of dedication to one's work and of Taylorist-Fordist rationality, of superstition, and of science. This temporal plurality should not be confused, however, with an objective, eternal condition that sees fragmentariness as a value in itself, and which consequently expresses a politics that tends to incorporate these diverse temporalities into one "harmonious plurality".[15] The Gramscian approach, linked to a progressive, unifying vision of emancipation – whether this is to be considered an advantage or a limitation makes little difference here – on the other hand, is characterised by the acknowledgement of a struggle aimed at temporal uniformity:

> Having established that the contradictory nature of the system of social relations implies that people's consciousness is inevitably contradictory, the question arises as to the manner in which this contradiction manifests itself, and how unification can be gradually achieved.[16]

This urge for temporal unity is characteristic of all the forces at play within the hegemonic struggle, each of which tries to bring its adversaries into its "own temporality". Even the working class has to move in this direction, through individual coherence, control over its own actions, the systematic and organic development of a "new Man", and consequently of a new order. The October Revolution was greeted by Gramsci as an epoch-making event also because it laid the basis for such possible unity:

> For a mass of people to be led to think coherently and in the same coherent fashion about the real present world, is a "philosophical" event far more

important and "original" than the discovery by some philosophical "genius" of a truth which remains the property of small groups of intellectuals.[17]

In this case, coherence is the result of that action designed to encompass the diverse temporalities within the temporality of revolution.

Of course, one should not underestimate the importance of Gramsci's willingness to accept plurality, compared to the monistic view of the working class in vogue during his time. One should not forget that Gramsci's innovation was radical, not only in considering the struggle within each formally perceived political unit (including the individual) to be fundamental but also in valorising this plurality in the phases of transition to the new order. The revolutionary process, as we have seen, is for this reason among others rethought on a longer timescale and in terms of its "consensual" characteristics. However, the ultimate purpose of Gramsci's politics remains that of social unity and individual coherency, to be achieved through a process that unfolds parallel to transformation.

The two types of temporality therefore manifest themselves through the coexistence of (1) diverse temporal layers and (2) a strained tendency towards unity, or rather, towards diverse, diverging unities. If one moves from the individual level to that of collective phenomena, this dual temporal structure emerges with equal force. Common sense, on the one hand, and language, on the other, in fact represent the collective forms of this temporal plurality that must tend towards unification.

Common sense is the plural "residue" that the intellectual history of humanity has rooted in popular consciousness, and it thus manifests itself as the incoherent stratification of world views, prejudices, and beliefs. It contains all and everything, from the most conservative and reactionary elements to the "intuitions of a future philosophy".[18] This latter aspect, identified as "good sense", is what interests Gramsci: "This is the healthy nucleus that exists in 'common sense', the part of it which can be called 'good sense' and which deserves to be made more unitary and coherent".[19] The plurality and incoherence of common sense contribute towards reproducing domination, because they fragment individual wills and prevent the formation of collective wills as an alternative to the dominant one. Such alternative collective wills, on the other hand, may emerge from the combination of the development of good sense and of criticism of common sense: "At those times in history when a homogeneous social group is brought into being, there comes into being also, in opposition to common sense, a homogeneous – in other words coherent and systematic – philosophy".[20] The time of common sense is of a plural character because it is within that time that a hegemonic struggle is fought; however, the time of the dominant group overdetermines this plurality because it forces it in a certain direction, at least until an opposing homogeneous social group forms.

Gramsci's writings in his *Notebook 29* reflect this same temporal structure in regard to the question of language. Language is also plural on two different levels: the internal level of the individual's linguistic capacity, which sees the individual sharing a dialect and the national language (if not more than one language); and on the level of the national and international communities, which sees dialects and languages take their respective shares of the territory, but also sees them superimposed to a certain extent.[21] The choice therefore is not between conserving a plurality of languages or imposing a single language but between two different ways of achieving unity. The opportunity to master a national language, in fact, is in Gramsci's view an essential prerequisite for the emancipation of the subalterns. It is something that cannot be sacrificed in the name of linguistic plurality.[22] Temporality comes to the fore once again here: this is a question of standardising languages at a national level – because only languages possess the instruments with which modern thought can be expressed in full[23] – rendering them translatable and thus getting away from the myth of the universality of language (Esperanto) in order to synchronise different national linguistic structures to the same (revolutionary) time. The temporality of duration, linguistically represented by the plurality of dialects and languages competing for prestige, is superimposed by the epochal temporality of national languages, which are the only ones that can enable a strong link to be established between popular culture and national politics, between the people and the leading groups.

One final consideration regarding the dual temporal nature of the *Prison Notebooks* concerns one of the most famous Gramscian distinctions, the one that makes reference to the diverse relationship between State and civil society in the East and in the West. In the East, Gramsci writes, society was "primordial and gelatinous", whereas in the West it was "a succession of sturdy fortresses and emplacements".[24] In reality, this spatial division refers to a temporal division, that is, it points to the development of Western societies. In the West, power cannot be taken by attacking the "places" of power, because power has been disseminated throughout society, rendering society a conservative inertial force within which the revolutionary use of the war of manoeuvre is no longer sufficient. Often scholars have insisted on this idea of the contemporaneity of the non-contemporary, that is, on the multiplicity of temporal levels in the diverse functional spaces globally dominated by capitalism, in particular in relation to theories of uneven development.[25] There are undoubtedly good reasons in support of this interpretation, and the identification of plural temporalities remains, even within the context of our insistence on the duality of Gramscian time, a significant feature of Gramscian analysis. However, in analysing this distinction, perhaps too much attention has been paid to the "Western" side of the process, that is, to the changes displayed by Western societies having resisted the challenge of "revolution in the West". Nevertheless, in keeping with Gramsci's work, the focus should also be in the other direction, that of the East described in this famous quotation.

In Gramsci's analysis, "Eastern" civil society was certainly considered more primordial and gelatinous at the end of the war, when the Bolsheviks dealt the fatal blow to Russia's Tsarist regime. However, the advent of the Worker's State, with the intense period of politicisation of the masses right through the 1920s, had radically changed the political panorama. In particular, with the attempt to stabilise the relationship between workers and peasants through the NEP (New Economic Policy) was created that social fabric subject to the hegemony of the workers that had been missing before[26] (Fitzpatrick, Rabinowitch, Stites 1991; Tagliagambe 1978; Cacciari 1975). It was this very process that led Gramsci to use the concept of hegemony, and to consider Lenin as its precursor, being the first person to put it into practice:

> the theoretical-practical principle of hegemony has also epistemological significance, and it is here that Ilich's [Lenin] greatest theoretical contribution to the philosophy of praxis should be sought. . . . The realisation of a hegemonic apparatus, in so far as it creates a new ideological terrain, determines a reform of consciousness and of methods of knowledge: it is a fact of knowledge, a philosophical fact.[27]

Gramsci was thus aware that the transition to mass politics had changed the scenario not only in the West, in relation to the liberal order, but also in the East in relation to the forms through which the revolution had been achieved. The post-revolutionary era in the USSR started in 1923, just like mass politics in the West (Fascism and Americanism), thus both presented the scenario of a war of position in which neither side was any longer characterised by a primordial and gelatinous civil society. For this reason, Gramsci was able to translate the social bloc from the economic terms of the USSR at the time of the NEP to superstructural terms, that is, of the intellectual blocs of the capitalistically stabilised Western countries. While in the writings of Bukharin – the greatest theoretician of the NEP – the formation of the bloc is driven first and foremost by the economic forces politically manoeuvred by the Workers' State, in Gramsci it is hegemony, specifically that of an intellectual and cultural nature, that underlies the formation of that bloc[28] (Buci-Glucksmann 1980, 261–264; Cohen 1975; Filippini 2016, 103–149). In this case, it was the "economically backward" Soviet Russia (albeit more advanced politically, as the first experimental Workers' State) that dictated the guiding principles and the theoretical-political problems to the international communist movement.

Thus, the global scenario is one of diverse, competing hegemonic times that massively effect the synchronisation of the plural temporalities to be found within each of the blocs. Planism,[29] Corporatism, and Soviet planning all represent different, competing "temporal rhythms" whereby States endeavour to hegemonically (but also coercively) unify their respective societies.

5.3   The Shape of Duration: The Passive Revolution

Having thus illustrated the bases for the dual structure of time in the *Prison Note-books*, we can now turn to the concept that Gramsci uses to analyse the temporal nature of duration as characterised by the hegemonic force that prevails, operating as a "temporal unifying device". The concept in question is that of passive revolution. As often is the case in the *Prison Notebooks*, Gramsci does not coin a new word out of nothing. Instead, he utilises a concept previously formulated by others and shifts its meaning,[30] thus actually formulating a new concept.

Gramsci takes the term from the *Historical Essay on the Neapolitan Revolution of 1799* by Vincenzo Cuoco, where the expression indicated the absence of popular involvement in the revolution due to the gap between the leaders and the people. Thus, the French Revolution, which established a clean break with the feudal past, was compared with the passive revolutions witnessed in the other European States, in which

> the needs that found a Jacobin-Napoleonic expression in France were satis-fied in small doses, legally, in a reformist manner, thereby managing to safe-guard the political and economic positions of the old feudal classes, avoiding agrarian reform and making especially sure that the popular masses did not go through a period of political experience such as occurred in France in the Jacobin era.[31]

The masses' non-involvement in politics, together with the slow, partial accept-ance of certain revolutionary demands on the part of the leading groups, may be considered those features of the hegemonic programme known as passive revolution.

According to Gramsci, this manner of historical development, characterised by the temporality of duration, conceals a "domesticated dialectic because it 'mechanically' presupposes that the antithesis should be preserved by the the-sis in order not to destroy the dialectical process".[32] The thesis (the hegemonic group) determines the antithesis (the subaltern group) and guides the actions, and eventually incorporates the demands, of such. Thus, the situation that arises is that of "historical inertia", where time flows homogeneously and politics is transformed from subjective action aimed at changing the world to the admin-istration of the existing power structure. The only undisciplined movement that remains in society is the inconsequential (in terms of power) "sporadic and inco-herent rebelliousness of the popular masses".[33]

The unification of Italy is the historical example of this flowing of time: "the Action Party [Garibaldi and Mazzini] was led historically by the Moderates [Cavour]",[34] who proved ideologically appealing to the Party, and succeeded in controlling, and taking advantage of, the fragmented nature of the Party's political action. Thus, the Moderates managed to impose the temporality of unification thanks to their unity of purpose, to the close bond they had with their social group of reference, and to the "ideological" attraction exercised on traditional intellectuals. Therefore, the exclusion of the great peasant masses from the newly founded Italian State resulted in a territorial and social divide between a South that created savings from the exploitation of the peasants and a North that drained these resources to finance industrial development. This is how Gramsci interpreted the onset of the "Southern question": he saw it basically as the failure to synchronise revolutionary developments, thus leaving a contradictory temporal plurality in place within the framework of the dominance of the Moderates,[35] this was the time of duration and of passive revolution. This process will continue in a unified Italy through transformism, which Gramsci considers an actual "form of historical development".[36] By preserving power relations and the specific interests on the basis of which national unity had been built, transformism operates as a filter for the new demands of a changing society, progressively broadening the bases of the State. The new industrial and financial bourgeoisie is in this way gradually included in the mechanisms of representation of interests within the political system, through the dynamics of inclusion "from above". Thus, transformism renews the basis of the State's consensus without compromising its power structure, and therefore avoids involving the masses – "*simultaneously*"[37] in Gramsci's words – in this process of reorganisation.

5.4   The Form of Epoch: Gramsci and Benjamin on How Novelty Emerges

We have seen how Gramsci views the passive revolution as representing the bourgeois model of the "historical management" of development and change: a model that was implemented immediately after the French Revolution, with the formation of the Nation-States in Europe in reaction to these upheavals. The characteristic temporality of this development is that of the passive revolution, which unfolds across a linear timescale, the development of which is controlled by a "false" dialectic in which the thesis presupposes the antithesis prior to conflicting with it.

Just a few years after Gramsci had formulated these reflections, Walter Benjamin wrote his thesis *On the Concept of History*, containing a similar criticism of bourgeois time:

> The concept of mankind's historical progress cannot be sundered from the concept of its progression through a homogeneous, empty time. A critique of the concept of such a progression must underlie any criticism of the concept of progress itself.[38]

The homogeneous, empty time described by Benjamin seems to copy that of the passive revolution described by Gramsci: homogeneity entails conformism, just as emptiness precludes any chance of an alternative subjective construction. This comparison, in addition to being fascinating due to the fact that the two writers did not know each other's work,[39] could be useful in particular when investigating the features of the second temporality that Gramsci alludes to: "epochal time". However, it should be said that this is an aspect that is not specifically dealt with in the *Prison Notebooks*, but one that emerges every now and then without being formulated in full. The problem of how the "time of revolution" emerges in Gramsci's writings, and in particular how it is to be triggered – apart from its phenomenology, which as we have seen is characterised by the synchronisation of different times – remains unresolved. Certain cues for a reflection on the question – which do not purport to include Gramsci in present-day discussions regarding immanence/transcendence or articulation/event – may be found, nevertheless, when comparing the *Prison Notebooks* with Benjamin's *Theses*. In Thesis XIV, Benjamin states that

> History is the subject of a construction whose site is not homogeneous, empty time, but time filled full by now-time [*Jetztzeit*]. Thus, to Robespierre ancient Rome was a past charged with now-time, a past which he blasted out of the continuum of history.[40]

The first thing to be said here is that for Benjamin, "epochal time" – his *Jetztzeit*, the messianic now-time introducing the novelty – is the time that makes history. History that sees a subject refer to fragments of the past in order to break the continuity of bourgeois time: the Jacobins could thus trace themselves back to the ancient Romans in order to break the homogeneous, empty time of the feudal system. Materialist historiography is thus called upon to oppose historicism (that of the Second International) that culminates in universal history, and whose "procedure is additive: it musters a mass of data to fill the homogeneous, empty time".[41] Historical materialism, on the contrary, develops a historiography contemplating radical interruptions in the temporal linearity of a dominion: "Thinking involves not only the movement of thoughts, but their arrest as well".[42] For materialists, historical time is that full of *Jetztzeit*, in which the present recalls fragments of the past in order to redeem and revive them. The link between two moments in time thus disrupts the linearity of bourgeois time and reveals a different movement.

This image of non-linear temporality constituted by historical highs and lows of particular intensity appears to be present in the *Prison Notebooks* as well: for example, in the relationship that Gramsci portrays between Machiavelli and the Jacobins. Both are treated as "fragments" of the past that may be reactivated within the context of a history that proceeds with an oscillating intensity rather than through any process of accumulation. Along this new temporality, even the historical sequence is questioned. With regard to the need for a simultaneous incursion of the peasant masses into political life, Gramsci wrote

> That was Machiavelli's intention through the reform of the militia, and it was achieved by the Jacobins in the French Revolution. That Machiavelli understood it *reveals a precocious Jacobinism* that is the (more or less fertile) germ of his conception of national revolution.[43]

Thus, in Gramsci's writings, the relationship between the Jacobins and Machiavelli marks a break in the linearity of bourgeois time. Not only did the Jacobins evoke Machiavelli but the reference also holds if the normal sequence of time is inverted: while the "Jacobins . . . were certainly a 'categorical embodiment' of Machiavelli's Prince",[44] Machiavelli also shared a "precocious Jacobinism". Their destinies were also similar from the historiographical point of view: both were "used" by the history of the victors – Machiavelli becoming a symbol of political cynicism and imprisoned in a political science synonymous with the administration of power, while the Jacobins were reduced to symbolising extremism and fanaticism – but both could also live on in the temporality of a revolutionary force capable of identifying itself with them.[45] Gramsci's references to the Jacobins and to Machiavelli thus served the following purpose in the *Prison Notebooks*: to force the present to identify itself with their actions, thus offering the working class the key to an alternative historical time to that of passive revolutions.

A further example of this "intense" non-linear temporality is regarding the problem of the relationship between town and countryside, between factory workers and peasants. Besides, this was the point on which the Workers' State that emerged from the October Revolution hinged. In criticising the Action Party's indifference towards the peasant masses – unlike the Jacobins, who had imposed a radical agrarian reform[46] – Gramsci pointed out how it also possessed a specific historical "tradition to which it could go back and attach itself" in order to promote this synchronisation. This was the medieval tradition of the Communes that bore witness to a "nascent bourgeoisie [that] seeks allies among the peasants against the Empire and against the local feudalism".[47] The historical bloc of town and countryside, the synchronisation of these two times to revolutionary time, was already the key to democratic revolution at the time, and this is one of those aspects of "epochal time" that chronologically links distant events on the basis of their intensity:

> the most classic master of the art of politics for the Italian ruling classes, Machiavelli, had also posed the problem – naturally in the terms and with the preoccupations of his time. In his politico-military writings, the need to

subordinate the popular masses organically to the ruling strata, so as to create a national militia capable of eliminating the companies of fortune, was quite well understood.[48]

In Gramsci's view, an alternative historical time to that of passive revolution is thus potentially ever-present, even within the context of the linear development of a time that is over-determined by the practice of the hegemonic subject. It is up to the revolutionary subject that wishes to establish hegemony to be able to reconnect with those moments in history that have expressed such intensity, and to bring to contemporaneity those attempts made to overturn the old organic system in order to create a new one. The hegemony of an emergent subject thus always presupposes the urge to synchronise the diverse temporalities of the subaltern groups. This is the only way that the latter may get free from the depoliticising uniformity of bourgeois time. In this sense, Gramsci views con-temporariness as the product of political endeavour: it does not exist originally but needs to be created.

How such a process is to be started, that is, how the synchronisation of the times of the subaltern groups is to disrupt the unity of homogenous, empty time, is a question that is destined to remain unanswered in the *Prison Notebooks*. Gramsci does not manage to (or perhaps cannot) illustrate the forms by means of which "novelty" is to be produced within an organic system. The only epoch-making event that had seen the working class as protagonist had been triggered, in fact, by a war of manoeuvre (the October Revolution), within the context of a weak civil society that no longer existed following the advent of mass politics. It is likely that this "unspoken aspect" of Gramsci's work corresponds to an "unspoken" structural aspect of political theory, an aspect that remains unspeak-able for the simple reason that it cannot be rationalised within the categories of politics. It comes as no surprise that all of the classical dichotomies of Marxist thought – theory and practice, structure and superstructure, ideology and class consciousness – bear witness to the impossibility of rationally defining the tran-sition from one to the other. At this point, the fact that Gramsci's writings permit a reflection on this question without forcing a solution is a strength, and not a weakness, for all those who wish to utilise his open Marxism to interpret and change contemporary society.

Notes

1 See Nicola Badaloni, *Il marxismo di Gramsci: dal mito alla ricomposizione politica* (Torino: Einaudi, 1975). In the late 1960s, Althusser had criticised Gramsci on the basis of a reading of the *Prison Notebooks* heavily influenced by this political use; see Louis Althusser, et al., *Reading Capital* (London: New Left Books, 1970), 126–138. The relationship between Althusser and Gramsci is more complex than this initial criticism led people to believe, however. Indeed, in 1965, Althusser also wrote, "Who

has *really* attempted to follow up the explorations of Marx and Engels? I can only think of Gramsci." Louis Althusser, *For Marx* (London and New York: Verso, 2005), 114. During the 1970s, Althusser returned once again to Gramsci in Louis Althusser, *Machiavelli and Us* (London and New York: Verso, 2000). For the dating of the manuscripts, see the *Editorial Note* written by François Matheron, in Althusser, *Machiavelli and Us*, VII–IX.

2 The most well-known criticism of this temporal structure is that offered by Althusser in *Reading Capital* (94). This criticism of Gramscian historicism divulged through the PCI (Italian Communist Party) also led to the emergence of a difficult relationship between the Italian workerist tradition (*operaismo*) and the thought of Antonio Gramsci; see Mario Tronti, "Tra materialismo dialettico e filosofia della prassi", in *La città futura. Saggi sulla figura e il pensiero di Antonio Gramsci*, ed. Alberto Caracciolo and Gianni Scalia (Milan: Feltrinelli, 1959), 139–186; Antonio Negri, *Books for Burning* (London and New York: Verso, 2005), 90ff.

3 See Peter Thomas, "Gramsci e le temporalità plurali" and Fabio Frosini, "Spaziotempo e potere alla luce della teoria dell'egemonia", in *Tempora multa: il governo del tempo*, ed. Vittorio Morfino (Milan: Mimesis, 2013), 191–224, 225–254, who criticise the two interpretations of time in Gramsci's work made, respectively, by Althusser and Laclau.

4 See Thomas' comparison of Gramsci's theory of personality and Deleuze's concept of "disjunctive synthesis" in Thomas, "Gramsci e le temporalità plurali", 208.

5 An example of this type is Gramsci's thoughts on subalterns: "The history of subaltern social groups is necessarily fragmented and episodic. There undoubtedly does exist a tendency to (at least provisional stage of) unification in the historical activity of these groups, but this tendency is continually interrupted by the activity of the ruling groups; it therefore can only be demonstrated when an historical cycle is completed and this cycle culminates in a success." Antonio Gramsci, *Selections from the Prison Notebooks*, ed. Quintin Hoare and Geoffrey Nowell Smith (London: Lawrence and Wishart, 1971), 54–55 (Q25§2).

6 Antonio Gramsci, *Further Selections from the Prison Notebooks*, ed. Derek Boothman (London: Lawrence & Wishart, 1995), 179 (Q10II§8).

7 See Alberto Burgio, *Gramsci storico* (Rome and Bari: Laterza, 2003), 18–21; Alberto Burgio, *Gramsci: il sistema in movimento* (Rome: DeriveApprodi, 2014), 112–118.

8 See Burgio, *Gramsci storico*, 122; Reinhart Koselleck, *Futures Past* (New York: Columbia University Press, 2004), 95.

9 Michele Filippini, *Using Gramsci* (London: Pluto Press, 2017), 95–97.

10 This interpretation of Gramscian time does not necessarily imply an "aleatory" interpretation of his Marxism. The way in which political novelty is produced, in fact, remains an "unspoken" feature of Gramscian discourse.

11 Gramsci, *Selections from the Prison Notebooks*, 357 (Q10II§48). The translation has been modified with regard to the term *mentalità* ("mentality"), which Hoare and Smith translate as "consciousness".

12 See Michele Filippini, *Una politica di massa. Antonio Gramsci e la rivoluzione della società* (Rome: Carocci, 2016), 67–102.

13 Gramsci, *Selections From the Prison Notebooks*, 324 (Q11§12).

14 Max Weber, "Science as a Vocation", in *The Vocation Lectures* (Cambridge: Hackett, 2004), 13.

15 See Thomas, "Gramsci e le temporalità plurali", 208. The emphasis on plurality that characterises this reading is linked to the pre-eminence of the "immanentist" interpretative approach to the *Prison Notebooks*. In reading Gramsci's works solely in the light of the immanentist view of philosophy, history, and politics, there is a risk, however, that the other elements, which we could call "historically teleological", and

which refer to another temporality, are ignored. On this point, Gramsci wrote that "teleology . . . means something that, following Kant's qualifications, can be defended by historical materialism". Antonio Gramsci, *Prison Notebooks: vol. 3*, ed. Joseph A. Buttigieg (New York: Columbia University Press, 2007), 194 (Q7§46).

16 Antonio Gramsci, *Quaderni del carcere*, ed. Valentino Gerratana (Torino: Einaudi, 1975), 1875 (Q16§12) (our translation).

17 Gramsci, *Selections From the Prison Notebooks*, 325 (Q11§12).

18 Gramsci, *Selections From the Prison Notebooks*, 324 (Q11§12).

19 Gramsci, *Selections From the Prison Notebooks*, 328 (Q11§12).

20 Gramsci, *Selections From the Prison Notebooks*, 419 (Q11§13).

21 See Franco Lo Piparo, *Lingua, Intellettuali, Egemonia in Gramsci* (Bari: Laterza, 1979); Peter Ives, *Gramsci's Politics of Language* (Toronto: University of Toronto Press, 2006); Alessandro Carlucci, *Gramsci and Languages: Unification, Diversity, Hegemony* (Leiden and Boston: Brill, 2013).

22 However, this does not exclude his "positive relationship with linguistic diversity [that] was crucial for his awareness of the perils inherent in imposing cultural and political unification". Carlucci, *Gramsci and Languages: Unification, Diversity, Hegemony*, 15–16; see also Ives, *Gramsci's Politics of Language*, 32.

23 Gramsci, *Selections From the Prison Notebooks*, 325 (Q11§12).

24 Gramsci, *Prison Notebooks: vol. 3*, 169 (Q7§16).

25 Adam David Morton, *Revolution and State in Modern Mexico: The Political Economy of Uneven Development* (Lanham, MD: Rowman & Littlefield, 2011).

26 See Sheila Fitzpatrick, Alexander Rabinowitch and Richard Stites, eds., *Russia in the Era of Nep: Explorations in Soviet Society and Culture* (Bloomington and Indianapolis: Indiana University Press, 1991); Silvano Tagliagambe, *Scienza, filosofia, politica in Unione Sovietica 1924–1939* (Milan: Feltrinelli, 1978); Massimo Cacciari, "Preobraženskij e il dibattito sull'industrializzazione durante la Nep", in *Piano economico e composizione di classe*, ed. Massimo Cacciari and Paolo Perulli (Milan: Feltrinelli, 1975), 11–143.

27 Gramsci, *Selections From the Prison Notebooks*, 365–366 (Q10II§12).

28 See Christine Buci-Glucksmann, *Gramsci and the State* (London: Lawrence & Wishart, 1980), 261–264; Stephen Cohen, *Bukharin and the Bolshevik Revolution* (New York: Random House, 1975); Filippini, *Una politica di massa*, 103–149.

29 See Henri De Man, *Au-delà du marxisme* (Bruxelles: L'Églantine, 1927). Gramsci had a 1929 Italian translation of this book when he was in prison, see Dirk Pels, "Hendrik de Man and the Ideology of Planism", *International Review of Social History* 32 (1987): 206–229.

30 This observation holds for many of the most important concepts contained in the *Prison Notebooks*: "hegemony" is taken from Lenin, see Peter Thomas, *The Gramscian Moment* (Leiden: Brill, 2009), 57–58; "civil society" from the classical economists and from Marx, see Jacques Texier, "Gramsci, Theoretician of the Superstructures: On the Concept of Civil Society", in *Gramsci and Marxist Theory*, ed. Chantal Mouffe (London: Routledge, 1979), 48–79; "historical bloc" from Sorel (*Reflections on Violence*), "intellectual and moral reform" from Renan (*La réforme intellectuelle et morale*), "modern Prince" from Machiavelli (*The Prince*), "philosophy of praxis" from Antonio Labriola, "Letter to G. Sorel 14 May 1897", in *Socialism and Philosophy*, www.marxists.org/archive/labriola/works/al04.htm (here translated as "philosophy of practice"); "Fordism" from the European debate, see von Friedrich Gottl-Ottlilienfeld, *Fordismus: Paraphrasen über das Verhältnis von Wirtschaft und technischer Vernunft bei Henry Ford und Frederick W. Taylor* (Jena: G. Fischer, 1924). See Anne Showstack Sassoon, "Gramsci's Subversion of the Language of Politics", in *Gramsci, Language, and Translation*, ed. Peter Ives and Rocco Lacorte (Lanham, MD: Lexington Books, 2010), 243–254.

31 Gramsci, *Further Selections From the Prison Notebooks*, 349 (Q10I§9).
32 Gramsci, *Prison Notebooks: vol. 3*, 372 (Q8§225).
33 Gramsci, *Prison Notebooks: vol. 3*, 252 (Q8§25).
34 Gramsci, *Selections from the Prison Notebooks*, 57 (Q19§24).
35 See Antonio Gramsci, "Some Aspects of the Southern Question", in *Pre-Prison Writings*, ed. Richard Bellamy (Cambridge: Cambridge University Press, 1994), 313–337.
36 Gramsci, *Selections From the Prison Notebooks*, 109 (Q15§11).
37 Gramsci, *Selections From the Prison Notebooks*, 132 (Q13§1).
38 Walter Benjamin, "On the Concept of History", in *Selected Writings, Volume 4 (1938–1940)*, ed. Howard Eiland and Michael W. Jennings (Cambridge, MA and London: Harvard University Press, 2003), 394–395 (Thesis XIII).
39 The theses were written between 1939 and 1940, and were conceived as an introduction to the *Passagen-Werk*; see Gianfranco Bonola and Michele Ranchetti, "Introduzione" and "Sulla vicenda delle tesi 'sul concetto di storia'", in Walter Benjamin, *Sul concetto di storia*, ed. Gianfranco Bonola and Michele Ranchetti (Turin: Einaudi, 1997), vii–xix, 5–13. The *Prison Notebooks* and the *Theses*, despite being very different writings from many points of view, nevertheless share certain specific characteristics: both are unfinished and were not published by their respective authors; both were written in dangerous situations, under the looming Fascist and Nazi regimes; and both were the last works written by their respective authors.
40 Benjamin, "On the Concept of History", 395 (Thesis XIV).
41 Benjamin, "On the Concept of History", 396 (Thesis XIV). See Benedict Anderson's use of this Benjaminian concept in regard to the construction of nationalism, in *Imagined Communities* (London and New York: Verso, 2006), 24–26.
42 Benjamin, "On the Concept of History", 396 (Thesis XIV).
43 Gramsci, *Selections From the Prison Notebooks*, 132 (Q13§1) (our italics). Gramsci repeats on several occasions in this note his thoughts on the precocious Jacobinism of Machiavelli: "Machiavelli did not merely abstractly desire the national unification of Italy; he had a programme, and it was one which revealed his 'precocious Jacobinism'." Gramsci, *Selections From the Prison Notebooks*, 132 (Q13§1).
44 Gramsci, *Selections From the Prison Notebooks*, 130, 123 (Q13§1). The same temporal structure also emerges in the following passage: "There is the 'passion' of the 'Jacobin' in Machiavelli, and that is why he must have been so popular with both the Jacobins and the followers of the Enlightenment." Gramsci, *Quaderni del carcere*, 1929 (Q17§27) (our translation).
45 Benjamin, "On the Concept of History", 391 (Thesis VI).
46 Gramsci in fact points out that "Without the agrarian policy of the Jacobins, Paris would have had the Vendee at its very doors." Gramsci, *Selections From the Prison Notebooks*, 79 (Q19§24).
47 Gramsci, *Selections From the Prison Notebooks*, 64 (Q19§24).
48 Gramsci, *Selections From the Prison Notebooks*, 64 (Q19§24).

Bibliography

Althusser, Louis, et al. *Reading Capital*. London: New Left Books, 1970.
Althusser, Louis. *Machiavelli and Us*. London and New York: Verso, 2000.
Althusser, Louis. *For Marx*. London and New York: Verso, 2005.
Anderson, Benedict. *Imagined Communities*. London and New York: Verso, 2006.
Badaloni, Nicola. *Il marxismo di Gramsci: dal mito alla ricomposizione politica*. Torino: Einaudi, 1975.
Badaloni, Nicola. "Gramsci and the Problem of the Revolution". In *Gramsci and Marxist Theory*, edited by Chantal Mouffe, 80–109. London: Routledge & Kegan Paul, 1979.

Benjamin, Walter. "On the Concept of History". In *Selected Writings, Volume 4 (1938–1940)*, edited by Howard Eiland, and Michael W. Jennings, 389–400. Cambridge, MA and London: Harvard University Press, 2003.

Bonola, Gianfranco, and Ranchetti, Michele. "Introduzione". In Walter Benjamin, *Sul concetto di storia*, edited by Gianfranco Bonola, and Michele Ranchetti, vii–xix. Turin: Einaudi, 1997.

Bonola, Gianfranco, and Ranchetti, Michele. "Sulla vicenda delle tesi 'sul concetto di storia'". In Walter Benjamin, *Sul concetto di storia*, edited by Gianfranco Bonola, and Michele Ranchetti, 5–13. Turin: Einaudi, 1997.

Buci-Glucksmann, Christine. *Gramsci and the State*. London: Lawrence & Wishart, 1980.

Burgio, Alberto. *Gramsci Storico*. Rome-Bari: Laterza, 2003.

Burgio, Alberto. *Gramsci: il sistema in movimento*. Rome: DeriveApprodi, 2014.

Cacciari, Massimo. "Preobraženskij e il dibattito sull'industrializzazione durante la Nep". In *Piano economico e composizione di classe*, edited by Massimo Cacciari, and Paolo Perulli, 11–143. Milan: Feltrinelli, 1975.

Carlucci, Alessandro. *Gramsci and Languages: Unification, Diversity, Hegemony*. Leiden and Boston: Brill, 2012.

Cohen, Stephen. *Bukharin and the Bolshevik Revolution*. New York: Random House, 1975.

De Man, Henri. *Au-delà du marxisme*. Bruxelles: L'Églantine, 1927.

Filippini, Michele. *Una politica di massa. Antonio Gramsci e la rivoluzione della società*. Rome: Carocci, 2016.

Filippini, Michele. *Using Gramsci*. London: Pluto Press, 2017.

Fitzpatrick, Sheila, Rabinowitch, Alexander, and Stites, Richard, eds. *Russia in the Era of Nep: Explorations in Soviet Society and Culture*. Bloomington and Indianapolis: Indiana University Press, 1991.

Gottl-Ottlilienfeld, Friedrich von. *Fordismus: Paraphrasen über das Verhältnis von Wirtschaft und technischer Vernunft bei Henry Ford und Frederick W. Taylor*. Jena: G. Fischer, 1924.

Gramsci, Antonio. *Selections From the Prison Notebooks*, edited by Quintin Hoare, and Geoffrey Nowell Smith. London: Lawrence and Wishart, 1971.

Gramsci, Antonio. *Quaderni del carcere*, edited by Valentino Gerratana. Torino: Einaudi, 1975.

Gramsci, Antonio. "Some Aspects of the Southern Question". In *Pre-Prison Writings*, edited by Richard Bellamy, 313–337. Cambridge: Cambridge University Press, 1994.

Gramsci, Antonio. *Further Selections From the Prison Notebooks*, edited by Derek Boothman. London: Lawrence & Wishart, 1995.

Gramsci, Antonio. *Prison Notebooks: Vol. 3*, edited by Joseph A. Buttigieg. New York: Columbia University Press, 2007.

Ives, Peter. *Gramsci's Politics of Language*. Toronto: University of Toronto Press, 2006.

Koselleck, Reinhart. *Futures Past*. New York: Columbia University Press, 2004.

Labriola, Antonio. "Letter to G. Sorel 14 May 1897". In *Socialism and Philosophy*, 1907. www.marxists.org/archive/labriola/works/al04.htm.

Lo Piparo, Franco. *Lingua, Intellettuali, Egemonia in Gramsci*. Bari: Laterza, 1979.

Morfino, Vittorio, ed. *Tempora multa: il governo del tempo*. Milan: Mimesis, 2013.

Morton, Adam David. *Revolution and State in Modern Mexico: The Political Economy of Uneven Development*. Lanham, MD: Rowman & Littlefield, 2011.

Negri, Antonio. *Books for Burning*. London and New York: Verso, 2005.

Pels, Dirk. "Hendrik de Man and the Ideology of Planism". *International Review of Social History* 32 (1987): 206–229.

Sassoon, Anne Showstack. "Gramsci's Subversion of the Language of Politics". In *Gramsci, Language, and Translation*, edited by Peter Ives, and Rocco Lacorte, 243–254. Lanham, MD: Lexington Books, 2010.

Tagliagambe, Silvano. *Scienza, filosofia, politica in Unione Sovietica 1924–1939*. Milan: Feltrinelli, 1978.

Texier, Jacques. "Gramsci, Theoretician of the Superstructures: On the Concept of Civil Society". In *Gramsci and Marxist Theory*, edited by Chantal Mouffe, 48–79. London: Routledge, 1979.

Thomas, Peter. *The Gramscian Moment*. Leiden: Brill, 2009.

Tronti, Mario. "Tra materialismo dialettico e filosofia della prassi". In *La città futura. Saggi sulla figura e il pensiero di Antonio Gramsci*, edited by Alberto Caracciolo, and Gianni Scalia, 139–186. Milan: Feltrinelli, 1959.

Weber, Max. "Science as a Vocation". In *The Vocation Lectures*, 1–31. Cambridge: Hackett, 2004.

6

CHARLES BAUDELAIRE IN THE AGE OF PASSIVE REVOLUTION

Benjamin and Gramsci[1]

Dario Gentili

6.1 Passive Revolution, Yesterday and Today

The fiftieth anniversary of 1968 reminded us to take stock of that social and political experience that lasted an entire decade in some countries, including in Italy. Much of the debate centred on the revolutionary value of the 1968 movement.[2] Was it a revolutionary movement that was then defeated or neutralised, or, with hindsight, would we say that its most significant outcome was the "counter-revolution"[3] that lay the ground for the affirmation of the so-called neoliberalism? To answer this, and to gain a more general understanding of the conservative distortion of the idea of revolution, we must return to Antonio Gramsci's category of "passive revolution".[4]

In *Notebook 8*, Gramsci defines "passive revolution" as the dynamic according to which, in a given historical conjuncture, "progress" does not proceed from "popular initiative" but is a "reaction of the dominant classes to the sporadic, elementary and non-organic rebelliousness of the popular masses together with 'restorations' that accepted a certain part of the demands expressed from below, and were thus 'progressive restorations' or 'revolutions-restorations' or even 'passive revolutions'".[5] He uses the category of "passive revolution" to interpret the historical and political events of the nineteenth century, in particular the Italian Risorgimento. Gramsci identifies in Gioberti and the theorists of the passive revolution "the necessity for the 'thesis' to achieve its full development, up to the point where it would even succeed in incorporating a part of the antithesis itself — in order, that is, not to allow itself to be 'transcended' in the dialectical opposition. The thesis alone in fact develops to the full its potential for struggle, up to the point where it absorbs even the so-called representatives of the antithesis: it

DOI: 10.4324/9781003457039-9

is precisely in this that the passive revolution or revolution/restoration consists".[6] In both definitions, only "a certain part" of the subversive demands of the subaltern class is captured and neutralised. There is thus a remainder, a residue.

At several points in the *Prison Notebooks*, Gramsci considers whether this category could also aid in the interpretation of phenomena in the period that followed. In *Notebook 22*, titled *Americanism and Fordism*, Gramsci asks "whether Americanism can constitute an historical 'epoch', that is, whether it can determine a gradual evolution of the same type as the 'passive revolution' examined elsewhere and typical of the last century, or whether on the other hand it does not simply represent the molecular accumulation of elements destined to produce an 'explosion', that is, an upheaval on the French pattern".[7] Today we might be inclined to say that Americanism, as a form of social regulation, and Fordism, as a capitalist mode of production, have turned out to be a "passive revolution": the height of their development did not lead to an "explosion" in the West as it did with the French Revolution.

To answer the question of whether Americanism represents an age of passive revolution, we have to look more closely at the events of the period from which Gramsci drew for his definition of "passive revolution". We must return to the "sporadic, elementary and non-organic rebelliousness of the popular masses" during the second half of the nineteenth century, also identifying how their "popular demands" gave the restoration of order the stamp of progress. Walter Benjamin's depiction of Paris as the capital of the nineteenth century, which begins from the figure of Charles Baudelaire, provides us with some important clues, particularly for understanding how Americanism took root in the Parisian metropolis in the aftermath of the revolutionary phase that culminated in 1848.

In the forms of life that characterised the post-revolutionary restoration in Paris, Benjamin identifies a process which prefigures that "psycho-physical adaptation" that for Gramsci was instead produced by Fordism in the early twentieth century. We could consider Benjamin's position here as a modification and integration of Gramsci's concept of passive revolution, giving anthropological change and changes in forms of life an autonomy that precedes and takes precedence over their capture within Fordism, for he already glimpses a form of Americanism in Baudelaire's behaviour. At times Benjamin even seems to find the prehistory of post-Fordist intellectual labour in the *Hochkapitalismus* of nineteenth-century Paris.[8] It is also worth remembering that Gramsci's and Benjamin's experiences of the world of work were different: for the former, it was Turin in the midst of Fordist development, for the latter, it was the intellectual precariat in 1930s' Paris.

6.2   The Passive Revolution in the Nineteenth Century: Paris, la bohème, la flânerie, and Baudelaire

The category of "passive revolution" is mainly used by Gramsci to analyse Italian history, in particular the Risorgimento. However, it is through comparison with events in nineteenth-century France that he arrives at its definition. It would therefore be interesting to consider whether Benjamin recognises phenomena in the Paris of that time that could in some way be traced back to the dynamics of passive revolution. Benjamin's analysis focuses on the form of life that took shape following the "explosive" revolutionary phase in the first half of the nineteenth century. Starting with the defeat of the proletariat in 1848, the phase of the "counter-revolution" began, to use Marx's expression, culminating in Louis Bonaparte's coup d'état and the establishment of the Second Empire. In the archaeology of nineteenth-century Paris that he laid out, using Baudelaire's life and work as a test case, Benjamin saw this form of life emerge and subsequently be captured and put to work within a new "advanced" phase of capitalism, which then made that form of life its prototype. This form of life consisted in a series of figures such as the *flâneur*, the *bohémien*, the idler, the professional conspirator, the gambler, the night owl, the detective, the rag picker, the prostitute, the poet, and the artist. This is the bohemian group against which Marx expressed a very severe judgement – "scum, offal, refuse of all classes" – because he recognised a basic ambiguity in it, its lack of class belonging meant it was sensitive to the flattery of power:

> Alongside decayed roués with dubious means of subsistence and of dubious origin, alongside ruined and adventurous offshoots of the bourgeoisie, were vagabonds, discharged soldiers, discharged jailbirds, escaped galley slaves, rogues, mountebanks, lazzaroni, pickpockets, tricksters, gamblers, maquereaus, brothel keepers, porters, literati, organgrinders, rag-pickers, knife grinders, tinkers, beggars – in short, the whole indefinite, disintegrated mass, thrown hither and thither, which the French term la bohème. . . . This Bonaparte, who constitutes himself chief of the lumpenproletariat, who here alone rediscovers in mass form the interests which he personally pursues, who recognises in this scum, offal, refuse of all classes the only class upon which he can base himself unconditionally, is the real Bonaparte, the Bonaparte sans phrase.[9]

But neither does the bohemian find a home within formal citizenship, the most fundamental result of the bourgeois revolution. In short, it is neither subjectivised within the people nor within the class. Instead the "crowd" of the nineteenth-century metropolises would end up being the mass that would become susceptible to Nazi-fascism's calls for the unity of the people: "This 'crowd', in which the flaneur takes delight, is just the empty mold with which, seventy years later, the *Volksgemeinschaft* (people's community) was cast".[10] For Gramsci, on the other hand, bohemianism represented those "viscous parasitic sedimentations"[11] that hindered the implanting of Americanism within the European production system. Benjamin also highlighted the highly unproductive character of this form of life when it appeared in the metropolis, describing the *flâneur* at home in the *passages* of Paris:

> In Baudelaire's Paris . . . Arcades where the *flâneur* would not be exposed to the sight of carriages that did not recognize pedestrians as rivals were enjoying undiminished popularity. There was the pedestrian who wedged himself into the crowd, but there was also the *flâneur* who demanded elbow room and was unwilling to forego the life of a gentleman of leisure. His leisurely appearance as a personality is his protest against the division of labor which makes people into specialists. It is also his protest against their industriousness.[12]

A few decades later, it was Fordism that set the pace of progress: "But this attitude did not prevail; Taylor, who popularised the watchword 'Down with dawdling!' carried the day".[13] Benjamin held that this was how the metamorphosis took place, when this form of life – which had been born outside the market – became a commodity among others and was put to work and valorised:

> In these conditions, . . . the gesture of the *flânerie* becomes meaningless for the free intelligentsia and therefore loses all meaning. Now the type of the *flâneur* so to speak shrinks, as if a bad fairy had touched him with a magic wand. At the end of this process of shrinking is the sandwich-man: here the identification with the commodity is complete. The *flâneur* is now really a commodity. He now goes for a walk for money, and his inspection of the market has become, almost overnight, a job.[14]

Benjamin claimed that rather than being an obstacle to the rise of Americanism, the unproductiveness of the bohemian ways of life that emerged from the 1848 revolution offered an opportunity for capitalism to valorise and profit from metropolitan lifestyles. Indeed, Benjamin understood with extraordinary shrewdness that, in nineteenth-century Paris, the metropolis became a factory, that is, the main site for the extraction of value. As he repeatedly wrote, everywhere the labyrinthine space of the metropolis takes on the function of the market: "The labyrinth is the right path for the person who always arrives early enough at his destination. This destination is the marketplace".[15] In this way, the marketplace provided the *flâneur* and Baudelaire himself with the possibility of feeling that their individuality was recognised and valued, whereas it would be nullified in class or citizenship. For Benjamin, Baudelaire is in fact the "prototype" par excellence of the individual as he would be constituted in the age of the masses, when "lifestyle" became one with artistic production. Indeed, for his poetry to have a market, Baudelaire's own life had to become the commodity to be promoted on the market. Benjamin had already found in Baudelaire the Americanism of making one's lifestyle a mass commodity: "The mass-produced article was Baudelaire's model. His 'Americanism' has its firmest foundation here".[16] His dandyism was thus an enhancement of his individuality, that individuality that had to stand out from the uniform crowd. But this happened not *against* the rise of mass society but *because* of it. The market is the sphere in which the individual has the possibility of standing out and distinguishing themselves from the masses. On the one side, as Marx argued in his analysis of Bonapartism, the charismatic leader, on the other, the market: these are the temptations to which the individual is susceptible in the metropolitan crowd and in mass society. This dynamic following the defeat of the potentially "explosive" revolution of 1848 – when Baudelaire had been on the same side as the proletariat and its leader Louis-Auguste Blanqui – and traced by Benjamin in nineteenth-century Paris, can even be found today, albeit with some differences, in capitalism's continued ability to extract value from the commodification of forms of life. The expression that Benjamin uses to define Baudelaire's attitude, becoming "his own impresario", bears striking resemblance to the "entrepreneur of the self" with which Michel Foucault describes the individual brought to market and valorised in the neoliberal era[17]:

> No study of Baudelaire can fully explore the vitality of its subject without dealing with the image of his life. This image was actually determined by the fact that he was the first to realize, and in the most productive way, that the bourgeoisie was about to annul its contract with the poet. Which social contract would replace it? That question could not be addressed to any class; only the market and its crises could provide an answer. . . . But the medium of the market through which it revealed itself to him dictated a mode of production and of living which differed sharply from those known to earlier poets. Baudelaire was obliged to lay claim to the dignity of the poet in a society that had no more dignity of any kind to confer. . . . In Baudelaire, the poet for the first time stakes a claim to exhibition value. Baudelaire was his own impresario.[18]

"Exhibition value" – which precisely at that time for Benjamin began to take precedence over the "cult value" of the auratic work of art[19] – thus entered the capitalist market and found its peculiar sphere of valorisation. It was thus Baudelaire who first conferred an exhibition value on his own life; he "was perhaps the first to conceive of a market-oriented originality",[20] long before today's regime of visibility and self-promotion, in which, through the use of technologies such as social media, it has become everyone's prerogative. Lifestyle is the last outpost of individuality in globalised society, and it is the market that determines the success or otherwise, and at what price, of the aspiration to stand out from the masses.

6.3 Psycho-Physical Adaptation

Although, unlike Gramsci, Benjamin understood that the "progressive" element of Americanism's passive revolution consisted in making metropolitan forms of life productive, they both nevertheless completely agreed that the peculiarity of Americanism lay in its requiring a general "psycho-physical adaptation" to the new system of production. But whereas for Benjamin this "psycho-physical adaptation" was already driven by life in the metropolis in the second half of the nineteenth century, so much so that it became a sort of training ground for a subsequent adaptation to the productive rhythms of the Fordist factory, for Gramsci the opposite was true: it was the industrial Fordist system that required psycho-physical adaptation, which then found its living environment in the metropolis. And yet, for both, Fordism required the elaboration of a new type of human:

> In America rationalization has determined the need to elaborate a new type of man suited to the new type of work and productive process. This elaboration is still only in its initial phase and therefore (apparently) still idyllic. It is still at the stage of psycho-physical adaptation to the new industrial structure, aimed for through high wages. Up to the present (until the 1929 crash) there has not been, except perhaps sporadically, any flowering of the "superstructure". In other words, the fundamental question of hegemony has not been posed.[21]

This adaptation required constant training and "apprenticeship", so that forced and "non-natural" disciplining could gradually be perceived by the worker as a voluntarily chosen and thus "natural" way of life: "Life in industry demands a general apprenticeship, a process of psycho-physical adaptation to specific conditions of work, nutrition, housing, customs, etc. This is not something 'natural' or innate, but has to be acquired".[22] The hegemony of Americanism finally bears fruit when this disciplining takes on a "superstructural" aspect, that is, when it becomes self-coercion and self-disciplining to conform to a general and widespread lifestyle: the "new type of man" is thus the outcome of a process of standardisation.[23]

Benjamin sees this same process of standardisation at work in the metropolitan space, it is here – on the superstructural level, before it arrives at the structural level of Fordism – that the hegemony of Americanism asserts itself. For it is here that psycho-physical adaptation finds the motivation to become self-disciplining, and this motivation is the enjoyment promised by the market:

> insofar as a person, as labour power, is a commodity, there is no need for him to identify himself as such. The more conscious he becomes of his mode of existence, the mode imposed on him by the system of production, the more

he proletarianizes himself, the more he will be gripped by the chilly breath of the commodity economy, and the less he will feel like empathizing with commodities. But things had not yet reached that point with the class of petty bourgeoisie to which Baudelaire belonged. On the scale we are dealing with here, this class was only at the beginning of its decline. Inevitably, many of its members would one day become aware of the commodity nature of their labour power. But this day had not yet come; until then, they were permitted (if one may put it this way) to pass the time. The very fact that they share could, at best, be enjoyment, but never power, made the period which history gave them a space for passing time.[24]

It is on this basis that Benjamin finds an analogy between the inhabitant of the great metropolis in the second half of the nineteenth century and the Fordist factory worker in the twentieth century. Whereas for the Fordist factory worker, the motivation for self-discipline comes from high wages, for the individuals in the metropolitan crowd it comes from the spectacle of the commodity. In both cases, there is a promise of enjoyment: that arising from having a greater amount of money to use for consumption and the narcissistic enjoyment of being able to promote oneself on the market. And it is precisely those metropolitan forms of life that are unproductive, and therefore potentially subversive to the capitalist system (the *flâneur*, the *bohémien*, and Baudelaire) that for Benjamin represented the main vantage point from which to grasp the apparatuses of capture and disciplining in what he called *Hochkapitalismus*. Thus the metropolis itself was the training ground for the psycho-physical adaptation to Americanism. In Baudelaire's Paris, Benjamin sees the very first manifestations of a phenomenon that had already come into its own in the "Americanised" London of Edgar Allan Poe's *The Man of the Crowd* and had now been perfected in the metropolises of his time:

> The unskilled worker is the one most deeply degraded by machine training. His work has been sealed off from experience; practice counts for nothing in the factory. . . . Poe's text helps us understand the true connection between wildness and discipline. His pedestrians act as if they had adapted themselves to machines and could express themselves only automatically. Their behavior is a reaction to shocks. . . . The shock experience [*Chockerlebnis*] which the passer-by has in the crowd corresponds to the isolated "experiences" of the worker at his machine.[25]

6.4 Americanism and Fascism

The fact that both Gramsci and Benjamin analysed the revolutionary uprisings in nineteenth-century France in order to read their own contemporaneity – the 1920s and 1930s – already seems a good enough basis to justify a comparison

between them. To add to this, both Benjamin and Gramsci were attentive readers of Marx's *Eighteenth Brumaire of Louis Bonaparte*, in which they found a
key to interpreting their own era. In Marx's analysis of Bonapartism – of which
we might also detect some traces in today's "populisms"[26] – each thinker finds
elements that were present in the rise of fascisms in Europe within the economic
context of the 1929 crisis. This is clear in Gramsci's definition of a "non-organic
crisis", that is, in the authoritarian form that the "organic crisis" assumes when
"a single party" (what Marx calls the "party of order"), "which better represents
and resumes the needs of the entire class",[27] is no longer able to cope with and
govern the economic crisis by itself and so gives way to a charismatic leader.
So, on the basis of his reading of Marx's *Eighteenth Brumaire* and the events
of post-1848 France, Gramsci pointed out that the category of "passive revolution" could also be applied to fascism. He asked, "In modern conditions, is
not 'fascism' precisely a new 'liberalism'? Is not fascism precisely the form of
'passive revolution' proper to the twentieth century as liberalism was to the nineteenth?".[28] In hindsight, we can see that the "new liberalism" that emerged from
the irreversible crisis of classical liberalism following the Wall Street Crash of
1929 was not in fact fascism. It could instead be glimpsed ten years later in the
1938 Walter Lippmann Colloquium in Paris, which laid the foundations for the
development of neoliberalism several decades later.[29]

Although conceived in the context of nineteenth-century Europe, Gramsci
did not limit the category of "passive revolution" to a specific historical conjuncture, but instead hypothesised that it could also be applied to different eras
and historical contexts, as an *affirmation* of an idea of revolution *alternative*
to the paradigm of the French Revolution, that is, a revolution led by the ruling classes. For Gramsci, fascism, which he defined as "a new liberalism", was
an example of this alternative, insofar as it performed the function that liberalism had performed following the French Revolution of restoring and preserving
class hegemony, as Marx argued happened in the bourgeois revolutions of the
nineteenth century (Marx, 1852). In some ways, fascism and Nazism were also
bourgeois revolutions for Benjamin. It is important for us to try to understand
whether Americanism and fascism represented two separate forms of passive
revolution or whether they converged to form a unitary phenomenon.

6.5   Passive Revolution Today

In answer to Gramsci's question as to whether Americanism was a passive revolution, both Benjamin and Gramsci argued that it was. But this was not only due
to its ability to capture the demands and forms of life that were produced in the
revolutionary ferments preceding it but also because, even in the passive revolution's capacity to impose adaptation, a residue was left in the persistence of revolutionary power. Gramsci calls this formless and indeterminate power – to which

Americanism gave its own form, both in order to govern it and to make it productive – "animality": "The history of industrialism has always been a continuing struggle (which today takes an even more marked and vigorous form) against the element of 'animality' in man. It has been an uninterrupted, often painful and bloody process of subjugating natural (i.e. animal and primitive) instincts to new, more complex and rigid norms and habits of order, exactitude and precision which can make possible the increasingly complex forms of collective life which are the necessary consequence of industrial development".[30] Gramsci takes prohibitionism and the "crisis of libertinism" as examples. According to Benjamin, Baudelaire himself foresaw this crisis of libertinism, seeing his drive for enjoyment constantly disappointed by the market, which promised enjoyment only to leave it frustrated: "he envisioned the day on which even the fallen women, the outcasts, would readily espouse a well-ordered life, condemn libertinism, and reject everything except money".[31]

However, for both Gramsci and Benjamin, the revolutionary chance lay in preventing Americanism from having the initiative on the anthropogenesis of the new human and in orienting this power to shape our own lives in the opposite direction to that offered by adaptation. Gramsci makes this clear: "It is not from the social groups 'condemned' by the new order that reconstruction is to be expected, but from those on whom is imposed the burden of creating with their own suffering the material bases of the new order. It is they who 'must' find for themselves an 'original', and not Americanised, system of living, to turn into 'freedom' what today is 'necessity'".[32] This applies to the passive revolution of the nineteenth century, to that of Americanism, and also to today's neoliberal revolution. And we must keep in mind that in the past each of these passive revolutions of the capitalist system of production implied a complementary authoritarian passive revolution in politics. It is this "non-organic" articulation of the "organic crisis" that we also find in neo-populisms and neo-sovereignisms, which, instead of representing a response to the economic crisis that began in 2007–2008 (and is still ongoing) and a political alternative to neoliberalism, rather play an internal function in the preservation of existing power relations. It might be worth exploring whether the Benjaminian state of exception as rule could be rethought as passive revolution as rule.

And so the question arises as to whether now, in an era of widespread crisis (in all its social, economic, environmental, and cultural forms) that becomes increasingly hard for the capitalist order to govern, we find the failure of the persuasive capacity of "progress". If so, this would mean the failure of that "dialectic of conservation and innovation",[33] beginning from the affirmation of bourgeois hegemony, that Gramsci claims supported – and I believe still supports – every form of "passive revolution". Already in his time Gramsci had diagnosed the crisis of progress not so much as a crisis of "faith in the possibility of rationally dominating nature and chance" but as a result of the fact that "the official 'standard bearers' of progress have become incapable of this dominating, because they have brought into being in the present destructive forces like crises and unemployment, etc., every bit as dangerous and terrifying as those of the past".[34] Benjamin was no less clear on this subject. At the outbreak of the Second World War, after analysing the emergence of the idea of progress in Baudelaire's Paris, he not only firmly criticised its "official standard bearers", those "politicians in whom the opponents of fascism had placed their hopes", and their "stubborn faith in progress, their confidence in their 'base in the masses', and, finally, their servile integration in an uncontrollable apparatus"[35], but also pointed to the unsustainability of the concept itself: "The concept of progress must be grounded in the idea of catastrophe".[36] Who's to say whether that catastrophe that was avoided thanks to "popular initiative" – certainly at the end of the Second World War, but maybe we could also argue after the crisis of Fordism in the 1970s – is not back on the agenda today, in the twilight of the age of progress and perhaps also of passive revolutions.

Notes

1 This essay is a more in-depth reproposal of Dario Gentili, "Charles Baudelaire im Zeitalter der passiven Revolution: Benjamin und Gramsci", in "Gramsci und Benjamin – Passagen: Gramsci and Benjamin – Bridges", ed. Birgit Wagner and Ingo Pohn-Lauggas, Special Issue, *International Gramsci Journal* 3, no. 4 (2020): 31–44.

2 See Ilaria Bussoni and Nicolas Martino, eds., *È solo l'inizio. Rifiuto, affetti, creatività nel lungo '68* (Verona: ombre corte, 2018).

3 See Paolo Virno, "Do You Remember Counterrevolution?", in *Radical Thought in Italy: A Potential Politics*, ed. Paolo Virno and Michael Hardt (Minneapolis and London: University of Minneapolis Press, 1996), 241–259.

4 For an analysis of the category of "passive revolution" in Gramsci, see Giuseppe Cospito, Gianni Francioni, and Fabio Frosini, eds., *Crisi e rivoluzione passiva. Gramsci interprete del Novecento* (Como and Pavia: Ibis, 2021); Marcello Mustè, *Rivoluzioni passive. Il mondo tra le due guerre nei Quaderni del carcere di Gramsci* (Rome: Viella, 2022).

5 Antonio Gramsci, *Further Selections from the Prison Notebooks*, ed. Derek Boothman (London: Lawrence & Wishart, 1995), 523 [Q 10, § 41].

6 Antonio Gramsci, *Selections From the Prison Notebooks*, ed. and trans. Quintin Hoare and Geoffrey Nowell Smith (New York: International Publishers, 1992), 110 [Q 15, 11].

7 Gramsci, *Selections from the Prison Notebooks*, 279–280 [Q 22, 1].

8 Especially in his notes for the project *Charles Baudelaire: A Lyric Poet in the Era of High Capitalism*, although less so in the essay "On Some Motifs in Baudelaire", published in 1940 in the *Zeitschrift für Sozialforschung*.

9 Karl Marx, "The Eighteenth Brumaire of Louis Bonaparte", in *The Collected Works of Karl Marx and Frederick Engels* (New York: International Publishers, 1975), vol. 11, 149.

10 Walter Benjamin, *The Arcades Project* (Cambridge, MA: The Belknap Press, 1999), 345.

11 Gramsci, *Selections from the Prison Notebooks*, 285 [Q 22, 2].

12 Walter Benjamin, *Charles Baudelaire: A Lyric Poet in the Era of High Capitalism* (London: Verso/NLB, 1973), 53–54.

13 Benjamin, *Charles Baudelaire*, 54.
14 Walter Benjamin, *Baudelairiana. Unveröffentlichte Fragmente zu einer Neufassung des Flaneurs*. Frankfurter Adorno Blätter IV (München: edition text + kritik, 1995), 13–14 (trans. by CP).
15 Walter Benjamin, "Central Park", in *Selected Writings, Volume 4 (1938–1940)*, ed. Howard Eiland and Michael W. Jennings (Cambridge, MA and London: Harvard University Press, 2006), 170.
16 Benjamin, "Central Park", 188.
17 See Michel Foucault, *The Birth of Biopolitics: Lectures at the Collegè de France, 1978–1979* (London: Palgrave Macmillan, 2008). I have gone into more detail on the Benjaminian figure of Baudelaire as an intellectual prototype of the neoliberal "entrepreneur of the self" in Dario Gentili, "Cosmo e individuo. Per una genealogia del lavoro intellettuale in epoca neoliberale", *aut aut*, no. 365 (2015): 21–36.
18 Benjamin, "Central Park", 168–169.
19 This is the dialectical dyad that Benjamin analyses in *The Work of Art in the Age of Its Technological Reproducibility*. See Walter Benjamin, "The Work of Art in the Age of Its Technological Reproducibility: Second Version", in *Selected Writings, Volume 3 (1935–1938)*, ed. Howard Eiland and Michael W. Jennings (Cambridge, MA and London: Harvard University Press, 2006). On this aspect, see Marina Montanelli and Massimo Palma, eds., *Tecniche di esposizione. Walter Benjamin e la riproduzione dell'opera d'arte* (Macerata: Quodlibet, 2016).
20 Benjamin, "Central Park", 168.
21 Gramsci, *Selections From the Prison Notebooks*, 286 [Q 22, 2].
22 Gramsci, *Selections From the Prison Notebooks*, 296 [Q 22, 3].
23 See Michele Filippini, *Una politica di massa. Antonio Gramsci e la rivoluzione della società* (Rome: Carocci, 2015), 151–185.
24 Walter Benjamin, "The Paris of the Second Empire in Baudelaire", in *Selected Writings, Volume 4 (1938–1940)*, ed. Howard Eiland and Michael W. Jennings (Cambridge, MA and London: Harvard University Press, 2006), 33–34.
25 Walter Benjamin, "On Some Motifs in Baudelaire", in *Selected Writings, Volume 4 (1938–1940)*, ed. Howard Eiland and Michael W. Jennings (Cambridge, MA and London: Harvard University Press, 2006), 329.
26 See Martin Beck and Ingo Stützle, eds., *Die neuen Bonapartisten. Mit Marx den Aufstieg von Trump & Co. verstehen* (Berlin: Dietz, 2018); Francesca Antonini, *Caesarism and Bonapartism in Gramsci: Hegemony and the Crisis of Modernity* (Leiden: Brill, 2021).
27 Gramsci, *Selections From the Prison Notebooks*, 211 [Q 13, 23].
28 Antonio Gramsci, "Fascism as Passive Revolution: First Version", in *The Gramsci Reader: Selected Writings 1916–1935*, ed. D. Forgacs (New York: New York University Press, 2000), 264 [Q 8, 236].
29 See Foucault, *The Birth of Biopolitics*; Quinn Slobodian, *Globalists: The End of Empire and the Birth of Neoliberalism* (Cambridge, MA and London: Harvard University Press, 2018).
30 Gramsci, *Selections From the Prison Notebooks*, 298 [Q 22, 10].
31 Benjamin, "On Some Motifs in Baudelaire", 343.
32 Gramsci, *Selections From the Prison Notebooks*, 317 [Q 22, 15].
33 Gramsci, *Further Selections From the Prison Notebooks*, 374 [Q 10, 41].
34 Gramsci, *Selections From the Prison Notebooks*, 358 [Q 10, 48].
35 Benjamin, "On the Concept of History", in *Selected Writings, Volume 4 (1938–1940)*, ed. Howard Eiland and Michael W. Jennings (Cambridge, MA and London: Harvard University Press, 2006), 393.
36 Benjamin, "Central Park", 184.

Bibliography

Antonini, Francesca. *Caesarism and Bonapartism in Gramsci: Hegemony and the Crisis of Modernity*. Leiden: Brill, 2021.

Beck, Martin, and Stützle, Ingo, eds. *Die neuen Bonapartisten. Mit Marx den Aufstieg von Trump & Co. verstehen*. Berlin: Dietz, 2018.

Benjamin, Walter. *Charles Baudelaire: A Lyric Poet in the Era of High Capitalism*. London: Verso/NLB, 1973.

Benjamin, Walter. *Baudelairiana. Unveröffentlichte Fragmente zu einer Neufassung des Flaneurs*. Frankfurter Adorno Blätter IV. München: edition text + kritik, 1995.

Benjamin, Walter. *The Arcades Project*. Cambridge, MA: The Belknap Press, 1999.

Benjamin, Walter. "Central Park". In *Selected Writings: Volume 4 (1938–1940)*, edited by Howard Eiland, and Michael W. Jennings. Cambridge, MA and London: Harvard University Press, 2006.

Benjamin, Walter. "On Some Motifs in Baudelaire". In *Selected Writings: Volume 4 (1938–1940)*, edited by Howard Eiland, and Michael W. Jennings. Cambridge, MA and London: Harvard University Press, 2006.

Benjamin, Walter. "On the Concept of History". In *Selected Writings: Volume 4 (1938–1940)*, edited by Howard Eiland, and Michael W. Jennings. Cambridge, MA and London: Harvard University Press, 2006.

Benjamin, Walter. "The Paris of the Second Empire in Baudelaire". In *Selected Writings: Volume 4 (1938–1940)*, edited by Howard Eiland, and Michael W. Jennings. Cambridge, MA and London: Harvard University Press, 2006.

Benjamin, Walter. "The Work of Art in the Age of Its Technological Reproducibility: Second Version". In *Selected Writings: Volume 3 (1935–1938)*, edited by Howard Eiland, and Michael W. Jennings. Cambridge, MA and London: Harvard University Press, 2006.

Bussoni, Ilaria, and Martino, Nicolas, eds. *È solo l'inizio. Rifiuto, affetti, creatività nel lungo '68*. Verona: ombre corte, 2018.

Cospito, Giuseppe, Francioni, Gianni, and Frosini, Fabio, eds. *Crisi e rivoluzione passiva. Gramsci interprete del Novecento*. Como and Pavia: Ibis, 2021.

Filippini, Michele. *Una politica di massa. Antonio Gramsci e la rivoluzione della società*. Rome: Carocci, 2015.

Foucault, Michel. *The Birth of Biopolitics: Lectures at the Collegè de France, 1978–1979*. London: Palgrave Macmillan, 2008.

Gentili, Dario. "Cosmo e individuo. Per una genealogia del lavoro intellettuale in epoca neoliberale". *aut aut*, no. 365 (2015): 21–36.

Gentili, Dario. "Charles Baudelaire im Zeitalter der passiven Revolution: Benjamin und Gramsci". *International Gramsci Journal* 3, no. 4 (2020): 31–44.

Gramsci, Antonio. *Selections from the Prison Notebooks*, edited by Quintin Hoare, and Geoffrey Nowell Smith. New York: International Publishers, 1992.

Gramsci, Antonio. *Further Selections from the Prison Notebooks*, edited by Derek Boothman. London: Lawrence & Wishart, 1995.

Gramsci, Antonio. "Fascism as Passive Revolution: First Version". In *The Gramsci Reader: Selected Writings 1916–1935*, edited by David Forgacs. New York: New York University Press, 2000.

Marx, Karl. "The Eighteenth Brumaire of Louis Bonaparte". In *The Collected Works of Karl Marx and Frederick Engels*, vol. 11. New York: International Publishers, 1975.

Montanelli, Marina, and Palma, Massimo, eds. *Tecniche di esposizione. Walter Benjamin e la riproduzione dell'opera d'arte*. Macerata: Quodlibet, 2016.

Mustè, Marcello. *Rivoluzioni passive. Il mondo tra le due guerre nei Quaderni del carcere di Gramsci*. Rome: Viella, 2022.

Slobodian, Quinn. *Globalists: The End of Empire and the Birth of Neoliberalism*. Cambridge, MA and London: Harvard University Press, 2018.

Virno, Paolo. "Do You Remember Counterrevolution?". In *Radical Thought in Italy: A Potential Politics*, edited by Paolo Virno, and Michael Hardt, 241–259. Minneapolis and London: University of Minneapolis Press, 1996.

Translated by Clara Pope

7

GRAMSCI, BENJAMIN, AND PASSIVE REVOLUTIONS

Marcello Mustè

7.1 Gramsci and Benjamin: Similarities and Differences

Can Gramsci and Benjamin be understood as expressions of a common need for theoretical Marxism? As we shall see, the answer to this question is partly yes and partly no. What unites these two authors is above all their belief that a significant continuity exists between the Marxism of the Second International and the new orthodoxy of the Stalinist period (the so-called Marxism-Leninism), a continuity marked by a deterministic view of history and a merely "progressive" conception of revolutionary struggle. Benjamin developed this concept through a radical critique of the three main principles of historicism (the idea of universal history, narrativity, and identification with the past)[1] and with a denial of the "concept of progress itself", of "homogeneous, empty time", which was the keystone of "social democratic theory" in the nineteenth and twentieth centuries.[2] Gramsci made a similar criticism, albeit using a different lexicon, of the reformist socialism of the early twentieth century and of Bucharin's scholasticism. Both identified the root of the problem in Marx's own thought. In the notes accompanying the theses On the Concept of History, Benjamin found it in the idea of revolutions as the "locomotives of world history" (to which he opposed the image of the "emergency brake").[3] He also refuted the "theory of progress in Marx", defined, in the preface to *A Contribution to the Critique of Political Economy*, as the "development of the productive forces".[4] Even Gramsci, from his early article on the "revolution against Capital",[5] recognised Marx's "scientific" spirit as the root of various deformations that would become manifest after his death in the Marxism of the Second International. Moreover, both rejected the image of communism as a

DOI: 10.4324/9781003457039-10

normative and finalistic ideal,[6] were convinced of the importance of translation and translatability,[7] with a shared critique of Esperanto, and above all affirmed the connection between historiography and politics (and philosophy), which, Benjamin explained, "is identical to the theological connection between remembrance and redemption".[8]

The similarities in their thought also follow a similar trajectory. However, at a certain point, in relation to their conceptions of the physiognomy of the revolutionary *subject*, the similarities end. For Benjamin, it is in the "moment" in which the past contracts into the present,[9] in the "state of emergency",[10] that revolutionary action redeems the past, representing a history of the oppressed that surpasses the "cultural treasures" (391, WB, SW) of the victors. The revolution is thus configured as a kind of "vendetta". He writes, "Marx presents it as the last enslaved class – the avenger that completes the task of liberation in the name of generations of the downtrodden. This conviction . . . has always been objectionable to Social Democrats. . . . The Social Democrats preferred to cast the working class in the role of a redeemer of future generations, in this way cutting the sinews of its greatest strength".[11] In the passage in which his detachment from Marx and Engels becomes most obvious (for whom the communist revolution was the "heir" of the bourgeois revolution and its world market, not of slaves or serfs, thereby overcoming the principle of alienated labour and exploitation), Benjamin paradoxically accepts the Marxian figure of the subject, the proletariat constituted as a class and, in the last instance, formed by the development of industry itself. The subject is still the class, which, due to its objective position in modern society, can create *discontinuum* in history, taking up the legacy of the vanquished of every epoch.

Gramsci takes the opposite path. He retains Marx's historical conception, rethinking the subaltern class as a folkloric figure (as the sedimentation of common sense, incapable of taking revolutionary initiative on its own) and transforms Marx's and Lenin's figure of the *subject*. With the theory of hegemony, the fundamental problem of the philosophy of praxis becomes that of the *constitution* of the political subject, in the combination of civil society and the state and of national and international levels. His reading of modernity and progress thus differs from Benjamin's paradigm, as we shall try to show through the example of the theory of passive revolutions.

7.2   A New Morphology of Politics

As with all the main categories in the *Prison Notebooks* (for instance, hegemony and war of position), the concept of passive revolution has a dual physiognomy. On the one hand, it is an *analytical* tool, necessary for reading reality and, in particular, history. On the other hand, it is a *strategic* tool, with a political and practical purpose, which allows us to consider the problems of a world revolution.

On the *analytical* level (as with all theoretical Marxism, starting with Marx himself), Gramsci engages in a reading of the cycle of bourgeois revolutions. Unlike Marx, however, who had identified 1848 as the climax, the *Höhepunkt* – the point of conversion from the "upward" to the "downward" trajectory of European movement[12] – Gramsci saw 1870 (also thanks to the analyses of Labriola and Croce) as the moment in which the contemporary and post-bourgeois age properly began (in which world capitalism separated from the progressive values of the revolutionary bourgeoisie).[13] He held that the bourgeois revolution had two main results in the period between 1789 and 1870: on the one hand, the construction of European nation-states as a modern form of politics; and, on the other, the cosmopolitan unification of the economy with the global expansion of the capitalist model into a world market.

After 1870, the "downward line" began, when these two results (the nation-state and economic cosmopolitanism) became the poles of an explosive contradiction, which dragged the world into a series of destructive wars. As Gramsci had already expressed in his early writings (evaluating Wilson's Fourteen Points), the nation-state was *out of step* with the global development of the economy. An irreducible antithesis arose between political nationalism and economic cosmopolitanism, which in many ways translated the Marxian contradiction between relations and forces of production into modern terms. It was about adjusting (*conguagliare*) politics to economics. To do this, it was necessary to overcome the modern morphology of politics, based on the theory of sovereignty (Hobbes) and its bourgeois form in the territorial state. Hence, the new "enlarged" theory of the state, including the Hegelian *bürgerliche Gesellschaft*, and the search for a new mix of the "national" and the "international", culminating in the theory of translatability and the "fantastical" figure of the modern Prince, as the germ of the collective will. As he writes in *Notebook 22*, the world today is engaged in a difficult transition "from the old economic individualism to the planned economy"[14]: that is, in the task of affirming a new form of politics adapted to the globalised world and of overcoming the classical conception of the sovereign state.

For this reason, the theory of crises acquires fundamental importance in the notebooks, which Gramsci focuses on in two notes found in *Notebook 13* and *Notebook 15*. In *Notebook 13*, the crisis is interpreted as the disintegration of the hegemonic apparatus, when "social groups break away from their traditional parties" and common sense no longer recognises the dominant world view as its own: "A 'crisis of authority' is spoken of: this is precisely the crisis of hegemony, or general crisis of the State".[15] Gramsci elaborates on this in *Notebook 15*, saying, with reference to the 1929 crisis, that crisis is not a single event but a complex process accompanying the entire development of modernity, manifesting itself in the fundamental contradiction between the cosmopolitanism of economic life and the nationalism of politics.[16]

7.3 What Are Passive Revolutions?

Gramsci used the category of passive revolution to represent the cycle of bourgeois revolutions. Only recently, thanks to the chronological method of reading the notebooks, has it been possible to accurately reconstruct the development of this concept.[17] The term derives from Vincenzo Cuoco in his 1801 essay *Saggio storico sulla rivoluzione di Napoli*, as well as from other authors (Michele Natale in 1799 and Francesco Lomonaco in 1800–1801), but it actually stretches back to an older tradition, beginning with Thomas Paine's *Rights of Man* in early 1792, in which the term "passive revolutions" was first used.[18] In his essay, Cuoco used the term (showing that he was unaware of Paine's precedent use of it) to indicate a revolution such as that in Naples, which, unlike in France in 1789, did not have a spontaneous and popular character but an *imitative one*, and was thus doomed to defeat. The term was taken up by Benedetto Croce in the 1896 preface to his *Studi storici sulla rivoluzione napoletana del 1799*, and Gramsci encountered it around November 1930 (the first occurrence is in *Notebook 4*) in the broader reworking that Guido De Ruggiero had made of it in the 1922 book *Il pensiero politico meridionale nei secoli XVIII e XIX*. Only later, in the miscellanea of *Notebook 8* (January–February 1932), did Gramsci establish the correspondence between the concept of passive revolution and that of restoration-revolution, which Daniele Mattalia had attributed to Edgar Quinet in the former's article on Giosuè Carducci.[19] But the most important connection (albeit not explicit in the notebooks) was with Antonio Labriola's fourth essay on historical materialism (*Da un secolo all'altro*), where, with reference to the Italian Risorgimento, a distinction was made between "active history" and "passive history" and between "active peoples" and "passive peoples".[20]

Whatever his sources, Gramsci adopted this concept (greatly expanding its meaning) to indicate the entire expansive process triggered by the French Revolution of 1789, in a form that was no longer active and Jacobinist, but passive. It was a national "translation" of global progress; a revolution from above, carried out by the ruling classes but capable of assimilating, realising, and even weakening the claims of the subaltern classes. It is important to remember that the Italian Risorgimento was just one example of the European process of passive revolution, in which the dialectic between moderates and democrats perfectly manifested the absence of the people-nation and of the active Jacobinist moment. Here too, Gramsci's gaze was global, never purely national. He was undoubtedly struck by the oxymoron of the term "passive revolution", capable of simultaneously indicating a real process of revolutionary transformation (a passive revolution is a *revolution*, in the full sense of the term) and the passive character that the subaltern classes maintain within it. Passive revolution accurately indicated not only the characteristic process of bourgeois revolutions but the epochal transition that Gramsci argued had taken place. The active revolutions (the French and

Soviet revolutions) were the last examples of a war of movement, especially after the failed uprising in Germany in March 1921. Gramsci went so far as to speak, in *Notebook 15* (March–April 1933), of "the absolute identity"[21] between passive revolution and the war of position. Now the epoch of the war of movement and of the concept of revolution in the classical and traditional sense was over, the workers' movement had entered the dimension of passive revolution, that is, of a conflict conducted in the trenches of civil society. This was also the underlying reason for his criticism of Trotsky (theorist "of frontal attack when this can only lead to defeat"[22]) and of Rosa Luxemburg's essay on *The Mass Strike* (1906).[23] The discovery of passive revolution was the synthesis of the morphological shift in the concept of revolution and of modern politics in general.

7.4 Between Marx and Max Weber

If what we have said is true, namely that the concept of passive revolution is an original reading of the process of bourgeois revolutions, it is understandable why the confrontation with Marx's work remains at the core of Gramsci's work. During his years in prison in Turi, he continuously engaged in an in-depth reading of Marx, beginning with translating various parts of his work from German between May 1930 and July 1931 in *Notebook 7*.[24] The old liberal criticism of Gramsci, of having developed a Marxism without Marx or without *Capital*, appears to be completely unfounded. In fact, the opposite is true: the entire dossier on passive revolutions shows us his decisive confrontation with Marx. The following texts were particularly significant to his concept of passive revolution: *The Holy Family*, which he recognised as the origin of the concept of translatability (the passive revolution is a figure of global translatability, in the sense that it translates the content of active revolutions to national spheres);[25] *The Poverty of Philosophy*, where Gramsci found in Marx's critique of Proudhon the idea of the domestication of the Hegelian dialectic, that is, the avoidance of opposition and social conflict in the context of a passive revolution;[26] and the 1859 *Preface to a Contribution to the Critique of Political Economy*, from which Gramsci derived, through reworking them, the two principles of modern politics: on the one hand, the idea (as translated by Gramsci) that "no social formation disappears as long as the productive forces which have developed within it still find room for further forward movement", and, on the other hand, the rule in which "society does not set itself tasks for whose solution the necessary conditions have not already been incubated".[27] As is clear, the two principles taken from the 1859 Preface established the precise theoretical basis for the transition from active revolution to passive revolution.

But Marx's text that most clearly influenced Gramsci's thinking was *The Eighteenth Brumaire of Louis Bonaparte*.[28] In addition to an article by Robert Michels on the oligarchic tendencies of democracy and charismatic power,[29] it was Marx's *Eighteenth Brumaire* and Max Weber's essay "Parliament and Government in Germany under a New Political Order"[30] that allowed Gramsci to point to a particular reading of Caesarism (what he called a "Caesarism without a Caesar"[31]) as the political form characteristic of passive revolutions. Gramsci could not find a theory of Caesarism in Marx, because, as we know, Marx had explicitly rejected this category, but he did find in Marx a theory of the crisis that went beyond the schematic vision of the *Manifesto*. In *The Eighteenth Brumaire*, Marx reread the process of bourgeois revolution by emphasising a "long crapulent depression"[32] (*ein langer Katzenjammer*), the long nausea that had taken possession of European society after the initial expansive phase of the revolutionary movement, making possible a power like that of Louis Bonaparte, which rested neither on the bourgeoisie nor on the proletariat, but on the consensus of the social classes that remained on the margins of capitalist development (the peasants and lumpenproletariat). It was the perfect image of the organic crisis, of the "interregnum" in which "the old is dying and the new cannot be born".[33] Gramsci united this Marxian theory of crisis with the teachings of Max Weber, who, in "Parliament and Government in Germany under a New Political Order", had identified Caesarism as the political destiny of modernisation processes, in a dialectical relationship with the development of parliamentary democracy and the "iron cage" of bureaucratisation.[34] Uniting Marx's analysis with that of Weber, in *Notebook 9*, Gramsci identified the political form characteristic of passive revolutions not in Caesarism in general (charismatic power and providential man) but in a "Caesarism without a Caesar", such as that which had asserted itself in the coalition governments in Italy between 1922 and 1926 and in Great Britain with the MacDonald cabinet, thus in the practice of *trasformismo*.

7.5 A Global Organic Crisis

Up to this point, we have considered passive revolution as an *analytical* category, capable of capturing the rhythm of bourgeois revolutions and inaugurating a new figure of politics and revolution, merging with the concepts of the war of position and hegemony. At a certain point, however, Gramsci predictably extended the discourse, raising the question of whether or not the present epoch – the global context of the 1930s – created a new situation of passive revolution. In *Notebook 10*, he directly posed the question, asking: "Can this 'model' for the creation of the modern states be repeated in other conditions?". He went on: "The question is of the highest importance, because the France – Europe model has created a mentality".[35] The answer required an analysis of the forces on the world stage, of the "great powers", as he called them: in particular Russia, America, and Europe. A new passive revolution should have manifested itself in the progressive potential of the 1917 Soviet revolution (on the model of the 1789 French Revolution), in the possibility of transforming its principle into a world revolution, in the form, specified in Notebook 22, of a passage from the "old economic individualism to the planned economy". As we shall now see, Gramsci ultimately rejected this hypothesis. Contrary to that previously argued by his most authoritative interpreters,[36] Gramsci did not understand the reality of the 1930s as a passive revolution, but as an epoch of *global organic crisis*, in which none of the subjects involved was capable of leading an epochal transition in a hegemonic sense. This meant war and unprecedented destruction were an inevitable destiny, as Gramsci predicted.

Gramsci's discourse primarily concerned the Soviet Union after Lenin's death, including the struggle for power and the beginning of Stalin's five-year plans. Gramsci had already expressed concern over the exhaustion of the Soviet state's expansive and propulsive capacity in his famous letter to the Russian party's central committee, written on 14 October 1926: "You today, are destroying your own work, you degrade and run the risk of nullifying the leadership function that the Communist Party of the USSR won through Lenin's impetus".[37] This judgement became even more severe and radical in the notebooks, finding a perfect metaphor in the image of the Reformation without Renaissance, that is, of a doctrine that had failed to develop on the superstructural and hegemonic level. But in Gramsci's eyes, America, the other great power, suffered from a similar malady, as a virgin nation "without tradition", "in which the 'structure' dominates the superstructures more immediately".[38] It is easy to see, therefore, that the whole discourse on Americanism and Taylorism was not about America but about Europe, or rather the possibility that Europe, which was weighed down by its "great historical and cultural traditions", could enter the terrain of modernity and exercise a hegemonic function in the world. But his analysis of Europe also revealed the limitations of the situation, because the strength of its tradition represented a set of "passive sedimentations" that the bourgeois revolution had produced and crystallised, starting with a political form limited to the figure of the nation-state.

None of the great powers appeared capable of taking up the challenge of the 1917 revolution and leading the shift to a planned economy. And so a new passive revolution appeared impracticable. The picture that was emerging was of a global organic crisis, a world without hegemony and without leadership, running head first towards catastrophe. It was a dramatic and painful paradox that Gramsci saw the seed of a passive revolution only in fascism or, more precisely, in corporatism. In *Notebook 8*, he wrote, "[W]ould fascism not be precisely the form of 'passive revolution' proper to the twentieth century, as liberalism was to the nineteenth century?".[39] The answer to this question was ultimately negative, because corporatism, as an attempt at a European-style Americanism, was born in fascism from the needs of "economic policing" and therefore reaffirmed, rather than overcame, the unproductive tendencies of the national economy. But the paradoxical and painful fact remained that only fascism indicated a tendency towards passive revolution, while the great powers – Russia, Europe, and America – proved incapable of leading an epochal transition.

7.6 Conclusion

After the Soviet rupture, an act of separation from capitalism but also an early brake on the progressive capacity to build a new world order, both Benjamin and Gramsci sought to define a new idea of revolution that went beyond the Stalinist schema but was still far removed from "social democratic theory". This was the point of convergence, the common problem, that united them. Benjamin had a more radical critique of the idea of progress, coming to understand revolution as the destruction of the evolutionary line of the past, of "cultural treasures", and, consequently, as the emergence of a hidden, latent subjectivity, capable of taking up the legacy of all of the oppressed and defeated of civilisation. Following Marx, revolution was a "dialectical leap",[40] a "messianic arrest of happening",[41] "a moment of danger"[42]: it is in "class struggle", as Benjamin repeated several times in the *Theses on the Philosophy of History*, that the oppressed class becomes the "subject of historical knowledge".[43] That is, it divides, rescues, and redeems the entire past: "The Messiah comes not only as the redeemer; he comes as the victor over the Antichrist. The only historian capable of fanning the spark of hope in the past is the one who is firmly convinced that even the dead will not be safe from the enemy if he is victorious. And this enemy has never ceased to be victorious".[44] In the same *Augenblick* of the revolution, the *class* is the "victor over the Antichrist", it terrifies the enemy and redeems history, reactivating the forgotten "spark" of "hope".

Like Benjamin, after the simultaneous victory and retreat of the Soviet novelty, Gramsci also set out in search of a new image of the revolution. Through his research on passive revolutions, thus through re-reading the entire cycle of bourgeois revolutions, Gramsci was convinced that the era of the "war of movement" was completely over, not only in the West but in the world history. The destiny of revolution was now entrusted to the "war of position" and hegemonic conflict, to the struggle for the affirmation of a new vision of the world within civil society and of an effective democratic pluralism. Gramsci no longer believed, like Benjamin, in the "moment of danger" and the "dialectical leap". As a result, in Gramsci's theory, social conflict could no longer be configured in the traditional terms of "class struggle". As we have already said, the nature of the subject was at stake. The new subject, the "organic intellectual" (or, as Togliatti would put it, the "collective intellectual"), was the result of complex combinations, it was the "modern prince" that held within itself the germ of the collective will. It would not redeem the past in a moment of exception, in the manner of the angel of history, but carried the past within itself as the consciousness of a still not completely realised modernity.

Notes

1 Walter Benjamin, "Paralipomena to 'On the Concept of History'", in *Selected Writings, Volume 4 (1938–1940)*, ed. Howard Eiland and Michael W. Jennings (Cambridge, MA and London: Harvard University Press, 2006).
2 Walter Benjamin, "On the Concept of History", in *Selected Writings, Volume 4 (1938–1940)*, ed. Howard Eiland and Michael W. Jennings (Cambridge, MA and London: Harvard University Press, 2006), 394–395.
3 Benjamin, "Paralipomena to 'On the Concept of History'", 402.
4 Karl Marx, *A Contribution to the Critique of Political Economy* (Moscow: Progress Publishers, 1977).
5 Antonio Gramsci, "La rivoluzione contro 'Il Capitale' (1 Dec. 1917)", in *Scritti (1910–1926): 2. 1917*, ed. Leonardo Rapone with the collaboration of Maria Luisa Righi (Rome: Istituto della Enciclopedia Italiana, 2015), 617–620.
6 Benjamin, "Paralipomena to 'On the Concept of History'", 401.
7 Benjamin, "Paralipomena to 'On the Concept of History'", 405–407.
8 Walter Benjamin, "Aufzeichnungen zum Thema", in *Gesammelte Schriften*, ed. Rolf Tiedemann and Hermann Schweppenhäuser (Frankfurt am Main: Suhrkamp, 1991), vol. 1/3, 1248 (trans. by CP).
9 Benjamin, "Paralipomena to 'On the Concept of History'", 403.
10 Benjamin, "On the Concept of History", 392.
11 Benjamin, "On the Concept of History", 394.
12 See Karl Marx, "The Eighteenth Brumaire of Louis Bonaparte", in *The Collected Works of Karl Marx and Frederick Engels* (New York: International Publishers, 1975), vol. 11.
13 Antonio Gramsci, *Quaderni del carcere*, ed. Valentino Gerratana (Turin: Einaudi, 1975), 1229.
14 Antonio Gramsci, *Selections From the Prison Notebooks*, ed. and trans. Quintin Hoare and Geoffrey Nowell Smith (New York: International Publishers, 1992), 279.
15 Gramsci, *Selections from the Prison Notebooks*, 210.
16 Gramsci, *Quaderni del carcere*, 1755–1759.
17 See, in particular, Fabio Frosini, "Rivoluzione passiva e laboratorio politico: appunti sull'analisi del fascismo nei Quaderni del carcere", *Studi storici* 2 (2017): 297–328; Antonio Di Meo, "La 'rivoluzione passiva' da Paine a Cuoco a Gramsci", in *Decifrare Gramsci. Una lettura filologica* (Rome: Bordeaux, 2020), 88–133; Fabio Frosini, "'Rivoluzione passiva': la fonte di Gramsci e alcune conseguenze", in *Crisi e rivoluzione passiva. Gramsci interprete del Novecento*, ed. Giuseppe Cospito, Gianni Francioni, and Fabio Frosini (Como and Pavia: Ibis, 2021), 181–217; Marcello Mustè, *Rivoluzioni passive. Il mondo tra le due guerre nei Quaderni del carcere di Gramsci* (Rome: Viella, 2022).
18 Thomas Paine, *Rights of Man, Common Sense, and Other Political Writings*, ed. Mark Philp (Oxford: Oxford University Press, 1995).
19 Gramsci, *Quaderni del carcere*, 957.
20 Antonio Labriola, *Scritti filosofici e politici*, ed. Franco Sbarberi (Turin: Einaudi, 1976), vol. 2, 854–855 (trans. by CP).
21 Gramsci, *Selections From the Prison Notebooks*, 108.
22 Gramsci, *Selections From the Prison Notebooks*, 107.
23 Gramsci, *Selections From the Prison Notebooks*, 233.
24 Antonio Gramsci, *Quaderni del carcere. 1. Quaderni di traduzioni (1929–1932)*, ed. Giuseppe Cospito and Gianni Francioni (Rome: Istituto dell'Enciclopedia Italiana, 2007), vol. 2, 799–808.
25 Gramsci, *Quaderni del carcere*, 1468–1473.

26 Gramsci, *Quaderni del carcere*, 1083.
27 Gramsci, *Selections From the Prison Notebooks*, 106.
28 This question has been studied in detail by Francesca Antonini in the first part of her book *Caesarism and Bonapartism in Gramsci: Hegemony and the Crisis of Modernity* (Leiden and Boston: Brill, 2020).
29 Robert Michels, "Les partis politiques et la contrainte sociale", *Mercure de France*, 1 May 1928, 513–535.
30 Max Weber, "Parliament and Government in Germany under a New Political Order: Towards a Political Critique of Officialdom and the Party System", in *Political Writings* (Cambridge: Cambridge University Press, 1994), 130 ss.
31 Gramsci, *Quaderni del carcere*, 1195 (trans. by CP).
32 Marx, "The Eighteenth Brumaire of Louis Bonaparte", 106.
33 Gramsci, *Selections from the Prison Notebooks*, 276.
34 Weber, "Parliament and Government in Germany Under a New Political Order: Towards a Political Critique of Officialdom and the Party System".
35 Gramsci, *Selections From the Prison Notebooks*, 115.
36 See, for example, Franco De Felice, "Rivoluzione passiva, fascismo, americanismo in Gramsci", in *Il presente come storia*, ed. Gregorio Sorgonà and Ermanno Taviani (Rome: Carocci, 2016), 315–368; Mario Telò, "Note sul futuro dell'Occidente e la teoria delle relazioni internazionali", in *Gramsci e il Novecento*, ed. Giuseppe Vacca (Rome: Carocci, 1999), 51–74.
37 Chiara Daniele, ed., *Gramsci a Roma, Togliatti a Mosca. Il carteggio del 1926* (Turin: Einaudi, 1999), 404–412 (trans. by CP).
38 Gramsci, *Selections From the Prison Notebooks*, 286.
39 Gramsci, *Selections From the Prison Notebooks*, 119.
40 Benjamin, "On the Concept of History", 395.
41 Benjamin, "On the Concept of History", 396.
42 Benjamin, "On the Concept of History", 391.
43 Benjamin, "On the Concept of History", 394.
44 Benjamin, "On the Concept of History", 391.

Bibliography

Antonini, Francesca. *Caesarism and Bonapartism in Gramsci: Hegemony and the Crisis of Modernity*. Leiden: Brill, 2021.
Benjamin, Walter. "Aufzeichnungen zum Thema". In *Gesammelte Schriften*, edited by Rolf Tiedemann, and Hermann Schweppenhäuser, vol. 1/3. Frankfurt am Main: Suhrkamp, 1991.
Benjamin, Walter. "On the Concept of History". In *Selected Writings, Volume 4 (1938–1940)*, edited by Howard Eiland, and Michael W. Jennings. Cambridge, MA and London: Harvard University Press, 2006.
Benjamin, Walter. "Paralipomena to 'On the Concept of History'". In *Selected Writings, Volume 4 (1938–1940)*, edited by Howard Eiland, and Michael W. Jennings. Cambridge, MA and London: Harvard University Press, 2006.
Daniele, Chiara, ed. *Gramsci a Roma, Togliatti a Mosca. Il carteggio del 1926*. Turin: Einaudi, 1999.
De Felice, Franco. "Rivoluzione passiva, fascismo, americanismo in Gramsci". In *Il presente come storia*, edited by Gregorio Sorgonà, and Ermanno Taviani, 315–368. Rome: Carocci, 2016.
Di Meo, Antonio. "La 'rivoluzione passiva' da Paine a Cuoco a Gramsci". In *Decifrare Gramsci. Una lettura filologica*, 88–133. Rome: Bordeaux, 2020.

Frosini, Fabio. "Rivoluzione passiva e laboratorio politico: appunti sull'analisi del fascismo nei Quaderni del carcere". *Studi Storici* 2 (2017): 297–328.

Frosini, Fabio. "'Rivoluzione passiva': la fonte di Gramsci e alcune conseguenze". In *Crisi e rivoluzione passiva. Gramsci interprete del Novecento*, edited by Giuseppe Cospito, Gianni Francioni, and Fabio Frosini, 181–217. Como and Pavia: Ibis, 2021.

Gramsci, Antonio. *Quaderni del carcere*, edited by Valentino Gerratana. Turin: Einaudi, 1975.

Gramsci, Antonio. *Selections from the Prison Notebooks*, edited and translated by Quintin Hoare, and Geoffrey Nowell Smith. New York: International Publishers, 1992.

Gramsci, Antonio. *Quaderni del carcere. 1. Quaderni di traduzioni (1929–1932)*, edited by Giuseppe Cospito, and Gianni Francioni, II. Rome: Istituto dell'Enciclopedia Italiana, 2007.

Gramsci, Antonio. "La rivoluzione contro 'Il Capitale' (1 Dec. 1917)". In *Scritti (1910–1926). 2. 1917*, edited by Leonardo Rapone, with the collaboration of Maria Luisa Righi. Rome: Istituto della Enciclopedia Italiana, 2015.

Labriola, Antonio. *Scritti filosofici e politici*, edited by Franco Sbarberi, vol. 2. Turin: Einaudi, 1976.

Marx, Karl. "The Eighteenth Brumaire of Louis Bonaparte". In *The Collected Works of Karl Marx and Frederick Engels*, vol. 11. New York: International Publishers, 1975.

Marx, Karl. *A Contribution to the Critique of Political Economy*. Moscow: Progress Publishers, 1977.

Michels, Robert. "Les partis politiques et la contrainte sociale". *Mercure de France* (1 May 1928): 513–535.

Mustè, Marcello. *Rivoluzioni passive. Il mondo tra le due guerre nei Quaderni del carcere di Gramsci*. Rome: Viella, 2022.

Paine, Thomas. *Rights of Man, Common Sense, and Other Political Writings*, edited by Mark Philp. Oxford: Oxford University Press, 1995.

Telò, Mario. "Note sul futuro dell'Occidente e la teoria delle relazioni internazionali". In *Gramsci e il Novecento*, edited by Giuseppe Vacca, 51–74. Rome: Carocci, 1999.

Weber, Max. "Parliament and Government in Germany under a New Political Order: Towards a Political Critique of Officialdom and the Party System". In *Political Writings*. Cambridge: Cambridge University Press, 1994.

Translated by Clara Pope

PART 3

Capitalist Modes of Production and Production of Subjectivity

8

THE LITTLE PRINCE

Sorel, Myth and Violence Between Benjamin and Gramsci

Massimo Palma

8.1 Prologue-Epilogue: Georges Sorel, a "Sociologist of Myth", a Forerunner of Fascism

In January 1938, the journal *Esprit* published a contribution by Paul-Ludwig Landsberg, a pupil of Scheler and Husserl, in which Georges Sorel was described as "the first sociologist of myth". Landsberg, who had recently emigrated from Germany, noted how Sorel, indebted *à la fois* to Nietzsche and Marx, Bergson and Lenin, had an idea of the collective myth as a pure form with "interchangeable content". Sorel, writes Landsberg, was responsible for a large part of the "mythomania" of the time, as well as for influencing the political turn taken by a certain post-surrealism, which in those years insisted on the need to invent new myths. A few months later, one who had more than a liaison with those circles, Raymond Queneau, spoke in this regard of a "thirst for myth" (*soif de mythe*).[1] Landsberg continued the article by recalling the old Sorel's meeting in 1912 with a young Mussolini, who was to be "greatly influenced" by him.[2]

In 1938, therefore, certain critical lines against the contradictory legacy of the syndicalist theorist had already been largely drawn. Antonio Gramsci and Walter Benjamin, the one having just died, the other two years before taking his life, were therefore on a path that had already been traced. Both could boast a remarkable sensitivity to the Sorelian concept of "myth" and its ambiguities. Almost in unison, in fact, Benjamin and Gramsci acknowledge Sorel's questionable merit of having generated monsters. Already in 1927, Benjamin had called him the "father" of Georges Valois, an exponent of syndicalism that is, with socialism, "the best nursery (*Pflanzschule*) of fascist leaders".[3] And in that very 1938, the year Landsberg's article came out, in a review dedicated to Julien

DOI: 10.4324/9781003457039-12

Benda, Benjamin likened Sorel to Céline, but also to Rosenberg and Goebbels.[4] The four names, listed on a perfidious downward scale, would present a common vein recognisable today as a *culte de la blague* with distinctly anti-Semitic traits, which even had its ancestor in Baudelaire.[5]

Years earlier, in the *Quaderni*, Gramsci had reserved equally harsh treatment for Sorel and his bad friends, but preferred to frame him in a sociological category: the intellectual.

> It must be kept in mind that Sorel's moral and intellectual "austerity" and "seriousness" have been somewhat exaggerated; . . . a certain vanity . . . results from the very awkward tone of the letter in which he wants to explain to Croce his adhesion (albeit platonic) to Valois' *Cercle Proudhon* and his flirtation with young elements of the royalist and clerical tendency. Again: there was a certain dilettantism in Sorel's "political" attitudes, which were never overtly political, but more coming from "cultural politics", "intellectual politics", "*au dessus de la mêlée*". . . . He himself was a "pure" intellectual.[6]

Echoing Romain Rolland's famous pacifist manifesto (1915's *Au-dessus de la mêlée*), Gramsci did not hesitate to call Sorel an amateur, never really political – a relevant actor in cultural politics, not anything else. Would Sorel therefore ultimately be politically useless, if not harmful, to both Gramsci and Benjamin?

Things are different. And in a way, the very definition of Sorel as the "first sociologist of myth" provided in Landsberg's upset article finds a fruitful and ambivalent development in the two. Both indeed question the penetration, effectiveness, and danger of social myths in reference to the construction of mass political action.

8.2   1921: The Reflections and the Critique of Violence

It was in 1921 that Benjamin finally read that "necessary book from France" that was to come to him, as he had announced in a letter to his friend Gerhard Scholem on 1 December 1920.[7] In all likelihood, in that message, he was talking about Sorel's *Réflexions sur la violence*. By the time Benjamin read them, the *Réflexions* were in their fourth edition. The first printing of the text came out for the Librairie de "Pages Libres" in 1908, it had 257 pages. Two years later, it came out for publisher Marcel Rivière with an additional chapter ("Unité et multeplicité") and 165 pages more. The third edition, for the same types, is from 1913 and also contains a new chapter, "Apologie de la violence". After the pause of the war, in which Sorel remained editorially silent for six years, the *Réflexions* reappeared in 1919 with the further addition of a *Pladoyer pour Lénine*, again for Rivière: they count 458 pages. It is the edition that will see Benjamin, reprinted identically in 1921.

In Italy, the text had been translated from the first edition in 1909 by Antonio Sarno, with an introduction by Benedetto Croce, with whom Sorel had corresponded since 20 December 1895 (the correspondence would end on 26 August 1921, a year before Sorel's death at the age of 74[8]). Again due to Croce's interest,[9] the work would be re-edited with additions in 1926: Gramsci must have been aware of both editions.

As for Benjamin, an early, enigmatic nod to the Sorelian work just read is in the obscure fragment called *Capitalism as Religion*, where a mere note appears in a list: "Capitalism and Law. The heathen character of law. Sorel: *Réflexions sur la violence*, p. 262".[10] It is worth noting that the point recalled is not exactly perspicuous. If we listen to the fourth edition – or to the fifth, unchanged in 1921 – the passage on p. 262 does not seem to call up any "heathen" traits of law, which is called into question, in the context of a passage on the supposed "natural laws" of the economy, only with a brief phrase: "laws can be stated in their simplest, surest, and most elegant formulas, since the law of contract dominates every country of advanced capitalism".[11]

Despite a less-than-clear first occurrence, in the same weeks, Sorel's presence in another historical site of the young Benjamin becomes more evident and clearer. Indeed, in *Toward the Critique of Violence*, Sorel emerges in rather heated and laudatory tones, although ultimately the judgement on his theory appears ambivalent. While Fredric Jameson has recently proposed reading the whole of *Zur Kritik der Gewalt* as a commentary on Sorel, sealed not by the constitutions and legal reflections of the Enlightenment but rather by "that 'divine violence' he finds in Sorel and in Bolshevism", and again "as a meditation on Georges Sorel's epoch-making *Reflections on Violence*",[12] it is true that in his text Benjamin states how the book certainly has the merit of having distinguished – "in relation to violence" – two different modes of general strike: the "political" and the "proletarian". The political general strike is aimed at building a "strong, centralised and disciplined" *Staatsgewalt*,[13] while the proletarian one aims at the sole task of the annihilation of state power. It "nullifies all the ideological consequences of every possible social policy; its partisans see even the most popular reforms as bourgeois".[14] The proletarian general strike would be, in Benjamin's terms, a "purely non-violent means" because it takes the "determination to resume to resume only a wholly transformed work, no longer enforced by the state".[15]

Sorel rejects all sorts of programmes, utopias, in short, positions of entitlement for the revolutionary movement: "With the general strike all these fine things go up in smoke; the revolution appears as a pure and simple revolt, without any place being left for sociologists, for elegant worldly people who are friends of social reform, for intellectuals who dedicate themselves to the profession of thinking for the proletariat".[16] This profound, ethical, and genuinely revolutionary conception cannot be countered with a consideration that would stigmatise such a general strike as violence because of its possible catastrophic consequences.

In the still pre-Marxist Benjamin of 1921, a positive appreciation of Sorel's palingenetic catastrophism is evident. And at the same time one can remark the appreciation of Sorel's revolutionary genuineness – an appreciation of the "moral" quality of his choice in favour of the category of "producers" (albeit ambivalent in the choice of terminology). Not a word, however, does Benjamin spend on the element that touched Gramsci, namely the mythical character of the general strike. Which appears in *Reflections on Violence* almost at the opening.

> Men who are participating in a great social movement always picture their coming action as a battle. . . . The syndicalist "general strike" and Marx catastrophic revolution are such myths.[17]

Myth is, therefore, first and foremost a collective image of a battle. Again in the letter to Daniel Halévy placed as an introduction to the *Reflections* we read:

> The revolutionary myths which exist at the present time are almost free from any such mixture: by means of them it is possible to understand the activities, the feelings and the ideas of the masses preparing themselves to enter on a decisive struggle: the myths are not description of things, but expressions of a determination to act. . . . Contemporary myths lead men to prepare themselves for a combat which will destroy the existing state of things.[18]

Now, it is well known how even Benjamin, in that masterpiece of anarchic "destructivism" that is *Toward the Critique of Violence*, does nothing but deal with "myth". But he does not speak of it in the Sorelian key, at all. Surely "myth" is a decisive term for Benjamin in that dense essay, perhaps written with too much eagerness and ended up by a lucky chance in one of the most prestigious publishing venues of the German academy.[19] But Benjamin heavily stigmatises it just a few pages later: "Mythic violence is in its archetypal form a mere manifestation of the gods".[20] Or again: "If this immediate violence in mythic manifestations proves closely related, indeed identical, to lawmaking violence".[21] The term "myth" – characterised by the eternal return of the same, muteness, destinality, and epiphany of iterated violence that strips life of all determination (making it "mere life") – thus finds its determined specification in the juridical *Gewalt*: the same juridical sphere, its sanctioning procedures, would be a transparent mythological operation for the "critique" of violence, which reveals its mythical matrix, ultimately aimed at re-proposing death as the only alternative – the hard substance – in the event of transgression.[22] A radically anti-Sorelian move, given that "myth" is a decisive term in Sorel from the outset. But where Benjamin's praise of Sorel seems to radically stall, Gramsci's interest begins at the same point.

8.3 Gramsci, the *Notebook 13* and Sorel as Mythopoiet

Gramsci's famous *Notebook 13*, dedicated to Machiavelli's politics, opens in fact with an open and all-Sorelian question.

> The basic thing about *The Prince* is that it is not a systematic treatment, but a "live" work, in which political ideology and political science are fused in the dramatic form of a "myth". Machiavelli . . . gave imaginative and artistic form to his conception by embodying the doctrinal, rational element in the person of a *condottiero*, who represents plastically and "anthropomorphically" the symbol of the "collective will".[23]

The "condottiero" – who will soon be compared to the "charismatic leader" in Robert Michels and Max Weber – would thus be the hero-myth, the dramatic "person" symbolising the collective will. But far from Gramsci – unlike Benjamin, who in the *Critique of Violence* thinks of him in the key of the "great criminal" – is any attention to the founding figure of the hero: Gramsci receives with annoyance Michels's waffling on "charisma" – it is relevant to remind that Michels in those years was an avowed supporter of the fascist regime, albeit having been a correspondent of both Sorel and Weber.[24]

The theme had already appeared several years earlier in the writing on the "leader" that appeared in memory of Lenin in *Ordine Nuovo*. Celebrating the recently deceased Bolshevik leader, Gramsci shunned the reading of the political representative as leader and personality. Rather, he noted how "in the question of the proletarian dictatorship, the essential problem is not that of the physical personification of the function of command. The essential problem consists in the nature of the relations that the leaders or the chief have with the party of the working class: . . . are they purely hierarchical, of a military type, or are they historical and organic in character?".[25] These words anticipate Benjamin in the essay on *The Work of Art in the Age of Its Technical Reproducibility*. More precisely, they prefigure a very dense note of the Third Version that dwells on the disappearance of the opposition, in the class struggle, between the individual and the masses: "Decisive as the masses are for the revolutionary leader (*für den revolutionären Führer*), therefore, his great achievement lies not in drawing the masses after him, but in constantly incorporating himself into the masses, in order to be, for them, always one among hundreds of thousands".[26]

A few years later in Gramsci, the Sorelian and "mythical" connection of the problem of the "prince" is immediately made explicit in famous words. The prince is in fact identified with a myth.

> Machiavelli's *Prince* could be studied as a historical exemplification of the Sorellian "myth" – i.e. of a political ideology expressed neither in the form of a cold utopia nor as learned theorising, but rather as a creation of concrete phantasy which acts on a dispersed and shattered people to arouse and organise its collective will.[27]

Gramsci thinks of a use of the political myth in the key of a non-spontaneist organisation of the collective will (and thus not an "immediate" manifestation of its violence, in Benjaminian terms). Defining the political will in the "modern sense" as an "operative awareness of historical necessity", Gramsci claims the role of will as "protagonist of a real and effective historical drama" for the party.[28] In this key, Gramsci imagines a "Jacobin" use of myth to affirm the collective political will, emphasising its concreteness, as opposed to the intellectualist, calculated abstraction of the Sorelian myth. In doing so, he thus vindicates the line that from Machiavelli would arrive precisely at the Jacobins of the eighteenth century first and the twentieth century later, to separate from Sorel precisely in his inability to structure the creator subjects of the political myth.

> A study might be made about how it came about that Sorel never advanced from his conception of ideology-as-myth to an understanding of political party, but stopped short at the idea of trade union. It is true that for Sorel the "myth" found its fullest expression not in the trade union but in its practical action – i.e. a "passive activity", so to speak, of a negative and preliminary kind (it could only been given a positive character by the realisation of a common accord between the various wills involved), an activity which does not envisage an "active and constructive" phase of its own.[29]

Sorel's hostility to party organisation is stigmatised by Gramsci as an "impulse of the irrational, of the 'arbitrary' (in the Bergsonian sense of 'vital impulse')", that is, of "spontaneity". But the interest of Sorel's formulae cannot stop at condemnation.

> Can a myth, however, be "non-constructive"? How could an instrument conceivably be ineffective, if, as in Sorel's vision of things, it leaves the collective will in the primitive and elementary phase of its mere formation, by differentiation ("cleavage") – even when this differentiation is violent, that is to say destroys existing moral and juridical relations? Will not that collective will, with so rudimentary a formation, at once cease to exist, scattering into an infinity of individual wills?[30]

To obviate the "elementary" dispersion of primitive, unmediated action, Gramsci calls for a party of a new type. A party that does not repudiate a priori the element of the irrational, but that knows how to organise it in its complexity, directing its tendency to the universal, to the total. Political passions must therefore be elaborated, and moulded through the party organism, so that they lose their dispersiveness without losing their diffusion. And in this, the mythical character, which pertains to the complex organism that Gramsci refers to as "myth-prince", can help.

> The modern prince, the myth-prince, cannot be a real person, a concrete individual. It can only be an organism, a complex organ of society, in which a collective will, which has already been recognized and has to some extent asserted itself in action, begins to take concrete form. History has already provided this organism, and it is the political party – the first cell in which there come together germs of a collective will tending to become universal and total.[31]

Yet the theme of "passion", or of the irrational as the matrix of the political act, has an indisputable duplicity. Valid as a metaphor for the party's commitment to organising hegemony, it runs the risk of vanishing as soon as it is enunciated, according to an easy Croce criticism, which – we shall see – a young Ernesto De Martino will take up. So what to do with the irrational? Of myth, of passion?

> The "passionate" element as the origin of the political act, as theorised by Croce, cannot be accepted as such. Croce says about Sorel: "the 'feeling of cleavage' had not guaranteed it (syndicalism) enough, perhaps also because a theorised cleavage is an outdated cleavage; nor did the 'myth' warm it up enough, perhaps because Sorel, in the very act of creating it, had dissipated it, giving its doctrinal explanation" (cf. *Cultura e vita morale* [Culture and Moral Life], 2nd ed., 158). The observations on Sorel are also right for Croce: is not the "theorised passion" of which a doctrinal explanation is given also "dissipated"? Nor should it be said that Croce's "passion" is something different from Sorel's "myth", that "passion" means the "category" or the "practical spiritual moment" while "myth" is a "determined" passion. . . . Sorel did not theorise a certain myth, but "myth" as the substance of practical action. He then fixed which myth was historically and psychologically adherent to a certain reality. His treatment therefore has two aspects: one properly theoretical, of political science, and one practical, political. . . . In any case, there remains the "theory of myths", which is no more than a "theory of passions" with a less precise and formally coherent language. If theorising myth means dissolving all myths, theorising passions means dissipating all passions.[32]

Gramsci's question in *Quaderno 13* could thus be summarised as follows: is it possible, in the key to the organisation of the collective political will, to have a less anti-philosophical consideration of the passions and, therefore, of myth itself? Is it possible to imagine a phase in which passions, even the particular ones, of the structure (the corporate interests, the economic instances that concern the social group, the class as it produces), become "political", to the point of "prevailing, imposing themselves, spreading over the entire social area, determining not only the unity of economic and political ends, but also intellectual and moral unity, placing all the questions around which the struggle ferments, not on a corporate level, but on a 'universal' level and thus creating the hegemony of a fundamental social group over a series of subordinate groups"?[33] The question of hegemony also passes through the administration of myth.

8.4   1934: De Martino, Benjamin, the Fairy Tale, and the Counsel

In a short contribution from 1934, *Criticism and Faith*, when that young 26-year-old scholar had quite different political ideas than the future anthropologist, first a socialist and then a communist, Georges Sorel was called into question also by Ernesto De Martino, with a critique that echoes those of Croce and Queneau, and of Gramsci himself.

> Consider Sorel: he proposed the myth of the general strike to the proletarian élites, but then he penetrated its character of function and myth so well that he declared it impossible, like all myths . . . [Sorel, like other] tormented spirits of our time, misses a simple truth: that there is no other way to have a faith but that of the Breton peasant woman. As long as one says: "I must believe in this myth because its function is necessary for me to act in a certain way", it is over, there is nothing to be done. The will to believe has not made a single believer.[34]

Thirty years later, in a passage from the "Mundus" chapter of the unfinished project called *The End of the World*, Ernesto De Martino, regarding the question "What is myth?", pointed out its "particular relevance in the current cultural conjuncture", and proffered a long list of scholars from various disciplines responsible for this "renewed interest" in myth: "in addition to historians of religions and ethnologists and anthropologists, also philosophers, historians and critics of contemporary literature, and even political ideologists such as Sorel (whose echo raised by the 'myth of the general strike' has certainly not died down)".[35]

Three decades after *Criticism and Faith*, De Martino therefore set out, in his notes and materials relating to *The End of the World*, to address the issue of the definition of myth (and thus mythical-ritual symbolism). The comparison, there, is established between historicity and myth. Myth serves to "attenuate" and "mask" human responsibility, to curb individual alienation, to "attenuate" and "mask" the historicity of the future. Myth, we read again, "dehistorifies becoming in the repetition of unchanging metahistorical permanence".[36] It is precisely "through this *pia fraus* that one is in history as if one were not there". The operating consciousness is "subordinated, protected and disclosed by the hegemonic mythical-ritual consciousness".[37]

Looking at Gramsci and Benjamin's grappling with the Sorelian myth, and on the basis of De Martino's cue with a Gramscian echo, the question to be asked is whether even within the relationship with the myth there is not an operative and productive consciousness, albeit subordinate, ready to reverse the hegemonic dynamic by constructing a different narrative from below, one that does not de-dehistorifies but increases the possibilities of political intervention within the historical framework.

In the text on the *Storyteller*, written in 1936 in perfect temporal coincidence with the reworking of the essay on the work of art, Benjamin finds in the fairy tale – with some differences from De Martino, who expresses himself differently in this regard around the quoted passage – an alternative and a prelude to what the overthrow can be. Fredric Jameson again offers a significant reading: "We remember that fairy tales are the anti-myth, their peasant optimism the antidote to the deathly aestheticizing rituals of a modern fascism, their storytelling a reminiscence and recovery of a non-alienated mode of being. Storytelling is essentially handicraft: it is a bodily activity, like the potter's wheel . . ., a kind of nonsensuous mimesis of this new 'poverty of experience' and a lesson in how to use it productively".[38] Fairy tale and storytelling, in the Benjaminian reading, tell of how man can have relationship with myth where its hegemony can be "treated" and, although not overturned, can at least be "managed", even through its mockery.

> The fairy tale (*Märchen*), which to this day is the first tutor (*Ratgeber*) of children because it was once the first tutor of mankind, secretly lives on in the story. The first true storyteller is, and will continue to be, the teller of fairy tales. Whenever good counsel was at a premium, the fairy tale had it, and where the need was greatest, its aid was nearest.[39]

But if the fairy tale is mankind's first counsellor in an anti-mythical key, if the narrative is to continue its role in completely changed historical conditions, it is perhaps promising to note that there is in the Benjaminian corpus at least one point where the counsellor – the man of advice – is treated as a dramatic figure and political character. This happens some ten years before the arguments about Leskov and the narrative. The theme posed by Gramsci in the 1930s – the political management of the sphere of passion that is affected by myth – had already been analysed by Benjamin in a key that also sees the name of Machiavelli appear. And this is a place where Benjamin speaks of dictatorship.

8.5 1925: Benjamin and Machiavelli, Dictatorship and Calculations of Affects

In *The Origin of German Tragic Drama*, Benjamin makes a big deal about princes. The absolute protagonists of the *Trauerspiel*, but absolutely inept at action, sovereigns are presented in the first chapter as constitutively indecisive figures. And "Indecisiveness" is the anti-Schmittian title of one of its clearest paragraphs, where the works of Gryphius (*Catharina*), Hallmann (*Mariamne*), and Lohenstein (*Agrippina* and *Sophonisbe*) are used to state that "the prince, who is responsible to take a decision to proclaim the state of emergency, reveals at the first opportunity, that he is almost incapable of making a decision".[40] The sovereign, creature, tyrant and sometimes martyr yield precisely where all dominion is in his hands, because he has no political connection with the world he is supposed to govern, guide, and administer.

If Benjamin deems, it is impossible to find in the *Herrschergewalt*, albeit fixed by the public law doctrine of the time, an effective capacity to intervene productively in the world, further on in the same chapter Benjamin speaks of another figure, close to the indecisive and incapacitated sovereign, who accompanies and overrules him. He speaks of the courtier, at once "saintly" and "scheming".

The drama of the German protestants emphasises the infernal characteristics of the councillor; in Catholic Spain, on the other hand, he is clad with the dignity of *sosiego*, "which combines both the ethos of Catholicism and the *ataraxia* of antiquity in an ideal of the religious and the worldly courtier". It is, moreover, the unique ambiguity of his spiritual sovereignty which provides the basis for the thoroughly baroque dialectics of his position. Spirit – such was the thesis of the age – shows itself in power; spirit is the capacity to exercise dictatorship (*Geist ist das Vermögen, Diktatur auszuüben*).[41]

Paradoxically, just as he proposes the impossibility of exercising sovereignty, thus overturning the incipit ("sovereign is he who decides on the state of exception") and the general Schmittian thesis of that 1922 *Political Theology* that he explicitly quotes in three famous notes in the first chapter,[42] Benjamin seems to open up more than a glimmer for Carl Schmitt's twin thesis, expressed in 1921 in parallel with *Toward the Critique of Violence*, on dictatorship.

To "use" the dictatorial institution would rather be the *Geist* of the courtier, closer to the world of the sovereign, more accustomed to the slow modification of relations. It is satanic for Lutherans; disciplined, slavish, and sad for Spanish Catholics. It is precisely to the councillor, and not to the prince, that the dictatorial spirit belongs. The councillor over the prince, then. Benjamin is talking of a commissary dictatorship, a dictatorship by mandate, as far more concrete than sovereignty. It was precisely Schmitt's *Dictatorship* that saw among the protagonists of its incipit Niccolò Machiavelli, standard-bearer of the "absolute technicality" of politics, of the "rational technique of political absolutism".[43]

In this key of the "possibility of dictatorship" (being able "without any appellation to execute its deliberations" – so the *Discorsi sopra la prima decade di Tito Livio* 33 cited by Schmitt), it is perhaps curious but not impertinent that the Florentine Secretary is mentioned, for the only time in a text that has much to do with his theories and characters, in this very paragraph of the *Ursprung* that we have just referred to.

> [The intriguer] stands as a third type alongside the despot and the martyr. His corrupt calculations awaken in the spectator of the *Haupt- und Staatsaktionen* all the more interest because the latter does not recognize here simply a mastery of the workings of politics, but an anthropological, even a physiological knowledge which fascinated him. The sovereign intriguer is all-intellect and will-power. And as such he corresponds to an ideal which was first outlined by Machiavelli.[44]

The councillor is therefore for the public the index of an anthropological and at the same time political cognition that is expressed in an anti-mythical key. He is the standard-bearer of a harsh pessimism about human animality that is flanked by an operational, all-political *Spielraum*: the intrigue is "intellect and will". After a long quotation from a work by Dilthey (from *Weltanschauung und Analyse des Menschen seit Renaissance und Reformation*), which emphasises "the uniformity of human nature, the power of animality and emotions", Benjamin continues.

> Human emotions as the predictable driving mechanism of the creature – that is the final inventory of knowledge which had to transform the dynamism of world-history into political action. It is at the same time the source of a set of metaphors which was destined to keep this knowledge as alive in the language of poetry as Sarpi and Guicciardini were doing in historiography.[45]

Even leaving aside the undoubtedly "sad" and "mournful" trait of the intriguer-courtier-councillor, Benjamin seems to indicate in this capacity that is both "poetic" and "political" the means to keep his knowledge alive: the calculability of the affections, of human animality, becomes an instrument of political power. "The superior intriguer", says Benjamin, is all intellect and will. Not the prince, but, behind, inside the automaton of the sovereign, a little councillor moulds myths and passions, and knows how to calculate. He is intellect. But by calculating, by devising strategies that do not disdain the involvement of non-rational spheres, he wants to "organise pessimism". And, like the storyteller of fairy tales, the counsellor – the party, in Gramscian terms, or the dictator, in the dramaturgical reading of Benjamin coeval with his ideological turning point of 1924 – can intuit (to an audience of readers, to "distracted" spectators, to a class) an action, a mode of production that does not rhyme with myth, nor with alienation, that mimics freedom.

Notes

1 Raymond Queneau, "Le mythe et l'imposture", *Volontés* 14 (February 1939): 14–17, then in *Le Voyage en Grèce* (Paris: Gallimard, 1973), 154.
2 Paul-Ludwig Landsberg, "Introduction à une critique du mythe", *Esprit* (January 1938), 518. Landberg's article is actually the transcript of a conference he had held in Brussels in December 1937. Landsberg, from personalist positions, was like Benjamin in contact with the Collège de Sociologie, whose prominent characters were Georges Bataille and Roger Caillois. The Collège was among the most active institutes in France in propagating the need for a recovery of myth. See Denis Hollier, ed., *Le Collège de Sociologie* (Paris: Gallimard, 1995²), 50–52 and 827. On the use of Sorel in the Collège (particularly in Caillois, as a sectarian praise of a mythopoetic *minorité agissante*), see Marcel Mauss' criticism in the letter to Elie Halévy (Hollier, ed., *Le Collège de Sociologie*, 848–849). On the same topic Rita Bischof, *Tragisches Lachen. Die Geschichte von Acéphale* (Berlin: Matthes & Seitz, 2010), 238–240.
3 Walter Benjamin, "Für die Diktatur. Interview mit Georges Valois", in *Gesammelte Schriften*, ed. Rolf Tiedemann and Hermann Schweppenhäuser (Frankfurt am Main: Suhrkamp, 1972 [1927]), vol. 4/1, 489: "As a pupil of Sorel, the great, truly significant theorist of syndicalism, [Valois] started from socialism which, judging by the most recent European experience, is the best breeding ground for fascist leaders. Under the influence of Sorel, Valois was confronted with economic-social studies and, on the occasion of an initial revision of his political convictions, he joined the editorial staff of *Action française* as a specialist in economic issues. It was just another watershed for him." That the fascist one was also only one among many "watersheds" is shown by Valois' end as a French resistance fighter, who finally died in Bergen-Belsen.
4 The recognition of a somewhat direct thread, under a Nietzschean aegis, between Sorel and the theorists of myth – even racists and national-socialists – is a constant remark in German *émigrés'* thought. As well as in Landsberg and Benjamin, the same list – Sorel, Mussolini, Gobineau, Rosenberg, with the significant addition of Pareto – can be found in another German Jew who became a Parisian in the 1930s, Eric(h) Weil. In Eric Weil, *Logique de la philosophie* (Paris: Vrin, 1950), 278, footnote 6, while handling the category of "Intelligence", he reconstructs the alliance between intellectuals and voluntarism, in the name of the mythology of creative force as the only "truth" to support. So did Thomas Mann in *Doctor Faustus*, reading Sorel's *Réflexions* as "a sardonic rift between truth and power, truth and life, truth and community" (Thomas Mann, *Doctor Faustus: The Life of the German Composer Adrian Leverkühn as Told by a Friend*, trans. John E. Woods (New York: Knopf, 1997 [1947]), 386. See all the beginning of chap. XXXIV, "continued").
5 Walter Benjamin, "Caillois, Benda, Bernanos, Fessard", in *Werke und Nachlaß. Kritische Gesamtausgabe* (Berlin: Suhrkamp, 2011 [1938]), vol. 13, tome 1514: "When [Benda] for example speaks of the *culte de la blague* in Sorel, he touches on a vein that can be discerned just as clearly today in an adept of fascism like Céline and his spokesmen Rosenberg or Goebbels." The link between Sorel and fascist propaganda is also to be found in Walter Benjamin, "The Paris of the Second Empire in Baudelaire", in *Selected Writings: Volume 4, 1938–1940*, ed. Howard Eiland and Michael W. Jennings (Cambridge, MA and London: The Belknap Press of Harvard University Press, 2006 [1938]), 5: "The seeds of the *culte de la blague*, which reappears in Georges Sorel and has become an integral part of fascist propaganda, are first found in Baudelaire. The spirit in which Celine wrote his *Bagatelles pour un massacre*, and its very title, go back directly to a diary entry by Baudelaire." On this point, see Stephanie Polsky, "Benjamin's Gamble: Commodifying Life in the Age of Heroic Demise", *Conserveries mémorielles* 7 (April 2010), http://journals.openedition.org/cm/441

6 Antonio Gramsci, *Quaderni del carcere*, 4, XIII, 1930–1932, § 44, 469. See also IV, 2558–2559: in the context of a bibliography on Sorel and the Action Française where also Valois can be found, the quotation from Pierre Lasserre, *Georges Sorel théoricien de l'impérialisme. Ses idées. Son action* (Paris: L'artisan du livre, 1928), 50: "Un antidémocrate de gauche, quelle fortune et quel argument pour les anti-démocrates d'extrême droite!". On Cercle Proudhon – which was founded in December 1911 – under "Sorel's moral presidency" (Pierre Lasserre, *Georges Sorel théoricien de l'impérialisme*, 50) – and had members of the Action Française taking part in it – see Mimmo Cangiano, *Cultura di destra e società di massa* (Milano: Nottetempo, 2022), 201–202. Cangiano stresses how the short period where Sorel and Charles Péguy got closer to each other in 1911–1912 was mainly based on a "narrative" use of myth, in order to preserve the autonomy of an alleged proletarian or popular culture against the bourgeois one. See Mimmo Cangiano, *Cultura di destra e società di massa*, 281–288, on the approximation in an anti-Dreyfusard and anti-bourgeois key (and also anti-Semitic), and the persistent distance.

7 Walter Benjamin, *Gesammelte Briefe*, ed. Christoph Gödde and Henri Lonitz (Frankfurt am Main: Suhrkamp, 1996), vol. 2, 109–113: "As soon as I get a book I need from France I will go to the second part of my *Politics*."

8 See Georges Sorel, *Lettere a Benedetto Croce*, ed. Salvatore Onufrio (Bari: De Donato, 1980): the epistolary consists of 343 letters. A selection thereof had been published in Croce's journal *La critica*, starting from number XXV in 1927 until number XXVIII in 1930.

9 In *Reflections on Violence*, Sorel speaks of Croce as a "writer (*écrivain*) . . . well known in Italy as a remarkably acute critic and philosopher": see Georges Sorel, *Reflections on Violence*, trans. Thomas E. Hulme (New York: Huebsch, 1975 [1915]), 261 footnote 1.

10 Walter Benjamin, "Capitalism as Religion", in *Selected Writings, volume 1, 1913–1926*, ed. Markus Bullock and Michael W. Jennings (Cambridge, MA and London: The Belknap Press of Harvard University Press, 1996), 290.

11 Sorel, *Reflections on Violence*, 199.

12 Fredric Jameson, *The Benjamin Files* (London: Verso, 2020), 67 and 140.

13 Walter Benjamin, "Critique of Violence", in *Selected Writings: Volume 1, 1913–1926*, ed. Markus Bullock and Michael W. Jennings (Cambridge, MA and London: The Belknap Press of Harvard University Press, 1996 [1921]), 246. The quote is from the 5th edition: Georges Sorel, *Refléxions sur la violence* (Paris: Rivière, 1919⁵), 250: "les politiciens préparent déjà les cadres d'un pouvoir fort, centralisé, discipliné". It is easy to remark how Benjamin translates *pouvoir* with *Gewalt*.

14 Sorel, *Refléxions sur la violence*, 195.

15 Benjamin, "Critique of Violence", 246.

16 Benjamin, "Critique of Violence", 233.

17 Sorel, *Reflections on Violence*, 22.

18 Sorel, *Reflections on Violence*, 32–33.

19 On the formally objectionable style of *Toward the Critique of Violence*, see Petar Bojanić, "Una critica filosofica della violenza", in *La grammatica della violenza. Un'indagine a più voci*, ed. Alessandra Sannella and Micaela Latini (Milano and Udine: Mimesis, 2017), 100. The essay, thanks to Emil Lederer, happened to be published in August 1921 on the prestigious *Archiv für Sozialwissenschaft und Sozialpolitik*, founded by Max Weber, Werner Sombart, and Edgar Jaffé.

20 Benjamin, "Critique of Violence", 248.

21 Benjamin, "Critique of Violence", 248.

22 We quote Furio Jesi on Karl Kerényi: "[M]ythology is that universal language that casts around man a circle from which it is not possible to get out without immediately

entering the circle of death." Furio Jesi, *Materiali mitologici. Mito e antropologia nella cultura mitteleuropea*, ed. Andrea Cavalletti (Turin: Einaudi, 2001 [1979]), 31.

23 Antonio Gramsci, *Selections From the Prison Notebooks*, ed. and trans. Quintin Hoare and Geoffrey Nowell Smith (New York: International Publishers, 1992), 125. Gabriele Pedullà, "L'arte fiorentina dei nodi", in *Il principe. Edizione del cinquecentennale*, ed. Niccolò Machiavelli (Roma: Donzelli, 2013), XXV, shows the novelty, noted by Gramsci, of *The Prince* in terms of its "mythical" (or prophetic and therefore prescriptive) character compared to the *specula principis* of the fifteenth-century tradition. Leo Strauss' entire and oriented reading rests on the identification between Machiavelli and the prophet: "he brings the true code, the code which is in accordance with the truth, with the nature of things": see Leo Strauss, *Thoughts on Machiavelli* (Chicago and London: The University of Chicago Press, 1958), 83.

24 See Antonio Gramsci, *Quaderni del carcere*, ed. Valentino Gerratana (Torini: Einaudi, 1975), Q2, § 75, 1, 231: "Michels made a lot of fuzz in Italy because of 'his' finding of the 'charismatic leader' that probably [one should check] already was in Weber; one should also see Michels' 1927 book on *Political Sociology*: he doesn't even mention that the idea of a leader by the grace of God already existed, and how." Reference is here to Roberto Michels, *Corso di sociologia politica* (Milano: Istituto Editoriale Scientifico, 1927). On the last Michels, and the "misunderstandings about the alleged Weberism in Michels", see Francesco Tuccari, *I dilemmi della democrazia moderna. Max Weber e Robert Michels* (Roma and Bari: Laterza, 1993), 317 and 337–339.

25 Antonio Gramsci, *Il moderno principe. Il partito e la lotta per l'egemonia. Quaderno 13. Noterelle sulla politica del Machiavelli*, ed. Carmine Donzelli (Roma: Donzelli, 2012 [1924]), 484.

26 Walter Benjamin, "The Work of Art in the Age of Its Technological Reproducibility", in *Selected Writings: Volume 3, 1935–1938*, ed. Howard Eiland and Michael W. Jennings (Cambridge, MA and London: The Belknap Press of Harvard University Press, 2002 [1936]), 129, footnote 24.

27 Gramsci, *Selections From the Prison Notebooks*, 125–126.

28 Gramsci, *Selections From the Prison Notebooks*, 130.

29 Gramsci, *Selections From the Prison Notebooks*, 127.

30 Gramsci, *Selections From the Prison Notebooks*, 128. The comparison between myth and historical bloc is analysed by Carmine Donzelli, "Introduzione" (1981), in Gramsci. *Il moderno principe*, 32–34, on the basis of *Notebook 10*, dedicated to Croce, § 41. Gramsci asks himself whether Croce's dialectics of the "distincts" may find a speculative or historical solution, "given by the concept of 'historical bloc' as supposed by Sorel" (Gramsci, *Quaderni del carcere*, II, 1316).

31 Gramsci, *Selections From the Prison Notebooks*, 129.

32 Gramsci, *Quaderni del carcere*, 7, § 39, 888. The reference inside the text is to the second edition of the "polemic" work by Croce.

33 Gramsci, *Quaderni del carcere*, 1586.

34 Ernesto De Martino, "Critica e fede", *L'Universale* 4 (1934): 282–283. Biscuso has recently recalled these links: Massimiliano Biscuso, "La questione del simbolismo civile nell'ultimo de Martino", *nostos* 5 (December 2020), 59–111.

35 Ernesto De Martino, *The End of the World: Cultural Apocalypse and Transcendence*, trans. Dorothy Louise Zinn (Chicago: University of Chicago Press, 2023 [1977]), 56.

36 De Martino, *The End of the World*, 57.

37 De Martino, *The End of the World*, 57.

38 Fredric Jameson, *The Benjamin Files* (London: Verso, 2020), 216–217.

39 Walter Benjamin, "The Storyteller: Considerations on the Works of Nikolai Leskov", in *Selected Writings: Volume 3, 1935–1938*, ed. Howard Eiland and Michael W. Jennings (Cambridge, MA and London: The Belknap Press of Harvard University Press, 2002 [1936]), 157.

40 Walter Benjamin, "The Origin of German Tragic Drama", trans. John Osborne, intr. George Steiner (London: Verso, Kindle edition, 2009 [1928]), loc. 1171.

41 Benjamin, "The Origin of German Tragic Drama", loc. 1650–1651. The internal quote is from Herbert Cysarz, *Deutsche Barockdichtung. Renaissance, Barock, Rokoko* (Hildesheim: Georg Olms, 1924), 248.

42 Carl Schmitt, *Politische Theologie. Vier Kapitel zur Lehre von der Souveränität* (München: Duncker & Humblot, 1922), 11–12 and 14, quoted in Benjamin, "The Origin of German Tragic Drama", loc. 1074, footnote 14 and 16, loc. 1086, footnote 17.

43 Carl Schmitt, *Die Diktatur. Von den Anfängen des modernen Souveränitätsgedankens bis zum proletarischen Klassenkampf* (Berlin: Duncker & Humblot, 2015 [1921]), 8–9. On the role of the Secretary in Schmitt, see Carlo Galli, "Schmitt e Machiavelli", in *Lo sguardo di Giano. Saggi su Carl Schmitt* (Bologna: il Mulino, 2008 [2005]), 83–106 (on the limits of the book of *Dictatorship*, see 85–86). Benjamin writes to Schmitt in 1930 (Benjamin, *Gesammelte Briefe*, III, 558) to have had some confirmation of his method from the *Dictatorship*. Dario Gentili underlines the concept of the "agent" (*Mandatar*) – analysed in Schmitt's *Dictatorship* – in Benjamin's *The Destructive Character*, which was actually written at the same time of Benjamin's letter to Schmitt: Dario Gentili, *Topografie politiche. Spazio urbano, cittadinanza, confini in Walter Benjamin e Jacques Derrida* (Macerata: Quodlibet, 2009), 135–142.

44 Benjamin, *The Origin of German Tragic Drama*, loc. 1588–1600.

45 Benjamin, *The Origin of German Tragic Drama*, loc. 1600–1611.

Bibliography

Benjamin, Walter. "Für die Diktatur: Interview mit Georges Valois". In *Gesammelte Schriften*, edited by Rudolf Tiedemann, and Hermann Schweppenhäuser, vol. 4, 1, 487–492. Frankfurt am Main: Suhrkamp, 1972 [1927].

Benjamin, Walter. *Gesammelte Briefe*, edited by Chistoph Gödde, and Henri Lonitz, vol. 6. Frankfurt am Main: Suhrkamp, 1995–2000.

Benjamin, Walter. "Capitalism as Religion". In *Selected Writings. Volume 1, 1913–1926*, edited by Markus Bullock, and Michael W. Jennings, 288–291. Cambridge, MA and London: The Belknap Press of Harvard University Press, 1996.

Benjamin, Walter. "Critique of Violence". In *Selected Writings: Volume 1, 1913–1926*, edited by Markus Bullock, and Michael W. Jennings, 236–252. Cambridge, MA and London: The Belknap Press of Harvard University Press, 1996.

Benjamin, Walter. "The Work of Art in the Age of Its Technological Reproducibility". In *Selected Writings: Volume 3, 1935–1938*, edited by Howard Eiland, and Michael W. Jennings, 101–133. Cambridge, MA and London: The Belknap Press of Harvard University Press, 2002 [1936].

Benjamin, Walter. "The Paris of the Second Empire in Baudelaire". In *Selected Writings: Volume 4, 1938–1940*, edited by Howard Eiland, and Michael W. Jennings, 3–92. Cambridge, MA and London: The Belknap Press of Harvard University Press, 2006 [1938].

Benjamin, Walter. *The Origin of German Tragic Drama*, translated by John Osborne, introduced by George Steiner, Kindle edition. London: Verso, 2009 [1928].

Benjamin, Walter. "Caillois, Benda, Bernanos, Fessard". In *Werke und Nachlaß. Kritische Gesamtausgabe*, vol. 13, tome 1, 513–517. Berlin: Suhrkamp, 2011 [1938].

Benjamin, Walter. "The Storyteller: Considerations on the Works of Nikolai Leskov". In *Selected Writings: Volume 3, 1935–1938*, edited by Howard Eiland, and Michael W. Jennings, 143–162. Cambridge, MA and London: The Belknap Press of Harvard University Press, 2022 [1936].

Bischof, Rita. *Tragisches Lachen. Die Geschichte von Acéphale*. Berlin: Matthes & Seitz, 2010.

Biscuso, Massimiliano. "La questione del simbolismo civile nell'ultimo de Martino". *nostos* 5 (December 2020): 59–111.

Bojanić, Petar. "Una critica filosofica della violenza". In *La grammatica della violenza. Un'indagine a più voci*, edited by Alessandra Sannella, and Micaela Latini, 99–108. Milano and Udine: Mimesis, 2017.

Cangiano, Mimmo. *Cultura di destra e società di massa*. Milano: Nottetempo, 2022.

Cysarz, Herbert. *Deutsche Barockdichtung: Renaissance, Barock, Rokoko*. Hildesheim: Georg Olms, 1924.

De Martino, Ernesto. "Critica e fede". *L'Universale* 4 (1934): 279–283.

De Martino, Ernesto. *The End of the World: Cultural Apocalypse and Transcendence*, translated by Dorothy Louise Zinn. Chicago: University of Chicago Press, 2023 [1977].

Donzelli, Carmine. "Introduzione". In Antonio Gramsci. *Il moderno principe. Il partito e la lotta per l'egemonia. Quaderno 13. Noterelle sulla politica del Machiavelli*, edited by Carmine Donzelli, 3–82. Roma: Donzelli, 2012 [1981].

Galli, Carlo. "Schmitt e Machiavelli". In *Lo sguardo di Giano. Saggi su Carl Schmitt*, 83–106. Bologna: il Mulino, 2008.

Gentili, Dario. *Topografie politiche. Spazio urbano, cittadinanza, confini in Walter Benjamin e Jacques Derrida*. Macerata: Quodlibet, 2009.

Gramsci, Antonio. *Quaderni del carcere*, edited by Valentino Gerratana, vol. 4. Torino: Einaudi, 1975.

Gramsci, Antonio. *Selections from the Prison Notebooks*, edited and translated by Quintin Hoare, and Geoffrey Nowell Smith. New York: International Publishers, 1992.

Gramsci, Antonio. "Capo". In *L'Ordine Nuovo III, 1 (March 1924) and in Scritti dalla libertà*, edited by Alessandro D'Orsi, 483–487. Roma: Editori Internazionali Riuniti, 2012.

Gramsci, Antonio. *Il moderno principe. Il partito e la lotta per l'egemonia. Quaderno 13. Noterelle sulla politica del Machiavelli*, edited by Carmine Donzelli. Roma: Donzelli, 2012.

Hollier, Denis, ed. *Le Collège de Sociologie*. Paris: Gallimard, 1995.

Jameson, Fredric. *The Benjamin Files*. London: Verso, 2020.

Jesi, Furio. *Materiali mitologici. Mito e antropologia nella cultura mitteleuropea*, edited by Andrea Cavalletti. Turin: Einaudi, 2001 [1979].

Landsberg, Paul-Ludwig. "Introduction à une critique du mythe". *Esprit* (January 1938): 512–529.

Lasserre, Pierre. *Georges Sorel théoricien de l'impérialisme. Ses idées. Son action*. Paris: L'artisan du livre, 1928.

Mann, Thomas. *Doctor Faustus: The Life of the German Composer Adrian Leverkühn as Told by a Friend*, translated by John E. Woods. New York: Knopf, 1997 [1947].

Michels, Roberto. *Corso di sociologia politica*. Milano: Istituto Editoriale Scientifico, 1927.

Pedullà, Gabriele. "L'arte fiorentina dei nodi". In Niccolò Machiavelli, *Il principe. Edizione del cinquecentennale*, V–CXVII. Roma: Donzelli, 2013.

Polsky, Stephanie. "Benjamin's Gamble: Commodifying Life in the Age of Heroic Demise". *Conserveries mémorielles* 7 (April 2010). http://journals.openedition.org/cm/441.

Queneau, Raymond. "Le mythe et l'imposture". *Volontés* 14 (February 1939): 14–17. Then in Queneau, Raymond. *Le Voyage en Grèce*. Paris: Gallimard 1973.

Schmitt, Carl. *Politische Theologie. Vier Kapitel zur Lehre von der Souveränität*. München: Duncker & Humblot, 1922.

Schmitt, Carl. *Die Diktatur. Von den Anfängen des modernen Souveränitätsgedankens bis zum proletarischen Klassenkampf*. Berlin: Duncker & Humblot, 2015 [1921].

Sorel, Georges. *Reflections on Violence*, translated by Thomas E. Hulme. New York: Huebsch, 1915.

Sorel, Georges. *Refléxions sur la violence*. Paris: Rivière, 1919.

Sorel, Georges. *Lettere a Benedetto Croce*, edited by Salvatore Onufrio. Bari: De Donato, 1980.

Strauss, Leo. *Thoughts on Machiavelli*. Chicago and London: The University of Chicago Press, 1958.

Tuccari, Francesco. *I dilemmi della democrazia moderna. Max Weber e Robert Michels*. Roma and Bari: Laterza, 1993.

Weil, Eric. *Logique de la philosophie*. Paris: Vrin, 1950.

9

"TO LIVE IN A GLASS HOUSE"

Gramsci and Benjamin, or What Becomes of Historical Materialism When the Personal Is Political

Elettra Stimilli

At first glance, it seems impossible to find any affinity between Antonio Gramsci and Walter Benjamin, two thinkers who, although contemporaries, were very different. One was born in the rural and economically underdeveloped island of Sardinia, from a large family of office workers and small landowners tied to popular culture and local religious traditions; the other, the oldest of three in a Jewish family that had been completely assimilated into Berlin's upper middle class. The one, stricken as a young child by a then unknown form of tuberculosis of the bones, supported in his studies by the belief and efforts of his mother after the premature death of his father; the other growing up amongst the elite, with servants and a French governess. The one educated in a traditional state school in Cagliari; the other in the best secondary school in Berlin, the Kaiser-Friedrich-Schule in the elegant Charlottenburg district. Gramsci discovered socialism while studying at the University of Turin, in Italy's most industrialised city. He played an active part in political life and was one of the founders, and later the secretary, of the Communist Party. Benjamin's adherence to Marxism, which was more theoretical than militant in the strict sense, developed as a result of meeting Asja Lacis, the revolutionary Latvian theatre director, who led him to Moscow. Thus his relationship with the city of the twentieth-century revolution began[1] in a very different way to that of Gramsci, who found it through his links to the Central Committee of the Russian Communist Party (although for him too, a woman played an important role: Giulia Schucht, the young Russian aristocrat whom he met in 1922 in the sanatorium where he was hospitalised with serious health problems and with whom he would have two children).[2]

And yet, despite their different class origins and geographical, social, and cultural backgrounds, they had many things in common, not least their work

DOI: 10.4324/9781003457039-13

as literary critics, both publishing work in various journals and newspapers in which they displayed a similar political sensitivity in relation to literature.

However, I am not interested here in comparing them in these terms, but will instead read them by starting from a specific point of view and a particular issue that also calls our present into play. Both were eloquent interpreters of the profound changes that, from a Marxist point of view, the capitalist modes of production underwent in the interwar period, and both understood this as the result of a wider process. Furthermore, in both of their attempts to define the field of political action, the classical distinction between structure and superstructure fell apart. For both thinkers, the ambiguity of the ongoing dissolution of the separation between public and private in the modern age emerged as simultaneously deeply worrying and a reservoir of political potential.

In the world of absolute transparency in which we live today, the private no longer exists, but the safeguarding of individual freedoms has paradoxically taken on new political force, first with the critique of the exceptional measures following the spread of the pandemic, then with the defence of "Western values" against Putin's Russia during the war in Ukraine. Attempting to compare the work of these similarly "heretical" Marxist authors from the point of view of this transparency could help us to focus on the contradictions and potential of the present.

9.1 Americanism, the Creation of a New Ethics

If labour is the modern institution at the threshold of the bourgeois definition of the private sphere of the impolitical and the public sphere of politics, it is with Karl Marx that it takes on the force and value of a *political* institution, as a social relationship of subordination to capital. According to a certain interpretation of Marx, the political overcoming of the structural contradictions of the capitalist economy would coincide with the organisation of centralised economic planning in a highly industrialised society. As is well known, this was the most widespread interpretation of Marx in the twentieth century, particularly in the context of the industrial development that characterised the post-war era and in areas under the influence of the Soviet Union.

Antonio Gramsci became a keen interpreter of Marx precisely when, in the interwar period, he witnessed the first formation of that "passage from the old economic individualism to the planned economy".[3] His analysis is unique in the extreme lucidity with which he shows how this passage simultaneously involved post-revolutionary Russia and, albeit in different ways, Europe, which was devastated by the First World War and the crisis linked to the reconversion of the war industry, as well as the United States. In doing so, he shows that there were close links between the different economic planning policies of the various world powers who were aiming at hegemony in the years leading up to the rise of fascism and the outbreak of the Second World War.

It seems that Gramsci's first reflections on "Americanism and Fordism" date from late 1929 and early 1930, thus in the immediate aftermath of the collapse of the New York Stock Exchange.[4] In these texts, he clearly aims to connect the causes of the world economic crisis to the possibility that "Americanism can constitute an historical 'epoch'",[5] as he believed. It is important to point out that Gramsci chose a completely different path to "those who want to find the origin and cause of the crisis in 'Americanism'",[6] instead demonstrating prophetic insight into the changes underway, in a similar way to Benjamin. For Gramsci, Americanism, which he summarised in *Notebook 22*, was in no way the origin of the crisis, but, on the contrary, was a response to it. It was a restructuring of capitalism in reaction to the critical phase, in an attempt to adapt the modes of production to the fact that bourgeois hegemony had come to its historical end. The end of bourgeois hegemony refers to the period in which capitalism freed itself from its class of origin to become global, thus losing almost all ties to the bourgeois world view. Thus, for Gramsci, Americanism was an attempt to elaborate a new "human type" that was appropriate to a capitalism liberated from the bourgeois form of life.

The rationalisation of labour at play in this process not only combines "force (destruction of working-class trade unionism on a territorial basis) and persuasion (high wages, various social benefits, extremely subtle ideological and political propaganda) (285)"[7] but also manages to pivot "the whole life of the nation" – at both the individual and societal levels – around production.

This results in a profound transformation of the modern institution of labour, and of its political role as the essential defining element of the difference between the public sphere of politics and the private sphere of the impolitical on which the modern institution of the state is based, providing the ground for the development of capitalist relations of production.

The adaptation of customs to the needs of work, of which Americanism was an expression, implied that the new methods of work were "inseparable from a specific mode of living and of thinking and feeling life. One cannot have success in one field without tangible results in the other".[8] This was the real "attempt to create a new ethic",[9] which implied a shifting of the boundaries on which bourgeois politics and morality were founded.

It is worth noting that here Gramsci pays particular attention to the sphere of reproduction, which he explicitly links to the domain of production. The centrality of the "sexual question" in Taylorism and in the organisation of Fordist production processes leads him to focus on "the economic function of reproduction"[10] and thus, in Marxist terms, on its political role. Puritanism, prohibitionism, the fight against prostitution, and the absolute control of private life fit perfectly into the Fordist project, with a view to creating a "new type of man and of citizen".[11]

> The expression "consciousness of purpose" might appear humorous to say the least to anyone who recalls Taylor's phrase about the "trained gorilla". Taylor is in fact expressing with brutal cynicism the real purpose of American society – developing in the worker to the highest degree automatic and mechanical attitudes, breaking up the old psycho-physical nexus of qualified professional work, which demands a certain active participation of intelligence, fantasy and initiative on the part of the worker, and reducing productive operations exclusively to the mechanical, physical aspect. But these things, in reality, are not original or novel: they represent simply the most recent phase of a long process which began with industrialism itself.[12]

The novelty at stake in the modes of Fordist production was the formation of a new "psycho-physical nexus" between worker and machine, with the aim of creating "a stable, skilled labour force, a permanently well-adjusted complex, because the human complex (the collective worker) of an enterprise is also a machine which cannot, without considerable loss, be taken to pieces too often and renewed with single new parts".[13] Gramsci was aware that this balance could not simply be "external and mechanical", but had to become "internalised", thus, "proposed by the worker himself, and not imposed from the outside".[14] This implied the particular control of sexuality and reproduction as essential prerequisites for the functioning of the general process. This would be the battlefield of the Marxist feminist movements in the 1970s.[15] Incidentally, we should remember that this aspect, clearly analysed by Gramsci in *Notebook 22*, unites the Fordist and Leninist projects, as demonstrated in the conversation Clara Zetkin had with Lenin in 1920, on the eve of the launch of the NEP, which was only made public after the latter's death.[16]

The indistinction between private and public life at the expense of individual freedoms, which characterises the transition from the "old economic individualism" of the bourgeoisie "to the planned economy" of the new forms of production, led Gramsci to see Americanism as the most striking result of the global restructuring of capitalism, in which life became universally economic, unified in a single world model.

9.2 At the Margins of Fordism

In February 1929, Gramsci, who was being held in Turi prison, obtained permission to write and thus began what would become the *Prison Notebooks*, in which "Americanism and Fordism" and the "sexual question" were from the outset presented as the main topics of his research. At the same time, Walter

Benjamin published "*Der Surrealismus*" in the *Literarische Welt*. In this essay, Benjamin quotes the definition that André Breton, the father of Surrealism, gave to his book *Nadja: "livre à porte battente*" (a book with a banging door).[17] Then, in order to express what the reader of this Surrealist text feels, he describes a memory of his from Moscow:

> In Moscow I lived in a hotel in which almost all the rooms were occupied by Tibetan lamas who had come to Moscow for a congress of Buddhist churches. I was struck by the number of doors in the corridors that were always left ajar. What had at first seemed accidental began to be disturbing. I found out that in these rooms lived members of a sect who had sworn never to occupy closed rooms. The shock I had then must be felt by the reader of Nadja.[18]

So he adds, "To live in a glass house is a revolutionary virtue par excellence. It is also an intoxication, a moral exhibitionism, that we badly need. Discretion concerning one's own existence, once an aristocratic virtue, has become more and more an affair of petty-bourgeois parvenus".[19]

Surrealism, an artistic movement born out of the trauma of the Great War, inherited from the Dadaist revolt a total rejection of bourgeois conventions. Its main aim was to merge the social and political revolution embodied by the Bolsheviks with the liberation of subversive unconscious and new artistic creations aimed at breaking the alienation of bourgeois existence, which the war had brought to light in all its tragedy.

According to Benjamin, Surrealism had rediscovered a "radical concept of freedom"[20] that Europe had lost, the same concept that Gramsci, in the same years, understood as definitively lost in the passage from the "old economic individualism" of the bourgeoisie "to the planned economy" of the new capitalist forms. What struck Benjamin about the Surrealists was the fact that they were "the first to liquidate the sclerotic liberal-moral-humanistic ideal of freedom".[21] For the Surrealists, "mankind's struggle for liberation in its simplest revolutionary form (which, however, is liberation in every respect), remains the only cause worth serving".[22] But harnessing "the energies of intoxication for the revolution",[23] as the Surrealists tended to do, was not sufficient for Benjamin. "But to place the accent exclusively on it would be to subordinate the methodical and disciplinary preparation for revolution entirely to a praxis oscillating between fitness exercises and celebration in advance".[24] In short, the reason Benjamin reproached the Surrealists' "gothic Marxism" was because of its bohemian inclination; the same inclination that he found in Charles Baudelaire in the unfinished genealogy of Paris in the nineteenth century.

The greatest risk to that form of life, seemingly external to the mechanisms of power and, in that sense, also potentially including a revolutionary aspect, was its being captured and put to work within the mechanisms that characterised that new phase of capitalism that, even more prophetically than Gramsci, Benjamin found in nineteenth-century Paris. Not Fordist capitalism, which Benjamin also saw at work behind the glimmer of commodities, but a form of capitalism that had not yet fully developed, essentially aimed at the valorisation of life in all its aspects and not just the functional machinic force of the factory.

In the preparatory materials for the unfinished book on Paris, his attention was drawn to figures that could be traced back to the *bohème*, of which Baudelaire was the prototype, and who for this reason became the core of the work. The *flâneur*, the idler, the professional conspirator, the gambler, the night owl, the detective, the rag picker, the poet, the artist, and the prostitute were figures outside of the market, whose production was in no way reducible to exchange value and Fordist or Taylorist commodification.

> In Baudelaire's Paris . . . Arcades where the flaneur would not be exposed to the sight of carriages that did not recognize pedestrians as rivals were enjoying undiminished popularity. There was the pedestrian who wedged himself into the crowd, but there was also the flc1neur who demanded elbow room and was unwilling to forego the life of a gentleman of leisure. His leisurely appearance as a personality is his protest against the division of labour which makes people into specialists. It is also his protest against their industriousness. . . . But this attitude did not prevail; Taylor, who popularized the watchword 'Down with dawdling!' carried the day.[25]

Seemingly at the margins of the process Gramsci called "Americanism" – as the *flâneur* seems unable to relinquish his private life – in the Paris of the *Arcades* described by Benjamin, the *flâneur* actually finds himself at the *centre* of a transformation that envelops him and, as if in a vortex, includes his whole life. This is the foundation of what Benjamin tellingly calls Baudelaire's "Americanism", which finds its model in the mass article.[26] The sandwichman is the best example of this process, which makes the *flâneur* himself a commodity and through which his very life takes on an "exhibition value", which transforms everything that is most intimate and private into the public dimension. These are the harbingers of that enormous change in the post-Fordist mode of production, in many senses still operating today, whose peculiarity, in the final analysis, is that of reducing everyone to "entrepreneurs of the self".

If Baudelaire was the emblem of "his own impresario",[27] Benjamin saw in the prostitute the most effective allegory of life becoming a commodity. Paris turns out to be the multifaceted space where, among the various commodities that are the new inventions of the century, the prostitute is inserted in her niche like a statue.[28] With her, not only does the commodity attempt to look itself in the eyes and celebrate its incarnation but in the act of selling herself, the prostitute exposes the threshold that the institution of the Fordist family described by Gramsci seeks to make invisible, that boundary between productive labour and the labour of reproduction and care, which merge in the prostituted body. The "sexual question" which Gramsci sees as a central problem in the Fordist modes of production, emerges in Benjamin with the prostitute as a prophetic figure of the further development of capitalist forms of production; the process defined as the "feminisation of labour" would become the general condition of post-Fordist production.[29] In the post-Fordist period, there would be a valorisation of the same inter-relational capacities, the ability to engage in "creative" and "versatile" collaboration, to mediate and seduce, that are the main talents of the prostitute as an effective "entrepreneur of the self". Benjamin quotes Marx on this subject:

> The factory workers in France call the prostitution of their wives and daughters the Xth working hour, which is literally correct. Karl Marx, *Der historische Materialismus*, ed. Landshut and Mayer.
>
> *(Leipzig 1932)*[30]

Benjamin makes reference to an expression in vogue at the height of the nineteenth century that clearly expresses the same phenomenon: prostitution is the "fifth quarter of the day".[31] This additional form of exploitation of the working class is obscured in the Fordist economic organisation analysed by Gramsci, in which it is only the family that has an "economic function" as the fulcrum of the "new ethic" for those "trained gorillas" that have to be programmed. Benjamin, on the other hand, brings its role to light in all its ambiguity, a role which is only apparently marginal. The prostitute, besides being an icon and a resident of the labyrinth of the city, is its guardian. After the initial shock, those who encounter her gain a knowledge and capacity for orientation that reveals what is normally hidden: the intrinsic connection between labour and prostitution that takes shape in the post-Fordist modes of production. As Benjamin writes,

The closer work comes to prostitution, the more tempting it is to conceive of prostitution as work – something that has been customary in the argot of whores for a long time now. This rapprochement has advanced by giant steps in the wake of unemployment; the "Keep smiling" maintains, on the job market, the practice of the prostitute who, on the love market, flashes a smile at the customer.[32]

The sale of the prostitute's body in shop windows, as well as being a canon of experience, is revealed in Benjamin's prophetic eyes as the historical form of the age of absolute transparency, where nothing is private any longer; an age built on the remains of the dream world of the bourgeoisie. This is a reconstruction in many ways analogous to that given by Gramsci, who, while lucidly confronting a capitalism liberated from the bourgeois form of life, nevertheless does not go so far as to prefigure, as Benjamin does, a transcending of the Fordist organisation of production.

9.3 Gramsci and Benjamin: Marxist Heretics

Unlike most of his critics, Benjamin presents the *Theses On the Philosophy of History*[33] – probably written in early 1940 and bequeathed to posterity as an unfinished text – not as an autonomous text but as "a theoretical framework"[34] elaborated as a historical-gnoseological premise for the materials he was gathering in view of writing his book on Baudelaire, an economic-political critique of the nineteenth century. At stake in the thesis is the possibility of articulating an idea of history capable of marking out the terrain of political intervention in a Marxist sense. This could be said to be the text in which the greatest affinities between Benjamin and Gramsci emerge. They share a critique of the Marxism of the Second International and the new Stalinist orthodoxy, between which both see a substantial relationship of continuity. Both oppose a deterministic view of history and a merely "progressive" conception of revolutionary struggle. Their positions in relation to the Marxism of their time were therefore similarly anomalous, so much so as to make them both "heretical" within Marxist thought.

It might seem – and in many respects, it is indeed true – that after the shared disappointment of the Soviet reality, their positions on the idea and function of revolution began to differ. Whereas for Gramsci the fate of the revolution was now in the hands of the hegemonic conflict that saw in the "modern Prince" a new subject capable of bringing together a collective tension as the consciousness of a yet-to-be-completed modernity, Benjamin continued to see the class struggle as the terrain of political conflict capable of mobilising the "subject of historical knowledge" that assumes the inheritance of the entire history of the oppressed and defeated.

Despite the attention he paid to the subaltern classes, which was given a lot of weight in the revival of Gramsci's thought by postcolonial studies,[35] it might seem that Gramsci is in fact only interested in defining a political subject in the classical terms of the relationship between state and civil society. We could argue that for Gramsci the classes marginalised by capitalist development could not become a political subject without the development of a hegemony able to bring them together. However, there would be no hegemony in the Gramscian sense without the possibility of a history written from the point of view of the oppressed. This is intimately connected with the perspective that emerges in Benjamin's Theses *On the Philosophy of History*.

For both thinkers, it was a matter of elaborating a materialistic concept of history, in which the past never presents itself as a closed continent and a definitively accomplished process, as Benjamin sees in historicism. Even modernity, which has tended to define the limits of what is political from the point of view of the victors, separating the public space of political action from the private sphere – which as such is only guaranteed to citizens – still contains unrealised possibilities. Like the doors left ajar in the Moscow hotel where Benjamin stayed and the pavement where the prostitute stands, modernity is the threshold of that dimension that makes political what is apparently only personal. This has nothing to do with the revival and defence of liberal bourgeois rights; those same rights that are also discussed today in the criticism, in defence of "individual liberty", of the exceptional measures following the spread of the pandemic or with the defence of "Western values" against Putin's Russia during the war in Ukraine without questioning the fact that Western democracies with liberal institutional structures are also promoters of hegemonic policies that continue to exploit 80% of the planet's resources for the benefit of a tiny part of the world's population, a condition that continues to produce inequality and exploitation.

Only the construction of a collective consciousness from the point of view of the oppressed would be capable of creating a future in which the defeated still found a place in history by starting from a radical transformation of the past. Benjamin proposes a different narrative, in which a Gramscian hegemony is still possible through the power of the subaltern to represent themselves as a political force in history.

Notes

1 See Walter Benjamin, "Diario moscovita" and "Mosca", in *Opere Complete. II. Scritti 1923–1927*, ed. Rolf Tiedemann, Hermann Schweppenhäuser, and Enrico Ganni (Turin: Einaudi, 2001), 506–612 and 624–653.
2 See Angelo D'Orsi, *Gramsci. Una nuova biografia* (Milano: Feltrinelli, 2017); Howard Eiland and Michael W. Jennings, *Walter Benjamin. Una biografia critica*, trans. Antonio La Rocca (Turin: Einaudi, 2015).
3 Antonio Gramsci, *Selections from the Prison Notebooks*, ed. and trans. Quintin Hoare and Geoffrey Nowell Smith (New York: International Publishers, 1992), 279 [Notebook 22(v) 1934, "Americanism and Fordism" § 1].
4 Marcello Mustè, *Rivoluzioni passive. Il mondo tra le due guerre nei Quaderni del carcere di Gramsci* (Rome: Viella, 2022), 128.
5 Gramsci, *Prison Notebooks*, 279. [Notebook 22(v) 1934, "Americanism and Fordism" § 1].
6 Gramsci, *Prison Notebooks* [Notebook 15(II) 1933, § 5; trans. Clara Pope].
7 Gramsci, *Prison Notebooks*, 285 [Notebook 22(v) 1934, "Americanism and Fordism" § 2, 16].
8 Gramsci, *Prison Notebooks*, 302 [Notebook 22(v) 1934, "Americanism and Fordism" § 11, 36].
9 Gramsci, *Prison Notebooks*, 296 [Notebook 22(v) 1934, "Americanism and Fordism" § 3, 21].
10 Gramsci, *Prison Notebooks*, 295 [Notebook 22(v) 1934, "Americanism and Fordism" § 3, 19].
11 Gramsci, *Prison Notebooks*, 268 [Notebook 22(v) 1934, "Americanism and Fordism" § 11, 36].
12 Gramsci, *Prison Notebooks*, 302 [Notebook 22(v) 1934, "Americanism and Fordism" § 11, 36].
13 Gramsci, *Prison Notebooks*, 303 [Notebook 22(v) 1934, "Americanism and Fordism" § 11, 37].

14 Gramsci, *Prison Notebooks*, 303 [Notebook 22(v) 1934, "Americanism and Fordism" § 11, 37].

15 See, amongst others, Mariarosa Dalla Costa and Selma James, *Potere femminile e sovversione sociale* (Venice: Marsilio, 1972); Leopoldina Fortunati, *L'arcano della riproduzione. Casalinghe, prostitute, operai e capitale* (Venice: Marsilio, 1981).

16 See Noemi Ghetti, *Gramsci e le donne. Gli affetti, gli amori, le idee* (Rome: Donzelli, 2020), 87.

17 Walter Benjamin, "Surrealism", in *Reflections: Essays, Aphorisms, Autobiographical Writings*, ed. and with intr. Peter Demetz, trans. Edmund Jephcott (New York: Schocken Books, 1986), 180.

18 Benjamin, "Surrealism", 180.

19 Benjamin, "Surrealism", 180.

20 Benjamin, "Surrealism", 189.

21 Benjamin, "Surrealism", 189.

22 Benjamin, "Surrealism", 189.

23 Benjamin, "Surrealism", 190.

24 Benjamin, "Surrealism", 189.

25 Walter Benjamin, *Charles Baudelaire: A Lyric Poet in the Era of High Capitalism*, trans. Harry Zohn (London: Verso, 1997), 53–54.

26 Walter Benjamin, "Central Park", in *Selected Writings, Volume 4: 1938–1940*, ed. Howard Eiland and Michael W. Jennings (Cambridge: Harvard University Press, 2006), 188.

27 Benjamin, "Central Park", 168–169.

28 Benjamin, "Central Park", 188.

29 See Angela McRobbie, *Reflections on Feminism, Immaterial Labour and the Post-Fordist Regime* (London: Newformation, 2010); Cristina Morini, *Per amore o per forza. Femminilizzazione del lavoro e biopolitiche del corpo* (Verona: OmbreCorte, 2010).

30 Walter Benjamin, *The Arcades Project*, trans. Howard Eiland and Kevin McLaughlin (Cambridge, MA: Harvard University Press, 2002), 209.

31 Benjamin, *The Arcades Project*, 706.

32 Benjamin, *The Arcades Project*, 360.

33 Walter Benjamin, "On the Concept of History", in *Selected Writings*, ed. Howard Eiland and Michael W. Jennings (Cambridge, MA: Harvard University Press, 2003), vol. 4, 389–400. For a detailed analysis of the text, see Dario Gentili, *Il tempo della storia. Le tesi Sul concetto di storia di Walter Benjamin* (Macerata: Quodlibet, 2019).

34 Walter Benjamin, *Gesammelte Briefe*, ed. Christoph Gödde and Henri Lonitz (Frankfurt: Surhkamp, 2000), vol. 4, 400.

35 See, amongst others, Neelam Srivastava and Baidik Bhattacharya, eds., *The Postcolonial Gramsci* (London: Routledge, 2012).

Bibliography

Benjamin, Walter. *Reflections: Essays, Aphorisms, Autobiographical Writings*, edited and with an introduction by Peter Demetz, translated by Edmund Jephcott. New York: Schocken books, 1986.

Benjamin, Walter. *Charles Baudelaire: A Lyric Poet in the Era of High Capitalism*, translated by Harry Zohn. London: Verso, 1997.

Benjamin, Walter. *Gesammelte Briefe*, edited by Christoph Gödde, and Henri Lonitz, vol. 4. Frankfurt am Main: Surhkamp, 2000.

Benjamin, Walter. *Opere Complete. II. Scritti 1923–1927*, edited by Rolf Tiedemann, and Hermann Schweppenhäuser, Italian edition by Enrico Ganni. Turin: Einaudi, 2001.

Benjamin, Walter. *The Arcades Project*, translated by Howard Eiland, and Kevin McLaughlin. Cambridge, MA and London: Harvard University Press, 2002.

Benjamin, Walter. *Selected Writings, Volume 4 (1938–1940)*, edited by Howard Eiland, and Michael W. Jennings. Cambridge, MA and London: Harvard University Press, 2006.

Dalla Costa, Mariarosa, and James, Selma. *Potere femminile e sovversione sociale*. Venice: Marsilio, 1972.

D'Orsi, Angelo. *Gramsci. Una nuova biografia*. Milano: Feltrinelli, 2017.

Eiland, Howard, and Jennings, Michael. *Walter Benjamin. Una biografia critica*, translated by Alvise La Rocca. Turin: Einaudi, 2015.

Fortunati, Leopoldina. *L'arcano della riproduzione. Casalinghe, prostitute, operai e capitale*. Venice: Marsilio, 1981.

Gentili, Dario. *Il tempo della storia. Le tesi Sul concetto di storia di Walter Benjamin*. Macerata: Quodlibet, 2019.

Ghetti, Noemi. *Gramsci e le donne. Gli affetti, gli amori, le idee*. Rome: Donzelli, 2020.

Gramsci, Antonio. *Selections from the Prison Notebooks*, edited and translated by Quintin Hoare, and Geoffrey Nowell Smith. New York: International Publishers, 1992.

McRobbie, Angela. *Reflections on Feminism, Immaterial Labour and the Post-Fordist Regime*. London: Newformation, 2010.

Morini, Cristina. *Per amore o per forza. Femminilizzazione del lavoro e biopolitiche del corpo*. Verona: OmbreCorte, 2010.

Mustè, Marcello. *Rivoluzioni passive. Il mondo tra le due guerre nei Quaderni del carcere di Gramsci*. Rome: Viella, 2022.

Srivastava, Neelam, and Bhattacharya, Baidik, eds. *The Postcolonial Gramsci*. London: Routledge, 2012.

Translated by Clara Pope

10

TECHNIQUE AND POLITICS

From Gramsci to Benjamin

Massimiliano Tomba

10.1   Intensification

Art and technique. This was the nexus that Benjamin began to query in the 1930s. More precisely, the object of his investigation was the relationship between art, the liquidation of the aura, and mechanical reproduction. His analysis was motivated by the political implications enclosed in that nexus. In the notes for the first edition of his text *The Work of Art in the Age of Its Technological Reproducibility*, he wrote, "The change noted here in the method of exhibition caused by mechanical reproduction applies to politics as well".[1] Benjamin's attention fell primarily on the changes in apperception produced by photography, radio, and film. These technical innovations had not only made the artistic object reproducible but, at the same time, also given rise to a kind of collective fruition. What's more, even artistic production, as is the case with film, could no longer be considered an individual product, but the result of industrial production organised according to modern criteria of the division of labour. The actor had become a tool. A replaceable medium. This is what Bertolt Brecht portrayed in 1926 in *Mann ist Mann*. At the core of the plot of this theatrical piece is the transformation of one man, Galy Gay, into another man. A transformation that is not at all complicated, because "one man is like the other. Man equals man". "You can do with a human being what you will".[2] Brecht's play, not just in content but especially in form, can be understood as an attempt to bring to conscious experience technical and economic modifications that made the individual fungible and comparable to a machine. Not to save the individual. But to reconfigure him in relation to the collective. And not only to the collective. Film had shown how the material, for example, a rainstorm or a clock, "acts" alongside the actor.

DOI: 10.4324/9781003457039-14

These are still open issues. It could be said that humanity is still trying to come to terms with technical modifications that need to be brought to consciousness and governed. Today, the so-called neo-materialism has extended the notion of "agency" to the non-human. But in this extension of the notion of agency, neo-materialism operates as materialism without self-reflection. The integration between the technical and the organic has been celebrated in many different ways. This would mark the end of "human" and the beginning of a new politics. This new politics appears today with characters similar to those that can be found in films. The politicians stop speaking to Congress and instead address the camera directly. Their interlocutors are not the elected representatives but the television audience and social media. Just as the fungibility of the actor has, through compensation, generated the star, similarly the fungibility of the politician has generated the authoritarian leader. Today, the analogy between the two fields is evident in the ever-increasing number of personnel transitions from the world of entertainment to the world of politics.

It is now a matter of investigating these changes in technique and politics not as signs of decadence and decline but as a field of possibility. To investigate this field of possibility, it is useful to broaden our view. It has a history that must be investigated starting with analyses of the major changes produced by the technique of mass production as early as the beginning of the twentieth century. Inspiration can be taken from a few conceptual figures. These include Ernst Jünger, Theodor Adorno, and Antonio Gramsci. I will discuss each of them as figures of a triptych.

In 1932, Jünger published *Der Arbeiter*. In a paragraph in which he discussed the end of the classical notion of the individual, Jünger wrote, "To the same degree in which individuality dissolves, so diminishes the resistance that the individual can muster against his mobilisation".[3] The degree of intensification and massification achieved by labour has made replaceable not only the individual worker, now likened to the unknown soldier but also the traditional human type for whom "the rules of the Nineteenth Century, in particular those of psychology, have become invalid".[4] The protest that arises from the private sphere is ineffective, because the classical terms of contradictions have failed: "the old and the new, . . . power and right, blood and spirit, war and politics, natural and human sciences, technology and art, knowledge and religion, organic and mechanical world" are no longer contradictory terms.[5] The laws of war also apply to economics. Its discipline applies to every human activity. Even the pair of freedom and obedience no longer operates as opposition.

On the basis of these transformations, which reach the innermost fibres of the human type, a new hierarchy takes shape, different from the traditional hierarchy of the nineteenth century but still based on individuality. The new hierarchical order of the twentieth century is decided, according to Jünger, by the new character of labour. Dictatorship is a phenomenon of this transition. A necessary phenomenon, but only as a temporary form of transition since for the new human type, freedom, and obedience are identified. The hierarchical order that takes shape is tripartite. The bottom rung is characterised by a general levelling to which, according to Jünger, men and things are equally subjected. This levelling is based on the worker's substitutability not only with any other worker but also with machines. On the second hierarchical rung, the worker is part of a multiplicity of planned functions. On the third and final rung, the individual worker merges with total labour. Jünger cautions against looking longingly at the loss of individuality. The new *Rangordnung* in the making requires a new politics and a new individual configuration. This is what is at stake. And not only for Jünger.

It is time to introduce the second conceptual character or the second figure of the triptych. In 1944, Adorno published *Minima Moralia*. In a paragraph in which he discusses the end of the classical notion of the individual, Adorno writes, "That the individual is being liquidated lock, stock and barrel, is still too optimistic a thought".[6] Adorno wants to investigate the decadence of the individual starting from the social tendencies of today's capitalist society. To do this, he develops and applies the category of organic composition of capital not only to the whole of society but also to the individual.[7] The idea is that the change in the technical composition of capital also affects the individual, his emotional, physical, and psychological sphere. Thus grows the "organic composition of human beings".[8] This should not be understood as a mechanisation and deformation operated on the individual. The individual, or human being, is not the static substratum of mutations or deformations that would operate from outside. This way of looking at it would still be reactionary, because it would consider the modification of the organic composition of the human being both in terms of the modification of an unchanging individual substratum and in terms of the loss of individuality. For Adorno, the individual is never separate from society. The deformation to which the individual is subject is a deformation of society onto itself. And this deformation also affects the moments of the natural. The whole living being is transformed into "equipage".[9]

The division of labour, penetrated within the individual, also transforms emotions into empty shells, something foreign and objective to which the subject, or what remains of it, turns. The individual is reduced to a heap of automatic, unresisting reflexes. This is, for Adorno, the psychotic nature that is also the anthropological condition of mass totalitarian movements.

Before turning to the third conceptual character, it is useful to highlight some elements that emerge from the juxtaposition between Adorno and Jünger. For both, the change in human type has political implications. For Adorno, it produces the anthropological material used by totalitarianisms. For Jünger, it produces the basis of a new hierarchical ranking in which the individual worker, liquidated at the lowest level, re-emerges in the form of total labour at the highest level. For both, the new levelling carried out by technology hybridises the human with the machine. The categories historically employed by psychology lose their value, as there would no longer be an individual psyche.

Gramsci is the third figure in this triptych. His analysis of the modification of technical processes of production is built on the possibility of their communist use. His analysis is structured around three main axes: the disintegration of the distinction between public and private; an anthropological transformation that prefigures the decline of the old individual and the rise of a "new human type"; and a new "mechanisation" that includes intellectual labour. In general, Gramsci's discourse is characterised by anti-romanticism and anti-Americanism.[10] For each of these aspects of the ongoing transformation, Gramsci seeks to provide a timely response: a response that works not against the transformation, but *within* the ongoing transformation, which is to be understood as a field of possibility and action. As we shall see, this is a point of affinity with Benjamin's analysis.

A letter dated 20 October 1930 to his sister-in-law Tatiana exemplifies Gramsci's perspective. The letter begins by discussing his wife Giulia, who was suffering from a nervous breakdown and cerebral anaemia. In describing Giulia's condition, Gramsci takes the opportunity to make a generalisation, writing that "this is no isolated phenomenon; unfortunately, it's growing increasingly common, as can be seen from the scientific publications concerning the new work systems introduced from America".[11] The generalisation made by Gramsci can certainly be understood as a lack of sensitivity towards the specific case of his wife's health. But, one might observe, Gramsci was consistent with his own assumptions and acted in the dissolution of the separation between the public and private spheres. Gramsci had taken seriously the practice of inspectors sent by Ford to check the private lives of employees and impose on them a new regimen of living in accordance with the new type of work. Here was the question. How to coordinate the new kind of work, both manual and intellectual, with a new regimen of life? The new "mechanisation", Gramsci concluded, "crushes us".[12] But it should be approached without nostalgia or romanticism.

These are the same reflections noted in the *Notebooks*: "The introduction of rationalization without change in the system of living can lead to rapid nervous attrition and result in crises of unprecedented morbidity".[13] These morbid backlashes, which constitute the object of study of Freudism, are politically manifest in fascism. At their basis is the emergence of a new human type, a "collective man" who, in his making, can unleash fanaticism of all kinds. It is a matter, for Gramsci, of orienting the construction of the new human type. And this orientation requires the discipline of the morbid backlashes generated by the transition. It requires the control of natural instincts so as to produce a new "psycho-physical nexus" of a "superior" type.[14] It requires, finally, control of the regimen of life, as evident in Fordism in terms of prohibition, control of housing, and control of workers' morality.[15] It is a conformism from above that must accompany and guide the construction of the new human type. It is the new *Rangordnung* of which Jünger spoke. If left and right liberals lingered in romantic praise of bourgeois individuality and anti-American stances, fascism was the wrong answer to a right question.

Not only were the new Fordist methods of mass production introduced in Nazi Germany, Fascist Italy, and the Soviet Union but the New Deal, Italian Fascism, German Nazism, and Bolshevik discipline were to be understood as manifestations of the decline of the liberal state and the birth of a new type of society.[16] This transition required a "new type of coercion".[17] Leone Davidovi's (Trotsky's) interest in Americanism was shared by Gramsci, who considered it right to introduce the principle of coercion, both direct and indirect, into the order of production and labour. But wrong in form.[18] Gramsci observed that, on the one hand, the attempt to accelerate discipline and order in production through external means could result in forms of Bonapartism, such as Stalinism; on the other hand, this rationalisation of labour had to operate not only in the direction of producing a new type of worker but also a new type of man. This second dimension was crucial for Gramsci. Americanism, the Fordist methods of control and intervention in workers' lives, had to be taken seriously. More so than Trotsky had done. The workers' nervous energies had to be kept under control. And that meant control of workers' alcohol use, sex and family life. In other words, it meant control over workers' "private" lives.

Right here, in the proximity of Fordism and Fascism, Gramsci opens up a field of possibilities and political intervention. The new labour methods mechanise the worker's gestures, but leave his brain free, which "far from being mummified, reaches a state of complete freedom".[19] The worker thinks and understands that he is to be reduced to a "trained gorilla". He has no immediate satisfaction in what he does, and this "can lead him into a train of thought that is far from conformist".[20] Here is the field of intervention. This train of "far from conformist" thoughts can give rise to a different kind of conformism, if one can still call it that. It is a "conformism from below" that can allow "new possibilities for self-discipline, that is, even for individual freedom".[21] It is, in other words, the collective man struggling to destroy the "authoritarian conformism" that has become cumbersome and backwards after accomplishing its work.[22] The authoritarian work of conformism and Americanism is characterised by the destruction of traditions, declining social forms, and all the "still unburied European oldness".[23] It is also characterised by the (Fordist) disciplining of the worker and his private life. A disciplining that is more advanced in the United States by virtue of its lack of tradition, which would instead generate phenomena of resistance and social passivity in Europe.

For Gramsci, Americanism and Fordism represented the future. The issue was to decide whether it constituted an era of gradual social and political change, or whether it might represent a molecular accumulation of elements capable of producing a revolutionary explosion along the lines of the French Revolution.[24]

Gramsci pursues both ideas. Herein lies his analytical strength. But also his weakness. This weakness takes the form of a historical teleologism that still forms the framework of his reflections. It is on the basis of this framework that Gramsci condemns the European oldness as an obstacle to be eliminated, speaks of the "passivity of the Chinese people", and regards the East as "stalled at the phase of the investigation directed only at the inner world".[25] One thinks of social upheaval starting from an intensification of a historical-economic trend. Not only did Gramsci not question the inherently capitalist nature of modern technology and the new mechanisation; he thought that the change of hands of the means of production, that is, their appropriation by workers, already meant control over production. As if Fordism could be employed, in the manner of the Bolsheviks in Russia, for the purposes of communism.

If Gramsci looked at unproductive traditions and social strata as "viscous parasitic sedimentations"[26] and obstacles along the path of progress, these "obstacles", against Gramsci, could also be understood as productive anachronisms, unsynchronised elements that right-wing movements generally know how to use much better than the left. To work with these sedimentations, a change of course is required both in theory and in politics.

10.2 Changes of Course

However different, politically on opposite sides, the positions of Ernst Jünger, Theodor Adorno, and Antonio Gramsci have something in common. Jünger *intensifies* the technique to the point of envisioning a total mobilisation of labour capable of giving rise to a new human type and social order. Adorno *intensifies* the "organic composition of man" to the total liquidation of the individual. Gramsci *intensifies* Fordism and Americanism to make them the basis for a total and molecular transformation of ways of thinking and operating.

Given these differences and the contributions of these conceptual figures, the question is whether it is possible, thinking *with* Benjamin, to offer a different angle on the transformations of the human type and capitalism in the early twentieth century. Benjamin works with tensions. His perspective is neither the Jüngerian perspective of the "unknown soldier" nor the Gramscian perspective of a new, superior human type. But neither is it that of the *flaneur* or the *bohème*. When he reads Baudelaire as a prefiguration of the capitalist value of metropolitan lifestyles, one must keep Blanqui in mind. When he investigates the nineteenth century, Benjamin works from neither Baudelaire's nor Blanqui's perspective, but in and with the tension between Baudelaire and Blanqui. If Taylor had the last word against the idlers of Paris,[27] it is a matter neither of intensifying Taylor with Ford nor of celebrating the end of "viscous parasitic sedimentations",[28] nor of glorifying the *flaneur* who idles away in the metropolitan labyrinth. Instead, it is about building a productive tension between the idler's protest against industriousness and the socialist struggle against the rationalisation of labour and instincts.

Henry Ford stated that "history is more or less bunk. It is tradition. We don't want tradition". Ford invited people not to study history. Nor to take it seriously. In saying this, he was not only asserting a personal point of view but voicing a form of self-representation of capitalist modernity characterised by an abso-lutisation of the present. When the steamroller of Fordist rationalisation wipes out idle forms of life and traditions not subsumed in the valorisation process, it not only eliminates parasitic sedimentations and historical residues but also eliminates idleness as an alternative image to a present and future dominated by industriousness. If Gramsci continues to see a way out of capitalist society through its intensification, Benjamin opens up tensions capable of generating new fields of possibility and changes of course. When Benjamin speaks of the idler's life, it is not to elevate it as a model. For Benjamin, the *flaneur's* idleness, insofar as it is anachronistic, contains images of possible liberation that can be activated by their encounter with Blanqui and socialism. If the life of the idler is lousy in contemporary society, it is because life is lousy in a society in which there is no place for idleness and everything is dominated by productivity. If even the last fragment of idleness that can be traced in the image of the *flaneur* is dismissed, there is almost nothing left to be able to consider a non-industrious life. There remains a kind of puritanism, a new work ethic, and a rationalisation of labour and sexual instincts. Gramsci believed that he could use all this for the purpose of creating a new human type.[29] According to Gramsci, this new human type would also be subject to a "new type of coercion", that is, a coercion exercised by the elite of a class over its own class. Self-discipline of the working class over the working class.

Here Gramsci's thinking stops. One could say that for him the solution lay in replacing the domination of the capitalist class with that of the workers. Today we know that this handover of domination is insufficient and can easily lead to the self-exploitation of workers instead of their liberation. Today we know that the factory, machines, and modern technology have an intrinsic capitalist use value that does not dialectically spill over into liberation. Domination and technique are not notions that can be handed over from the oppressor class to the oppressed class. American workers understood this. In the midst of a long struggle with the Ford Motor Company, workers in the 1930s used the term "Fordism" not as a new model but to attack Ford's autocratic regime of factory oppression.[30] The question, still relevant today, is whether and to what extent technique and present forms of domination can be used for emancipatory pur-poses. The question is whether their intensification and acceleration can dialecti-cally spill over into something radically different. Or whether, instead, technique and domination should be not simply criticised, but reconfigured in a completely different way.

This is what Walter Benjamin was trying to do by differentiating between a notion of technique[31] understood as the "domination of nature" and a "second technique (*zweite Technik*)" understood instead as interaction and play (*Zusammenspiel*) between nature and humanity.[32] The emphasis of this interaction (*Zusammenspiel*) is to be placed on play (*Spiel*) with nature, meaning a different way of relating to it, while maintaining distance with it. It is not about abolishing the distance between the human being and nature. It is not even about returning to nature. These were, *and are*, at best fascist lines of escape. Benjamin's reflections on the "second technique" are intertwined with those on "second nature" as the integration of the collective into the individual.[33] For Benjamin, the struggle between fascism and communism is decided by this intertwining.[34] A game of which form of domination will prevail is also being played out on the integration of the individual and the collective, or, perhaps one should say, on its shape and structure. On the one hand, there is the differentiation and distancing from nature as "play"; on the other, the biological-animal identification pursued by fascism.

These reflections of the 1930s echo in part what was proclaimed in the final pages of *One-Way Street* (1926). Here Benjamin referred to the domination of technique not in terms of "the mastery of nature" (first technique) but "mastery of the relation between nature and humanity".[35] There is a semantic difference between the two notions of domination (*Beherrschung*). The second type of domination, possible as a second technique, is collective and concerns not individuals or peoples, but humanity as a species. These terms must now be clarified.

Domination over nature is sick and destructive, not as domination but as chaotic or anarchic in the sense in which Marx spoke of capitalist market anarchy by independent and competing producers. This form of domination is also characterised by private ownership over a thing. This relationship, elevated to dogma in the formula of *ius utendi et abutendi*, makes each owner an absolute lord. Mastering this form of domination requires a second type of domination. A domination of the second degree. The first form of domination is destructive and chaotic. Overcoming it means overcoming its atomistic, individualistic, proprietary and capitalistic form. Here is the field of intervention outlined by Benjamin. It lies between the *second technique*, the second domination, and the second or, one should perhaps say, the third nature of man. If the first nature is the object of domination, be it an external or internal force such as compulsions and instincts; if the second nature is characterised by the system of law in Hegel's objective spirit or, in Lukács, by an alienated social world that dominates and opposes men; what Benjamin calls "second nature" in the annotations written for the third edition of *The Work of Art in the Age of Its Technological Reproducibility*[36] differs from the second nature of Hegel and Lukács to the extent that it would be more appropriate to speak of a "third nature". This has to do with a modification of perception made possible by technique.[37] Perception and its modifications constitute the crux of Benjamin's analysis of aura and politics. It is also the core of his self-reflexive materialist approach. If the subject-object dualism, and with it that between human being and nature, falls within the formal conditions of experience and the transcendental outlined by Kant, then it is on the basis of the historical nature of perception and forms of experience that that dualism can be called into question. The challenge can be represented in these terms: to what extent, and how, that which is fragmented for individuals, their experience as *Erlebnisse*, can be the basis of a new collective experience, an *Erfahrung* of a new kind.

It is a matter of investigating the different configurations of the relationship between individual and collective that underlies the perceptual apparatus integrated with the second technique. In this new configuration, neither the individual is liquidated, as Adorno claimed, nor, one could and should add, is the aura. Rather, it is subject to transformation and reconfiguration. Even in the loss of originality, uniqueness, cultural heritage, and historical and traditional authority of the object, aura and tradition do not disappear once and for all. Rather they are revolutionised. Corresponding to these revolutions are social and political revolutions. It is in this context that Benjamin defines revolutions as "innervations of the collective – or, more precisely, efforts at innervation on the part of the new, historically unique collective which has its organs in the new technology".[38] Benjamin is not referring to the individual and his fusion or hybridisation with technique. The issue is neither the celebration of the old individuality nor the death of human in the post-human. Nor a mystical-biological fusion with nature. The issue concerns the perceptual apparatus becoming collective. It is about the integration of the individual with the collective. And the technique as new organs of the collective.

This new type of collective perception began with radio, photography, and cinema. It is what Paul Valéry defined in terms of the ubiquity of works.[39] The same music can be heard at the same instant anywhere on the globe. And anywhere on the globe, the same musical work can be played at will, without the constraint of a date or place. Valéry also observed that these developments in technique have altered what we call matter, space, and time. Technique applied to art (cinema, second technique) allows art to work in a new field of perception (third nature) in which the senses, intelligence, and memory become collective. This is where politics comes in. This new collective space of perception is not liberating or emancipatory per se. It can only be so as part of a larger political project beyond the fragmentation characterised by modern individual private property.

These political implications need to be developed. Technique not only makes a work of art reproducible, it democratises it. Not only can everyone own an artistic reproduction but everyone can become an artist, a photographer, and, today, a video-maker and a journalist. This is a process that has a history. In 1857, Léon de Laborde published *De l'Union des Arts et de l'Industrie*, a text that Benjamin does not quote and probably did not know. But de Laborde's text can be put into dialogue with Benjamin.

> Christianity vulgarized the worship of God, printing vulgarized letters, true scholars have vulgarized science; industry, that is, the genius of the applied arts, is in the process of popularizing the arts. Are we less sincerely religious, for being in communion with our neighbors; less educated, because one reads his Cicero and his Virgil in print along with a hundred thousand other readers instead of owning the manuscript with ten or twelve colleagues; less deeply cultured, for being more practically so? Will the arts, finally, lose something of their elevation by lowering their gaze to the crowd, reduce their apex by expanding their base? Certainly not.[40]

Léon de Laborde used the term *"vulgariser"* not in a derogatory sense, but as a synonym for *"populariser"*. Democratise, one might say. Technique democratises art. But this is a possibility, not a necessary outcome. The term "democracy" is a political term, and not a quantitative measure. The democratic possibility must be built on the tension between art and technique. Not on their original unity. Democratised art shortens the distance between the work and the audience, it questions its aura, to the point where everyone can imagine her/himself as the author. If, for Benjamin, each person at the beginning of the last century *"can lay claim to being filmed"*,[41] today technique makes it possible for each person to put forth a demand to film and make his or her own short films public. Each reader can claim to be an author and publish his or her texts in a virtual platform. Anyone can become a journalist, a commentator, an expert, or a critic. Anyone can demand to become a politician. Not only does the distance between author and spectator diminish but so does the distance between the politician and the masses. It follows that the politician is replaceable in the manner of any television actor. But this very closeness and fungibility produces fragmentation and authoritarian phenomena. The fungibility of the individual is offset by the cult of the TV star and political leader. The fragmentation of the real into a multiplicity of points of view and pieces of reality subsisting as independent bubbles is compensated for by a unity authoritarianly imposed by another. Nationalism, which seemed to have slumbered after the disasters of World War II, is resurrected to new life.

Here is the challenge of the second technology. The game is played at the level of perception. It is on the basis of a new form of collective perception that what appears as fragmented at the individual level can be reconfigured into a meaning-rich whole at the collective level. Technique has made the existence of millions of readers-authors-artists possible. The task of the second technique is to work in the inexhaustible reservoir of experimentation made possible by the modification, in a collective sense, of perception. This work is play (*Spiel*).

Art and politics have a specific task here. If "film is the first form of acquisition of the collective", revolutions are "efforts at innervation" of the new collective, which "has its organs in the new technique".[42] This is the same level of experimentation that Benjamin glimpsed in the spread of Fourier's phalansteries: a beacon to guide the new innervation of the collective.[43] An experimentation with the collective. These experiments are still ongoing. It is on their basis, that is, on the possibility of making sense of fragmentation by means of a new technical-collective transcendental, that the contraposition between emancipation and authoritarianism is decided. Or, to put it in Benjamin's crudest terms, between the "cheerfulness of communism" and the "animal gravity of fascism".[44]

Notes

1 Walter Benjamin, "Das Kunstwerk im Zeitalter seiner technischen Reproduzierbarkeit", in *Kritische Gesamtausgabe* (Frankfurt am Main: Suhrkamp, 2012), vol. 16, 12.
2 Bertolt Brecht, "Man Equals Man", in *Brecht Collected Plays*, ed. Matheuen Drama (New York and London: Bloomsbury, 2015), vol. 2, 37–38.
3 Ernst Jünger, *The Worker: Dominion and Form* (Evanston: Northwestern University Press, 2015), 100.
4 Jünger, *The Worker*, 102.
5 Jünger, *The Worker*, 104.
6 Theodor W. Adorno, *Minima Moralia* (London: Verso, 2005), Aphorism 88.
7 Adorno, *Minima Moralia*, Aphorism 147.
8 Adorno, *Minima Moralia*, Aphorism 147.
9 Adorno, *Minima Moralia*, Aphorism 147.
10 See Antonio Gramsci, *Quaderni del carcere* (Turin: Einaudi, 2007), vol. 3, Q 22, par. 2; vol. 1, Q 5, par. 105.
11 Antonio Gramsci, *Lettere dal carcere* (Turin: Einaudi, 1965), 374.
12 Gramsci, *Lettere dal carcere*, 374–375.
13 Gramsci, *Quaderni*, Q 5, par. 41.
14 Gramsci, *Quaderni*, Q 22, par. 11.
15 Gramsci, *Quaderni*, Q 22, par. 1 e Q 22, par. 11.
16 Anne Showstack Sassoon, *Gramsci and Contemporary Politics: Beyond Pessimism of the Intellect* (London and New York: Routledge, 2000), 18; Stefan J. Link, *Forging Global Fordism* (Princeton and Oxford: Princeton University Press, 2020).
17 Gramsci, *Quaderni*, Q 22, par. 10.
18 Gramsci, *Quaderni*, Q 22, par. 11.
19 Gramsci, *Quaderni*, Q 22, par. 12.
20 Gramsci, *Quaderni*, Q 22, par. 12.
21 Gramsci, *Quaderni*, Q 7, par. 12.
22 Gramsci, *Quaderni*, Q 9, par. 23.
23 Gramsci, *Quaderni*, Q 22, par. 11.
24 Gramsci, *Quaderni*, Q 22, par. 1.
25 Gramsci, *Quaderni*, Q 4, par. 23 e Q 5, par. 29.
26 Gramsci, *Quaderni*, Q 22, par. 2.
27 "[G]uerre à la *flânerie*". This was Taylor's obsession. See Walter Benjamin, "Das Passagen-Werk", in *Gesammelte Schriften*, vol. 5/1 (Frankfurt am Main: Suhrkamp, 1982), M 10, 1, 547.
28 Gramsci, *Quaderni*, Q 22, par. 2.

29 Gramsci, *Quaderni*, Q 22, par. 3.
30 Carl Raushenbush, *Fordism, Ford and the Workers: Ford and the Community* (New York: League for Industrial Democracy, 1937), 3.
31 "A new meaning of the term technology was imported into the American English language by 20th century social scientists (Thorstein Veblen, for example), deriving from the German *Technik*. Moreover, it mismatches two terms ('technique' and 'technology') of the Continental languages, where technique refers to specific craft procedures and technology denotes a 'logos' relating to the same activities. . . . From a history of ideas point of view, the notions of *technology* and *aesthetics* may be considered sister disciplines of two connected and parallel rationalizations, which corresponded with changes in the character of the artist/artisan: the modern artist was supposed to be concerned with beauty only, and the artisan with the production of useful goods." See Guido Frison, "The First and Modern Notion of Technology: From Linnaeus to Beckmann to Marx", *Consecutio Rerum*, no. 6 (2019), www.consecutio.org/wp-content/uploads/2019/06/6-frison.pdf
32 Walter Benjamin, "Handwritten Notes for the Third Edition of 'the Work of Art in the Age of Its Technological Reproduction'", in *Kritische Gesamtausgabe*, ed. Burkhardt Lindner (Berlin: Suhrkamp, 2013), vol. 16, 150.
33 Benjamin, *Kritische Gesamtausgabe*, vol. 16, 143.
34 Benjamin, *Kritische Gesamtausgabe*, vol. 16, 146.
35 Walter Benjamin, "One-Way Street", in *Selected Writings*, ed. Marcus Bullock and Michael W. Jennings (Cambridge, MA and London: Harvard University Press, 1996), vol. 1, 487.
36 Benjamin, *Kritische Gesamtausgabe*, 143; Walter Benjamin, "The Work of Art in the Age of Its Reproducibility", in *Selected Writings*, ed. Howard Eiland and Michael W. Jennings (Cambridge, MA: Belknap Press, 2002), vol. 3, 107.
37 On perception (*Wahrnehmung*) and apperception (*Apperzeption*), see Walter Benjamin, "Das Kunstwerk im Zeitalter seiner technischen Reproduzierbarkeit", in *Kritische Gesamtausgabe* (Frankfurt am Main: Suhrkamp, 2013), vol. 16, (first draft) 14, 18, 42; (second draft) 59, 84, 89, 92; (third draft) 101–103, 131, 137, 138, 141; (fourth draft in French: "perception") 166, 168, 190, 194, 196, 199; (fifth draft) 214–216, 247, 250. Henceforth, I will indicate the page of the German edition (KG) and, when available, the English edition. When not otherwise indicated, I will refer to the third German version, which corresponds to the second version in the English translation. In each occurrence, the translations will be checked and modified according to the German original if necessary.
38 Benjamin, KG, 109; Benjamin, "The Work of Art", 124, footnote 10.
39 In the epigraph in the fifth edition of "The Work of Art", Benjamin cites Paul Valéry: "In all the arts, there is a physical component which can no longer be considered or treated as it used to be, which cannot remain unaffected by our modern knowledge and power. For the last twenty years, neither matter nor space nor time has been what it was from time immemorial." See Benjamin, KG, 207; Benjamin, "The Work of Art", 251.
40 Léon de Laborde, "De l'Union des Arts et de l'Industrie", in *L'avenir* (Paris: Imprimerie Impériale, 1857), vol. 2, 27.
41 Benjamin, KG, 125; Benjamin, "The Work of Art", 114.
42 Benjamin, KG, 109; Benjamin, "The Work of Art", 124, footnote 10.
43 Benjamin, "Das Passagen-Werk", W 7, 4.
44 Benjamin, KG, 146. The censorial "contributions" made by Max Horkheimer to Benjamin's French text are well known. Horkheimer replaced the term "fascism" with "état totalitaire" and the term "communism" with "forces constructives de l'humanité". See Benjamin, KG, 339.

Bibliography

Adorno, Theodor W. *Minima Moralia*. London: Verso, 2005.

Benjamin, Walter. "Das Kunstwerk im Zeitalter seiner technichen Reproduzierbarkeit". In *Werke und Nachlass. Kritische Gesamtausgabe*, edited by Burkhardt Lindner, vol. 16. Berlin: Suhrkamp, 2013.

Brecht, Bertolt. *Brecht Collected Plays*, edited by Matheuen Drama, vol. 2. New York and London: Bloomsbury, 2015.

de Laborde, Léon. "De l'Union des Arts et de l'Industrie". In *L'avenir*, vol. 2. Paris: Imprimerie Impériale, 1857.

Frison, Guido. "The First and Modern Notion of Technology: From Linnaeus to Beckmann to Marx". *Consecutio Rerum*, no. 6 (2019). www.consecutio.org/wp-content/uploads/2019/06/6-frison.pdf.

Gramsci, Antonio. *Lettere dal carcere*. Turin: Einaudi, 1965.

Gramsci, Antonio. *Quaderni del carcere*, edited by Valentino Gerratana. Turin: Einaudi, 2007.

Jünger, Ernst. *The Worker: Dominion and Form*. Evanston: Northwestern University Press, 2015.

Link, Stefan J. *Forging Global Fordism*. Princeton and Oxford: Princeton University Press, 2020.

Raushenbush, Carl. *Fordism, Ford and the Workers: Ford and the Community*. New York: League for Industrial Democracy, 1937.

Showstack Sassoon, Anne. *Gramsci and Contemporary Politics: Beyond Pessimism of the Intellect*. London and New York: Routledge, 2000.

11

SOCIAL REBELS AND RAG PICKERS

On the Theoretical Function of Marginalised People in Gramsci and Benjamin

Birgit Wagner

This chapter[1] focuses on two marginalised figures, the social rebel Davide Lazzaretti in Gramsci and the rag picker in Benjamin. It should be noted right away that Gramsci's social rebel is a historical figure of the nineteenth century, whereas Benjamin's rag picker originates from Baudelaire's famous poem "Le vin des chiffonniers" ("The Rag Picker's Wine"). Nevertheless, also Benjamin carefully attempted a socio-historical sketch of the situation of the rag pickers in nineteenth-century Paris. The two case studies are interesting because they realise precisely what Adorno called "singularity's claim to truth . . . taken literally, up to the point where its untruth becomes evident".[2] This is a premise that both Benjamin and Gramsci fulfil in an exemplary manner, insofar as the truths of singularities also find their way into their theorising. Two questions arise: Firstly, can the social rebel and the rag picker be understood in the sense of Gramsci's concept of the subaltern? Secondly, how does Benjamin fit the rag picker into his theoretical structure? By exploring these questions, significant differences but also parallels will come to light.

Let us begin with a reflection on the relevant biographical experiences of the two theorists. Gramsci's childhood and youth in a small town in Sardinia, and later his high school years in Cagliari, were characterised by physical disability, child labour, poverty, and, not least, inadequate nutrition. It is probably superfluous to recall his later fate as a political prisoner. In any case, he had been biographically familiar with the situation of the marginalised since his youth and affected by this social situation himself. Benjamin, on the other hand, was born into a wealthy Jewish middle-class family, with a nanny, a handmaiden ("eine Magd", a nowadays obsolete German term, which, however, was part of everyday language use in Benjamin's times), a city flat, and a country estate. In *Berlin*

DOI: 10.4324/9781003457039-15

Childhood around 1900, he paints a moving picture of these biographical experiences, characterised by the irretrievable loss of all these social privileges. In the first section of this beautiful text, he hopes to "suggest how thoroughly the person spoken of here would later dispense with the security allotted his childhood".[3] In the later years of his life, Benjamin experienced, again as is well known, extremely precarious living conditions; poverty and the threats of the rise of fascism were among the formative experiences of his adult years, conditions that certainly made him a marginalised person. The biographical experiences of the two theorists can therefore definitely be compared, particularly considering the differences.

This contribution follows Gramsci's premise of *filologia vivente* ("living philology"), a path of knowledge that does not reduce a case study to selective findings but attributes cognitive power to it in a larger context, which must of course be taken into account.

11.1 Benjamin and the Rag Picker

So, it may come as no surprise that Baudelaire became one of the preferred objects of Benjamin's thinking. In a way, Baudelaire offered him a figure of identification: not least because the poet and theorist had presented lucid analyses of the situation of the intellectual and writer in Paris during the first age of capitalism but also because Baudelaire shared a biographical experience with him: moving from a humble flat to an even more miserable one, exactly the same as Benjamin's stay in his Parisian exile turned out.[4] In other respects, Baudelaire's awareness of his social and political situation differs crucially from Benjamin's, insofar as the latter takes a critical look at the former's political positions and statements.

Baudelaire and his "chiffonnier" are discussed in "The Paris of the Second Empire in Baudelaire", namely in the first section with the heading "The Bohème". In the very first paragraph, the nineteenth-century phenomenon of the rag picker is compared to the lifestyle of "professional conspirators". Marx had already associated this "political type" with the bohemian and sharply distinguished his attitude from the class-consciousness of "real" working-class men.[5] Benjamin finds – in my opinion rightly so – the characteristics of this political type in Baudelaire's theoretical writings, including the poet's changing political and aesthetic positions. "Ultimately, Baudelaire's political insights do not go beyond those of these professional conspirators",[6] states Benjamin.

But what does this have to do with the rag picker? The "great poem", as Benjamin calls it (SW, 7), *Le vin des chiffonniers* was inspired by a social and legal reality that Benjamin had carefully researched. The city limits of Paris were customs borders around the middle of the nineteenth century, and this had an impact on the price of wine. In the city, this opium of the people was more expensive; on the other side of the customs border, it was cheaper. Incidentally, it should be noted that one can still get an impression of the customs borders of the time in the city-scape of Paris today, for example, on Place Denfert-Rochereau, where the custom buildings have been preserved. In any case, the historically real rag pickers correspond to Gramsci's definition of the subaltern, which will be discussed later.

Due to the difference in price, the poor townspeople moved outside the city limits on Sundays to consume the cheaper "vin de la barrière" (i.e. beyond the customs border), which is exactly what Baudelaire's rag picker does. This profession, at the bottom of the social pyramid, developed because waste had acquired a certain value in the early days of industrialisation, according to the recycling methods of the time. Benjamin quotes in detail two nineteenth-century studies that document the extremely modest income of a rag picker – early insights from the "first investigators of pauperism", who asked themselves "the mute question: Where does the limit of human misery lie?" (SW, 8).

Baudelaire's "chiffonier", a lyrical figure of art, is located precisely in this field which stretches between social reality and the mental constitution of the would-be professional conspirator who imagines himself an avenger. Let me quote the second and third stanzas of the poem, which, by the way, is not one of the pieces of the *Fleurs du mal* that Benjamin himself translated (presumably for metrical reasons since it is difficult to fit the German word "Lumpensammler" (rag picker) into a poem):

> On voit un chiffonnier qui vient, hochant la tête,
> Buttant, et se cognant aux murs comme un poète,
> Et, sans prendre souci des mouchards, ses sujets,
> Épanche tout son cœur en glorieux projets.
> Il prête des serments, dicte des lois sublimes,
> Terrasse les méchants, relève des victimes,
> Et sous le firmament comme un dais suspendu
> S'enivre des splendeurs de sa propre vertu.[7]

In prosaic words: the rag picker is drunk and indulges in fantasies of revenge and compensation, such as those popularised by Eugène Sue's feuilleton novel *Les Mystères de Paris*. It should be noted that his and similar texts also reached the lower classes in cities, for example, in the "cabinets de lecture", where serialised newspaper stories could be consulted at a low price and inspired popular fantasies, as Gramsci noted in his studies on the feuilleton novel.

Baudelaire's rag picker thus imagines himself a rebel under the influence of drunkenness, while the following day he will once again collect scraps of cloth. To paraphrase Gramsci, this type certainly represents the subaltern, who, due to a lack of educational opportunities, does not sufficiently understand his class situation and does not have the necessary information to grasp the fundamentals of the ruling system of capitalism, let alone possess a political organisation that could support his concerns.

But how does Benjamin comment on this figure that is both fictional and rooted in reality? He first notes, "This has nothing of the profound duplicity which animates Baudelaire's own poetry. His verse supported the oppressed, though it espoused not only their cause but their illusions as well" (SW, 12). This is less precise than what Gramsci wrote on the topic, but it is dead on in terms of the rag picker's circumstances: insufficient understanding of the class situation. However, then the rag picker, perhaps surprisingly for us today, appears in the third section of Benjamin's writing titled "Modernity" under the category of "heroes", which Benjamin again borrowed from Baudelaire: "the dispossessed person makes another appearance in the guise of the hero" (SW, 43), and "The hero is the true subject of *la modernité*. In other words, it takes a heroic constitution to live modernity" (SW, 44).

Now, who are these heroes? First and foremost, Baudelaire himself, who as a flâneur stands out from the crowd, which he needs in order to feel alive, through his distanced observer's gaze.[8] Furthermore, the proletarian suicide whose act is intended to make public his status as a dispossessed person – we can think of the Tunisian suicide whose self-immolation triggered the so-called Arab Spring. Moreover, some characters from Balzac's narrative universe, such as the lesbian, question the prevailing gender stereotypes of femininity and masculinity. And finally, the type of the "apache", who was to have a great future in French literature and film in the first decades of the twentieth century: the rebellious, undisciplinable, erotically interesting Parisian petty criminal.[9]

The rag picker shares traits of the hero, because he stands for "the thousands of marginal existences eked out in the basements of a big city by criminals and kept women" (SW, 47). All these heroes of modernity are thus characterised by a fundamental opposition to the victorious bourgeois-capitalist social order of the nineteenth century, albeit one that is inadequately understood. In this context, Benjamin quotes a passage from the poet's prose, which I reproduce here in the English translation[10]:

Here we have a man whose job is to gather the day's refuse in the capital. Everything that the big city has thrown away, everything it has lost, everything it has scorned, everything it has crushed underfoot he catalogues and collects. He collates the annals of intemperance, the capharnaum of waste. He sorts things out and selects judiciously; he collects, like a miser guarding a treasure, refuse which will assume the shape of useful or gratifying objects between the jaws of the goddess of Industry (SW, 48).

Benjamin – not without good reason – considers this in turn to be a metaphorical description of Baudelaire's poetic credo (I would like to call to mind the verse line "se cognant comme un poète"/"stumbling like a poet lost in dreams"). In other words: the rag picker is metaphorised in Benjamin, becoming an alter ego of the poet; it is probably not far-fetched to consider him a metaphor for Benjamin's own writing, especially in the *Arcades Project*. In the section "On the Theory of Knowledge, Theory of Progress" of this complex writing project, he writes, "I shall purloin no valuables, appropriate no ingenious formulations. But the rags, the refuse – these I will not inventory but allow, in the only way possible, to come into their own: by making use of them".[11] This certainly also holds true for Gramsci's method in the *Prison Notebooks* – for what is the collection of quotations from newspapers and magazines of the fascist era that seem unimportant at first glance but food for thought, just like Benjamin's numerous quotations in the *Arcades Project*?

However, the social and political reality of the rag picker as a subaltern, to use Gramsci's term once again, underwent a process of metaphorisation in Benjamin (but not without the social underpinning remaining present). This is a process that Benjamin can in no way be blamed for: his text is not called "History of the Marginalised", even if this theme is present throughout, but dedicated to the poet and thinker Baudelaire. Furthermore, he produced wonderful literary portrayals of marginalised men and women elsewhere, for example, in the sections dedicated to the Paris Passages.[12] And is not literature also a form of knowledge?

The question that remains for the second part of this chapter is: does the metaphorisation of the marginalised also apply to Gramsci's social rebels? This will now be the subject of discussion.

11.2 Gramsci and the Social Rebel

First, it is indispensable to note that Gramsci always maintained the boundaries between fictional and historically real figures. Moreover, one should remember that the rampant banditry in Sardinia in the first decades of the twentieth century was a social reality for the adolescent Antonio – or Nino, as his family called him – at least in the shape of popular narratives. This is comparable to how the Sardinian Nobel Prize winner Grazia Deledda describes the same experiences in her autofictional novel *Cosima* (1937). Nino, therefore, knew the myths and legends surrounding these figures and the different motivations of these social rebels, if you want to call them that. In his well-known study, Hobsbawm applies the term also to Sardinia,[13] although this is not necessarily appropriate, because a good deal of criminal energy was often involved. Nevertheless, it is safe to say that these figures were certainly regarded as "heroes" by many sections of the Sardinian population.

In any case, due to his biographical experience and cultural socialisation, Gramsci had been more familiar with the reality of the marginalised since childhood and youth than Benjamin. This resulted in his thoroughly anthropological view of such phenomena.[14] Benjamin's approach, on the other hand, was that of a social historian and philosopher trained in literature, albeit with an attention to material culture that one does not find in Gramsci to the same extent (which is understandable because the author of the *Prison Notebooks* had virtually no contact with the outside world).

Gramsci's social rebel Davide Lazzaretti is in many respects comparable to the *conspirateur*, the professional conspirator, a falsely politicised subaltern, so to speak. The notes about him can be found in the twenty-fifth *Prison Notebook* with the heading "On the Margins of History (The History of Subaltern Social Groups)".[15] Lazzaretti, like Benjamin's rag picker, is a nineteenth-century figure; he is not a bandit but shares some traits with this figure; Gramsci also associates him with "brigantaggio" (banditry).

First, let us begin with a few biographical remarks about Lazzaretti (1834–1878). Born into a poor farming family in the Tuscan village of Arcidosso (still a village today) in 1834, Lazzaretti initially practised the profession of a carter, which is comparable to that of a rag picker. However, he claimed early on to have religious dreams and visions. In the course of his short life, he founded the "Chiesa Giurisdavidica" (Jurisdavidic Church), a movement that followed the teachings of the biblical David. In accordance with these beliefs, he managed to raise a rebellious movement supported by the local lower classes which can be characterised as Christian-inspired utopian socialism: with a lifestyle modelled on the early Christian churches, common property, etc.[16] "It is a mixture of religious doctrines of the past with a heavy dose of vaguely socialist-sounding maxims and generic references to the moral redemption of man", notes Gramsci (PN25, 6). Not to forget: "Davide's flag was red, with the inscription 'The Republic and the Kingdom of God'" (PN25, 5).

Just a reminder: Italy was a kingdom after the end of the Risorgimento – and was to remain so for a long time. Under these circumstances, propagating a republic under the auspices of an idealised early Christianity was undoubtedly risky. All the aforementioned programmatic elements of Lazzaretti's teaching were naturally a thorn in the side of those in power. In 1878, he was labelled a heretic by the Catholic Church, excommunicated and his works – indeed, he had also published texts[17] – were placed on the Index. In August 1878, he and his followers were intercepted by a troop of *carabinieri* and military men, and Lazzaretti and some other members of his congregation were shot dead: "the killing of Lazzaretti was savage in its cruelty and coldly premeditated" (PN25, 4), as Gramsci noted. In this case, throne and altar worked together splendidly in the interests of shared political goals.

But why was the Sardinian philosopher interested in this, historically speaking, marginal figure? First of all, because for the proponent of *filologia vivente* ("living philology"), nothing is marginal, every experience is worthy of reflection.

Moreover, because Lazzaretti allowed him to think about the conditions of the subaltern and to develop his theory in this regard.

Some of Gramsci's reflections on this figure are summarised later. He once again notes the bizarre mixture of political and religious motivations that characterise Lazzaretti's actions and writings. He claims that the Lazzaretti case is comparable to banditry: "The same thing happened, on a larger scale, with regard to 'brigandage' in the South and the islands" (PN25, 4). Furthermore, he explains, "The drama of Lazzaretti must be linked to the 'exploits' of the so-called bands of Benevento that occurred at the same time: the views of the priests and peasants in the trial of Malatesta were very similar to those of Lazzaretti's followers" (PN25, 5). In other words: those men and women were motivated by social and economic misery, therefore guiding their actions with the help of religious or pseudo-religious elements of faith. The motivation of the social rebel, according to Gramsci (here he agrees with Hobsbawm, rightly so in the case of Lazzaretti), is thus comparable to that of the bandit, and the reaction of the authorities to both phenomena is just as similar. Following an early biographer of Lazzaretti, Gramsci also notes that the latter had drawn some of his key words and ideas verbatim from a historical novel by Giuseppe Rovani, *Manfredo Pallavicino* (1845). This is the result of the typical approach of a subaltern, who, for lack of comprehensive knowledge, sticks to the scripture to which he can relate. We know this from today's experience through the perhaps not-so-astonishing success of fake news.

At the end, Gramsci comes to refer to a macabre circumstance: Cesare Lombroso, a representative of the so-called positivist anthropology, had Lazzaretti's body exhumed. After measuring his skull, this researcher, who was widely esteemed in his day, came to the conclusion that – in line with his doctrine – the deceased had a hereditary tendency towards crime. Gramsci comments, "[T]his was the cultural custom of the day: instead of studying the origins of a collective event and the reasons why it was widespread, why it was collective, one isolated the protagonist and limited oneself to producing his pathological biography" (PN25, 3). The motive for such an approach is clear to him: "[t]o a social elite, the components of subaltern groups always have something barbaric or pathological about them" (PN25, 3). This can also be applied to today's judgements about people who are rightly or wrongly considered to be marginalised. It not only means that, from today's perspective, we have to classify Lombroso's scientific premises as untenable. Equally worthy of criticism are the tendencies of politicians to conveniently attribute rebellions to the biographical motivations of their leaders, thereby not only sparing themselves social-historical considerations but above all withholding them from the electorate.

Another section, dedicated to "methodological criteria", in which Gramsci outlines his theory of the subaltern, follows the first biographical-analytical paragraph. The history of the subaltern is necessarily always "fragmented and episodic" (PN25, 6), because it is only incompletely handed down, often through court records, that is, usually not through direct statements by the accused marginalised. Furthermore, the subalterns are subject to the hegemony of the ruling class, even and precisely when they revolt: just as Benjamin implies for Baudelaire's rag picker.

Lazzaretti is therefore someone who constructs his credo and his mission from a mixture of biographical experience and more or less random, autodidactic, non-contextualised, arbitrarily interpreted readings.[18] From this theorem, Gramsci derives the maxim – keyword: living philology! – that the history of the subalterns has to consider firstly the respective individual figures or individual movements and must not prematurely move on to generalisations. This is a warning that we can also take to heart today when we talk about or research the motivations of the world's far-right or far-left movements.

In the following section, Gramsci discusses social-rebellion movements of the Middle Ages in Italy, which I will omit here. At the end of the twenty-fifth Notebook, in paragraph eight, he returns to the topic of interest of this article. The question is why the sociology of his time (or what was then called sociology and which we now classify as positivist anthropology) was so intensively concerned with the phenomenon of crime: Lombroso and consorts. He wonders, particularly understandably from our current perspective, whether one is dealing with a professional deformation here or whether this is "a residue of late Romanticism of 1848 (Sue and his novelistic lucubrations on criminal law?)" (PN25, 14). Here he is again very close to Benjamin's rag picker, who might be imagined as a fictional reader or at least as someone who is acquainted with Sue's feuilleton novels and their oral distribution. In any case, Gramsci's conclusion is a thoroughly cultural-scientific one: Italian intellectuals would "'scientifically' (i.e. naturalistically)" (PN25, 14) describe the phenomenon of banditry as barbarism.

With this brief remark, he manages to get to the heart of the naturalisation of historical criminal phenomena without condoning these forms of criminality. The quoted passage can be read in connection with the famous essay "Alcuni temi della quistione meridionale" ("Some Aspects of the Southern Question") from 1926. In this essay, Gramsci states that writers and politicians who describe the social and political conditions in Southern Italy and the islands as "barbaric" do not seek a critical-historical understanding of the problems. Deliberately omitting these mostly disturbing reflections, their efforts (as, e.g. the repeated official investigation reports of the time – "inchieste" – on Southern Italy) make any attempt to eliminate the grievances seem futile. Their attitude thus goes hand in hand with the discrimination of entire sections of the local populations, triggering resentment and the difficulty of winning the working class of the North for a common front with the farmers of the South (which is the political goal of Gramsci's essay).

In the twenty-seventh Prison Notebook, titled "Observations on 'Folklore'", Gramsci returns to his analyses of the twenty-fifth Notebook and develops his theorem of "folklore",[19] although Lazzaretti no longer plays a role. "Folklore" should not be considered a picturesque element of the past, but "a 'conception of the world and life'. . . . Hence the strict relationship between folklore and 'common sense', which is philosophical folklore" (PN25, 189).[20] The thought process that leads from Notebook 25 (1934) to Notebook 27 (1935) enlightens in a paradigmatic way Gramsci's intellectual approach. It leads from "living philology", which today we would call a case study, to an elaborate theory that does not forget its empirical foundations.

In their "case studies" discussed here, Gramsci and Benjamin, apart from their respective biographical experiences, start from reports that they know from reading, including Benjamin, who actually tried to get a picture of the real living conditions of rag pickers in nineteenth-century Paris. Lazzaretti is certainly no "hero" for Gramsci (in Benjamin's understanding). Rather, he is an example of the misguided political ambitions of a subaltern, with all the conclusions that the author of the *Prison Notebooks* knows how to draw from this exemplary story. As I hope to have shown, Gramsci's analysis offers numerous possibilities for analysing today's precarious political conditions. Benjamin's rag picker, on the other hand, is a cipher that stands for the poet, but ultimately also for himself. His claimed heroism is certainly a revaluation, an appreciation of the marginalised, but ultimately a bit romanticising, despite all the socio-historical contextualisation. But is not literature, and therefore Baudelaire's famous poem, a relevant part of human history? And did not Benjamin do full justice to this fact with his commentary? Do not the rag picker and his fantasies of revenge and justice live in the dreams of many? And should not people who see themselves as intellectuals take them seriously and consider them, just as Benjamin took them seriously and considered them?

Notes

1 This is a revised version of an essay published in Italian in Dario Gentili, Elettra Stimilli, and Gabriele Guerra, eds., *Un incontro mancato: Walter Benjamin e Antonio Gramsci* (Macerata: Quodlibet, 2023), 191–203.
2 Theodor W. Adorno, "The Essay as Form", in *Notes to Literature*, ed. Rolf Tiedemann, trans. Shierry Weber Nicholson (New York: Columbia University Press, 2019), 43. Adorno's essay was written in German (1954–1958), but only published much later.
3 Walter Benjamin, *Berlin Childhood around 1900*, trans. Howard Eiland (Cambridge, MA: Harvard University Press, 2006), 38.
4 See my essay "Walter Benjamin de passage", in *À la rencontre: Affinités et coups de foudre. Hommage à Claude Leroy*, ed. Marie-Paule Berranger and Myriam Boucharenc (Paris: Presses Universitaires de Paris Ouest, 2012), 271–282.
5 See Dario Gentili's contribution to this volume.
6 Walter Benjamin, *Selected Writings*, ed. Howard Eiland and Michael W. Jennings (Cambridge, MA: Harvard University Press, 2006), vol. 4, 4. Hereafter, abbreviated to SW.

7 Charles Baudelaire, *Œuvres complètes I* (Paris: Bibliothèque de la Pléiade, 1975), 106. It should not go unmentioned that Benjamin wrote a very similar poem in German, published in Klaus Garber, *Zum Bilde Walter Benjamins: Studien, Porträts, Kritiken* (Munich: Fink, 1992), 89. See below an English version of the two stanzas, translated by Carlyle F. MacIntyre:

One sees a ragpicker knocking against the walls,
Paying no heed to the spies of the cops, his thralls,
But stumbling like a poet lost in dreams;
He pours his heart out in stupendous schemes.
He takes great oaths and dictates sublime laws,
Casts down the wicked, aids the victims' cause;
Beneath the sky, like a vast canopy,
He is drunken of his splendid qualities.
See www.poetryfoundation.org/poems/54376/the-ragpickers-wine (25 November 2023).

8 See the last sentences of the second section "The Flâneur": "While Victor Hugo was celebrating the crowd as the hero of a modern epic, Baudelaire was seeking a refuge for the hero among the masses of the big city. Hugo placed himself in the crowd as a *citoyen*; Baudelaire divorced himself from the crowd as a hero" (SW, 39).

9 See the serial films of Louis Feuillade: *Fantômas* and *Les Vampires*.

10 Note that this citation is the result of a double translation: from French to German (Benjamin) and from German to English.

11 Walter Benjamin, *Arcades Project*, trans. Howard Eiland and Kevin McLaughlin (Cambridge, MA: Harvard University Press, 1999), 460.

12 See the following text about an impoverished saleswoman in an arcade: "On the pale-colored wallpaper full of figures and bronze busts falls the light of a gas lamp. An old woman sits beside it, reading. For years, it would seem, she has been alone." Benjamin, *Arcades Project*, 872. Benjamin is a great writer, let me mention it.

13 Eric Hobsbawm, *Primitive Rebels: Studies in Archaic Forms of Social Movement in the 19th and 20th Centuries* (Manchester: Manchester University Press, 1959).

14 See the contributions in Sabrina Tosi Cambini and Fabio Frosini, eds., "Gramsci and Anthropology: A Round Trip", *International Gramsci Journal* 2, no. 3 (2017): Special issue.

15 I quote from the new critical edition of this single Notebook, hereafter abbreviated to PN25: *Subaltern Social Groups: A Critical Edition of Prison Notebook 25*, ed. and trans. Joseph A. Buttigieg and Marcus E. Green (New York: Columbia University Press, 2021). Thanks to Ingo Pohn-Lauggas, who made this critical edition available to me. See also the new German edition, *Südfrage und Subalterne*, ed. Ingo Pohn-Lauggas and Alexandra Assinger (Berlin: Argument, 2023). Both editions also publish and comment on the dispersed remarks on the subalterns found in other issues of the *Prison Notebooks*. The German edition also contains a brand-new translation of "Some Aspects of the Southern Question" (in Italian 1926, Gramsci's last article published before his imprisonment, hence not a part of the *Prison Notebooks*).

16 Information regarding Davide Lazzaretti is somewhat incomplete, but, on the other hand, there are rich hints in Gramsci's sources about Lazzaretti in PN25, 139–142.

17 Under the significant genre headings of "Sermons, Prophecies and Aphorisms" or "Dreams and Visions".

18 Incidentally, this makes him a relative of the miller Menocchio, whose (also real) destiny Carlo Ginzburg researched: *Il formaggio e i vermi; Il cosmo di un mugnaio del '500* (Turin: Einaudi, 1976) (English version: *The Cheese and the Worms: The Cosmos of a Sixteenth Century Miller*, 1980). Ginzburg returns to Gramsci's terminology several times in his foreword. He also discusses the difficulties of reading old sources

(especially court records) in an illuminating way – which is crucial for the history of subaltern men and women.
19 English version in Antonio Gramsci, *Selections from Cultural Writings*, 2nd ed., ed. David Forgacs and Geoffrey Nowell-Smith, trans. William Boelhower (London: Lawrence and Wishart, 2012), 188–194.
20 What is interesting here is Gramsci's insistence on widely shared legal concepts that contradict the established law of the state but are nevertheless widely accepted by the population. Here one can think of the "codice barbaricino", a Sardinian customary law that was more relevant to people's actions, especially in the interior of Sardinia, than state law for many decades. See Gramsci, *Cultural Writings*, 192–194.

Bibliography

Adorno, Theodor W. "The Essay as Form". In *Notes to Literature*, edited by Rolf Tiedemann, translated by Shierry Weber Nicholson, 29–47. New York: Columbia University Press, 2019.
Baudelaire, Charles. *Œuvres complètes I*. Paris: Bibliothèque de la Pléiade, 1975.
Benjamin, Walter. *The Arcades Project*, translated by Howard Eiland, and Kevin McLaughlin. Cambridge, MA: Harvard University Press, 1999.
Benjamin, Walter. *Berlin Childhood around 1900*, translated by Howard Eiland. Cambridge, MA: Harvard University Press, 2006.
Benjamin, Walter. *Selected Writings: Volume 4 (1938–1940)*, edited by Howard Eiland, and Michael W. Jennings. Cambridge, MA: Harvard University Press, 2006.
Garber, Klaus. *Zum Bilde Walter Benjamins: Studien, Porträts, Kritiken*. Munich: Fink, 1992.
Ginzburg, Carlo. *Il formaggio e i vermi: Il cosmo di un mugnaio del '500*. Turin: Einaudi, 1976.
Gramsci, Antonio. *Selections from Cultural Writings*, edited by David Forgacs, and Geoffrey Nowell-Smith, translated by William Boelhower, 2nd edition. London: Lawrence and Wishart, 2012.
Gramsci, Antonio. *Subaltern Groups: A Critical Edition of Prison Notebook 25*, edited and translated by Joseph A. Buttigieg, and Marcus E. Green. New York: Columbia University Press, 2021.
Gramsci, Antonio. *Südfrage und Subalterne*, edited by Ingo Pohn-Lauggas, and Alessandra Axinger. Berlin: Argument, 2023.
Hobsbawm, Eric. *Primitive Rebels: Studies in Archaic Forms of Social Movement in the 19th and 20th Centuries*. Manchester: Manchester University Press, 1959.
Tosi Cambini, Sabrina, and Frosini, Fabio, eds. "Gramsci and Anthropology: A Round Trip". Special issue, *International Gramsci Journal* 2, no. 3 (2017).
Wagner, Birgit. "Walter Benjamin de passage". In *À la rencontre: Affinités et coups de foudre. Hommage à Claude Leroy*, edited by Marie-Paule Berranger, and Myriam Boucharenc, 271–282. Paris: Presses Universitaires de Paris Ouest, 2012.

PART 4

Translation and Criticism, Avant-Garde and Popular Culture

12

CRITIQUE, MEDIATION, AND STRATEGY

From Gramsci to Benjamin

Marco Gatto

12.1 Against Specialism

The following contribution focuses on literary criticism. Indeed, narrowing down the scope of the analysis should not appear as a limitation, since for both Gramsci and Benjamin literary criticism more generally corresponds to a form of cultural critique or social philosophy. Within this purview, the critic plays the role of "specialist+philosopher" [*specialista+filosofo*],[1] that is, a human-ist-intellectual for Gramsci, and a philologist who is also a philosopher, as it emerges from Benjamin's writings. Just as both Gramsci and Benjamin agree on the role of the critic, they also call for the need to acknowledge "critique" as a space for meditation. In effect, critique should aim at reinvigorating the drive of a Marxism that seeks to escape the vulgar, flattening mechanism of the Second International – this is especially true for Gramsci – and at strengthening Marxist dialectics – as is the case with Benjamin.

The terms "mediation" and "strategy" belong to their vocabulary. While the former intimately emerges from Gramsci's Hegelism, the second derives from Benjamin's idea of "literary struggle" at the beginning of the famous thesis on the tasks of the critic.[2] However, I believe that both "mediation" and "strategy" can highlight some common objectives and trajectories. For this reason, I set out to highlight the similarities and the convergences existing between these two concepts, possibly overemphasising them, while at the same time reiterating the profound differences existing on the subject of aesthetic judgement.

To begin, one may affirm that both terms are deeply rooted in the two thinkers' respective cultures of origin. The literary question in the *Notebooks* is national in nature (with some scarce comparisons with other nations). Gramsci's interest lies

DOI: 10.4324/9781003457039-17

in the history of the Italian intellectuals and literati, their distinctive mentality, and their social distribution on the cultural scene, whose peculiarities he considers against the framework of the country's history and its contradictions. This is how we should read the *Problems of Italian National Culture* opening *Notebook 21* on Popular Literature.

If we compare Italy to other "literary nations" – in particular, France with its serial literature, and Russia with Tolstoj's and Dostoevsky's extraordinary works – Gramsci evidently aims at delving into all of the *deficits* afflicting Italian culture. In this context, the terminological juxtaposition "national-popular" fully reveals the poignancy of the expression (one that is not new, but which Gramsci borrows from Ruggiero Bonghi),[3] as does the force of the negation preceding it, which marks its critical and diagnostic value. Indeed, according to Gramsci, Italian literature is not national-popular in character, coming from intellectuals who do not possess any "sentimental connection"[4] with their people-nation.

Benjamin's literary and cultural horizon is that of Germany, although his openings to other nations are broader and richer, and by no means limited to an interested comparison. In a letter to Scholem, Benjamin nominates himself as "the foremost critic of German literature",[5] explicitly indicating if not Germany, then central Europe as his irreducible geography of action. In effect, in my view, it is not a paradox to affirm that their being rooted in their respective national cultures allows both Gramsci and Benjamin to overcome the contradiction of a sterile nationalism, and to delineate the materialistic direction of their thought.

This militant and geographically situated outlook allows for a productive comparison between the two thinkers by concentrating, for the purpose of analysis, on two main issues. The first is the relationship between literature and subalternity (i.e. between cultural expression and "the tradition of the oppressed"[6]); the second is the attack against the caste-like character of their respective national literatures and, thus, against the intellectuals and the dominant culture.

12.2 Criticism and Nation

First, let me extrapolate a few Gramscian passages, while always bearing in mind the profound sense of coherence informing Gramsci's reasoning. In the miscellaneous Notebook 15, note 58, from prison, Gramsci explicitly defines the objectives of his hegemonic-cultural programme: "The problem remains", Gramsci writes, as to "how to create a body of literary figures who artistically stand to serial literature as Dostoevsky stood to Sue and Soulié; or as Chesterton, in the police novel, stands to Conan Doyle and Wallace, etc."[7] This strategy consists in the emergence of a class of intellectuals who, like the literature they produce, "has its roots in the humus of popular culture"[8] thereby ensuring the emancipatory cultural growth of the subordinate strata. Without this body of literati, the latter are condemned to *suffer* the hegemony of other cultural productions, as is the case of Italy, where the people read serial literature from France because there is no literary production intended for their needs.

Yet, Gramsci demonstrates that applying such a strategy encounters several problems deriving from the fact that "the development of intellectual and moral renewal is not simultaneous in all social strata."[9] The reason lies in the fact that accentuated social stratification produces the coexistence of possible developments, simultaneous stops, and unexpected accelerations. However, at the bottom lies some common reason, some materialistic marker. Given the historical development of the Italian culture, writers do not fulfil a "national 'educative function'" [*funzione "educatrice nazionale"*].[10] In effect, the latter "have not and do not set themselves the problem of elaborating popular feelings after having relived them and made them their own."[11]

As a result, it is impossible to trigger a strategy of aesthetic emancipation, and stagnation ensues, instead. No one, continues Gramsci, realistically considers the issue of the subaltern classes' cultural consumption, concluding that "if people like the novels of a hundred years ago, it means that their taste and ideology are precisely those of a hundred years ago."[12]

Consequently, the popular classes fail to find representation in literature. The Italian people benefit from a literary production conceived of and written for an audience-other. Moreover, the Italian people are the subject neither of study nor of representation, except for those paternalistic and bookish narratives by writers from the upper classes. The typical modern intellectuals, as Gramsci famously quipped, because of their caste-like character "feel closer to Annibal Caro or Ippolito Pindemonte than to an Apulian or Sicilian peasant."[13] After all, "the current term 'national' in Italy is connected to this intellectual and bookish tradition"[14] and not to the general culture of the people-nation.

Quite surprisingly, Benjamin articulates a similar argument, although this is connected more generally to the question of consumer literature and, consequently, to that of literature as production, rather than to matters of literary sociology, in tones and accents that cannot fail to recall the pages of Gramsci.

In the *Fragments* of literary criticism, Benjamin confronts the Norwegian writer Knut Hamsun, the author of the famous novel *Hunger* (1890). Fragments 116 and 117, dating back to July 1929, offer a meditation on a similar narrative failure to represent certain existences that have been silenced and suppressed, thus replicating their social invisibility:

> nothing that lies at the core of such men's existence [is] accessible to us. . . .
> If we have understood this sense of foreignness and have been able to real-
> ise how long over the generations the peasant has been silent, then Hamsun

stands before us: the toothless mouth of countless generations of peasants, who now begins to open and slowly speak his word about our lives, and who for the first time and in his own language allows his judgement on us to be expressed.[15]

Again, in the second fragment, Benjamin's need to give voice to the oppressed clashes – almost Gramscianly, I would say – with the indolence and the sloth proper of the legitimised and renowned intellectuals:

> to his simplest and most miserable creatures such as peasants, settlers and beg-gars, he always attributed all the unspeakable fragility, complication and abys-mality that our 'great' novelists, who know nothing and have problems only in their heads, consider the curse and privilege of the decadent big-city man.[16]

Hence, both Gramsci and Benjamin ascribe the lack of representation of the "voiceless" to the myopia of the intellectuals, to the caste-like character of their cultural and artistic production, which often appears to comfort the audience rather than disorienting them. In fragment 118, Benjamin talks about a literature that is a source of tranquillity and quietism, aiming at a devious identification between its readers and the heroes it represents. As the philosopher argues, "the success of such works lies in the fact that they turn every reader into a 'little Napoleon' or an 'inner Goethe'".[17]

12.3   Criticism and Social Groups

The strategy to create a nexus between subalternity and the elitism of cultural tradition is evident in the "Program of Literary Criticism" (dating back to 1929 as well) and especially from Gramsci's attempt to identify those social groups that allow this nexus to be preserved. For Gramsci, this is a blatant example of the "sectarianism" he denounces in several passages of his *Notebooks*. As an example, see the corrosive pages on some "priests of art" [*sacerdoti dell'arte*],[18] on the omnipresence of "single popes" on that, "last access of illness"[19] that for Gramsci is Gabriele D'Annunzio, and so on; see, in short, the reflections on the exclusivist character of culture. Benjamin writes,

> Germany's reading public has a highly peculiar structure. It can be divided into two roughly equal parts: "the public" and "the literary circles". There is scarcely any overlap between the two. The public regards literature as an instrument of entertainment, animation, or the deepening of sociability – a pastime in a higher or lower sense. The literary circles regard books as books of life, as sources of wisdom, as the statutes of their small groups – groups that alone bring bliss.[20]

The passage certifies that German criticism has dealt only with the public as a general audience, but not with "circles", that is, those narrow, self-referential social groups that act as "sects". Benjamin adds that this is "the authentic form of the barbarism to which Germany will succumb if Communism fails to conquer".[21] This is, an autonomist ideology that produces cultural forms based on an absent relation to "collective activity",[22] as it were. Possibly, this description well fits the Italian context that, writing from prison, Gramsci depicts in order to launch a hegemonic counter-proposal. The latter may find its realisation in the militant and pedagogical exercise of criticism, in the necessary emergence of the figure of an intellectual-persuader able to reach the lowest strata to invigorate them humanistically, and to set them on the path of conscious emancipation. This is the well-known passage about the shift from "common sense" to "good sense" from superstition to criticism, from chaos to coherent order, in the extraordinary pages of *Notebook 11*.

This is the first stage, a materialistic critique that, as Benjamin writes again in the *Program*, "would lead to a new, dynamic, dialectical aesthetics",[23] one that is therefore heteronomous, hostile to any closure. In other words, if confrontation with the materiality of production processes ceases, the myth of aesthetic autonomy is reproduced or, worse, the proliferation of capitalist conformism at every level goes unseen.

Within this last insight, I see a further convergence between these fragmentary writings dated 1929–1930 (I refer now to the five points "Characterization of the New Generation") and Gramsci's positions. Indeed, the sectarianism of the intellectuals not only leads to the subjugation of the average public – or, as Gramsci would say, of the people-nation – and to an inadequate literary production. It also supports the elitist convictions of those who consider literature a thing for the few. In this regard, Benjamin thus expresses himself in an incisive passage:

> Popular literature has always existed – that is to say, a literature that acknowledges no obligations to the age and the ideas that move it, except perhaps the desirability of presenting such ideas in an agreeable, fashionably packaged form for immediate consumption. Such consumer literature of course has the right to exist; in bourgeois society at least, it has its place and its justification. But never before, in bourgeois or any society, has this literature of pure consumption and enjoyment ever been identical with the avantgarde at its technically and artistically most advanced. This is precisely the pass to which the latest school has now brought us.[24]

12.4 Mediation

Now, if we read *Notebook 23* carefully and the notes Gramsci devotes to the pathologies of the Italian literati, we realise that such homologous results involve two seemingly distant phenomena. Arguably, the preservation of an exclusivist social and cultural condition results from the literary populism of the "nephews of Father Bresciani" arising from an "anti-state and anti-national individualism" [*individualismo antistatale e antinazionale*][25] and, at the same time, from class paternalism, coupled with the aristocratic character of the "new laymen". These are the ones who speak only for themselves in a coven language comprehensible only to a few followers. On the one hand, we have entertainment arising from a reactionary simplification of content (with the inevitable production of aesthetically inadequate texts) and, on the other, the reification of language in a supposedly unattainable style (high because it is unintelligible): two sides of the same coin, communicating a situation of value stalemate.

One can therefore understand the urgency of a critical strategy that restores the necessity of materialistic judgement. In this sense, criticism is a mediation between the work of art and life, a battlefield where seemingly distant elements face each other, elements that the materialist must show in their unity, demystifying their immediacy. In short, the critical act involves the reconstruction of a totality made up of subtle and invisible mediations.

One should point out that Gramsci's approach to the problem sometimes diverges from Benjamin's, because in many respects, it remains anchored to a logic of distinction between aesthetic and political judgement. It is also true that there is a more profound and less obvious dialectics to be extracted from the *Notebooks* (but also from the *Letters*). Such a dialectics has as its cardinal principle in Gramsci's recognition of literary specificity, whose litmus test is the necessity for the aesthetic emancipation of the people, so that they can have access to more sophisticated forms of representation. This is already the case in other countries such as Russia, where people read Dostoevsky and certainly not the bad copy of feuilletons. Such a literary specificity, however, does not turn automatically into aesthetic autonomy. Rather, it coincides with the heteronomous and materialistic character of art which, in order to be understood, actually requires not simply an analytical but also a political and cultural set of tools.[26]

It remains a fact that, in Gramsci, critique grounds itself within a process of mediation that takes on the image of a path of inexhaustible unhinging of the immediacies, of the false appearances with which cultural texts are presented. Such a path must lead to the question of class determination, to the "concrete" that lies behind the forms. It is from such a result that a counter-hegemony can emerge. For Gramsci, I would argue, critical mediation unquestionably means the demystification of aesthetic autonomy and the unhinging of a populist-romantic idea of art as a separate sphere governed by laws accessible only to the few. Benjamin and his "Program of Literary Criticism" go in this same direction:

> The function of criticism, especially today: to lift *the mask of "pure art"* and show that there is no neutral ground for art. Materialist criticism as an instrument for this.[27]

12.5   Criticism of the depth

This idea of a materialistic *inside* of the text that needs to be brought to the surface forcefully emerges, I think, from Gramsci's preoccupation for the "criticism of the 'unexpressed'", "the non-existent"[28] of the text in the Dantesque notes of *Notebook 4*. I will quickly approach these notes, in the attempt to grasp a possible, and new, similarity with Benjamin and the pages the latter devotes to the relationship between real content and truth content (I am referring to the early essays on Hölderlin and, above all, to the essay on Goethe's *The Elective Affinities*). When Benjamin enunciates a "basic law of literature according to which the more significant the work, the more inconspicuously and intimately its truth content is bound up with its material content",[29] he manifests an idea of literature and of the text based on a dialectics of concealment and latency. Texts are the keepers of a depth that must be explored beyond any formal immediacy: "the works that prove enduring are precisely those whose truth is most deeply sunken in their material content".[30] In the diagnostic and critical journey that is the exploration of this underlying dimension of the text we come across the evidence that the truth content, in the historical life of the work of art, "always remains to the same extent hidden as the material content comes to the fore".[31] The statement that follows is famous: "One may compare [the critic] to a paleographer in front a parchment whose faded text is covered by the lineaments of a more powerful script which refers to that text".[32] Hence, the need for commentary as the first act in assessing "the basic critical question of whether the semblance/luster [*Schein*] of the truth content is due to the material content, or the life of the material content to the truth content".[33] The latter is, in another image typical of Benjamin, the "luminous kernel of redemptive content".[34]

Now, it seems to me that Gramsci posits such an analytical distinction, which must then give rise to a dialectical combustion of the one and the other moment.[35] The Sardinian communist devotes those pages to the relationship between aesthetic judgement and political judgement, a relationship that can also be conflicting, obscure, and difficult. Not only that: the kernel of the truth content is characterised by its location within a space that is not epidermal, but rather hidden. When Gramsci asks whether it is acceptable to see in the text what the latter does not verbalise, he presupposes the existence – problematic for the materialist – of a content that, because of its absence, he must reconstruct. This refers specifically to in *Inferno* X, Cavalcante's grief at the (misunderstood) news of Guido's death: a grief that we feel only as the thud of the soul in pain in his ark.

Unlike Benjamin, Gramsci does not go so far as to insert a median element to circumvent the problem; consequently, he remains entangled in a logic of distinction, albeit one that subtly opens to the *unconscious* dimension of the text. Benjamin grafts the question of "technique" as a *tertium* capable of establishing a boundary between the epidermal, an apparent, superior, verbalised layer, and a deeper layer of the work, in which the truth content is deposited (*depositum historiae*, says Franco Fortini).[36] It is the boundary between what can be neither seen nor read; methodologically, it is a median concept that allows us to rewrite the age-old dialectics between form and content.

This is very close to the concept of the *das Dichtete* that finds definition in the essays on Hölderlin, appearing in the long contribution on Goethe. As Michele Capasso has recently written, this concept highlights the internal form of the work of art, analysing the "intuitive and intellectual connections immanent in the work" and must be "deduced, posited from the work itself",[37] so that an ultimate foundation can be accessed, which is precisely hidden, not superficial. Here lies not the mystery of the work, but the reason for its realisation as a form, its technical and aesthetic problems.

It seems to me that this critique of the profound unites, albeit to different degrees of awareness, our two authors. This critique is linked to a strategy of knowledge that insists on the dialectical nexus between the immediate and the mediated in order to mark it materialistically. It places such a nexus within a further dimension, where the real content and the truth content meet, giving rise to new interrogations, as it were.

There is no doubt that, on the level of literary criticism and culture, this is very close to a much renewed Marxism, sustained by an idea of textual and ideological complexity that has not found many spaces of representation in the following decades, despite a few important exceptions.[38] However, the exhaustion of the superficialising thrusts of postmodernity, due to the overbearing return of conflicts on a global scale, suggests that a demystifying hermeneutics may find new grounds for legitimacy today. A patient work of reconstruction of the dialectical and materialistic alphabet therefore seems urgent and desirable, starting with the reinvigoration of those categories that bring about the intelligibility of nexuses all too cleverly covered and hidden by capitalist abstraction.

Notes

1 Antonio Gramsci, *Quaderni del carcere*, ed. Valentino Gerratana (Torino: Einaudi, 1975), vol. 3, 1551 (Q. 12, § 3). Subsequent references will be in the text marked by the letter Q, followed by the number of the notebook, paragraph, and page number.
2 Walter Benjamin, "The Critic's Technique in Thirteen Thesis", in *Selected Writings*, ed. Michael W. Jennings (Cambridge, MA and London: The Belknap Press of Harvard University Press, 1996–2002), vol. 1, 1913–1926, 460.
3 Ruggiero Bonghi, *Perché la letteratura italiana non sia popolare in Italia* (Milano: Sugarco, 1993 [1856]).
4 Gramsci, *Quaderni del carcere*, 1505 (Q. 11, § 67).
5 Walter Benjamin to Gershom G. Scholem on 20 January 1930, in *The Correspondence of Walter Benjamin: 1910–1040*, ed. Manfred R. Jacobson and Evelyn M. Jacobson (Chicago and London: Chicago University Press, 2012), 505.
6 Walter Benjamin, "On the Concept of History", in *Selected Writings*, vol. 4, 1938–1940, 391.

7 Gramsci, *Quaderni del carcere*, 1821–1822 (Q. 15, § 58).
8 Gramsci, *Quaderni del carcere*, 1822 (Q. 15, § 58).
9 Gramsci, *Quaderni del carcere*, 1821 (Q. 15, § 58).
10 Gramsci, *Quaderni del carcere*, 2114 (Q. 21, § 5).
11 Gramsci, *Quaderni del carcere*, 2114 (Q. 21, § 5).
12 Gramsci, *Quaderni del carcere*, 2114 (Q. 21, § 5).
13 Gramsci, *Quaderni del carcere*, 2116 (Q. 21, § 5).
14 Gramsci, *Quaderni del carcere*, 2116 (Q. 21, § 5).
15 Walter Benjamin, "Elementi di storia della cultura e della letteratura", in *Letteratura e strategie di critica. Frammenti I*, ed. Gabriele Guerra (Milano: Mimesis, 2012), 40.
16 Benjamin, "Elementi", 41.
17 Benjamin, "Elementi", 41.
18 Gramsci, *Quaderni del carcere*, 2190 (Q. 23, § 3).
19 Gramsci, *Quaderni del carcere*, 1738 (Q. 14, § 72).
20 Walter Benjamin, "Program of Literary Criticism", in *Selected Writings*, vol. 2, 1927–1939, 289–290.
21 Benjamin, "Program", 290.
22 Benjamin, "Program", 290.
23 Benjamin, "Program", 294.
24 Walter Benjamin, "Characterization of the New Generation", in *Selected Writings*, vol. 2, 1927–1939, 401–402.
25 Gramsci, *Quaderni del carcere*, 2197 (Q. 23, § 8).
26 On this issue, see my *Nonostante Gramsci. Marxismo e critica letteraria nell'Italia del Novecento* (Macerata: Quodlibet, 2016).
27 Benjamin, "Program", 292.
28 Gramsci, *Prison Notebooks*, ed. and trans. Joseph A. Buttigieg (New York: Columbia University Press, 1996), vol. 2, 248 (Q. 4, § 79).
29 Walter Benjamin, "Goethe's Elective Affinities", in *Selected Writings*, vol. 1, 1913–1926, 297.
30 Benjamin, "Goethe's Elective Affinities", 297.
31 Benjamin, "Goethe's Elective Affinities", 297.
32 Benjamin, "Goethe's Elective Affinities", 298.
33 Benjamin, "Goethe's Elective Affinities", 298.
34 Benjamin, "Goethe's Elective Affinities", 323.
35 See Romano Luperini, *Il dialogo e il conflitto. Per un'ermeneutica materialistica* (Roma and Bari: Laterza, 1999), 30.
36 Franco Fortini, "Opus servile", in *Saggi ed epigrammi*, ed. Luca Lenzini (Milano: Mondadori, 2003 [1989]), 1651.
37 Michele Capasso, "La critica come compito filosofico. Benjamin lettore di Hölderlin", *Il Pensiero* 60, no. 1 (2021): 110.
38 I refer primarily to Fredric Jameson, *The Political Unconscious: Narrative as a Socially Symbolic Act* (Ithaca: Cornell University Press, 1981).

Bibliography

Benjamin, Walter. *Selected Writings*, edited by Michael W. Jennings. Cambridge, MA and London: The Belknap Press of Harvard University Press, 1996–2003.
Benjamin, Walter. *The Correspondence of Walter Benjamin. 1910–1040*, edited by Manfred R. Jacobson, and Evelyn M. Jacobson. Chicago and London: Chicago University Press, 2012.
Benjamin, Walter. *Letteratura e strategie di critica. Frammenti I*, edited by Gabriele Guerra. Milano: Mimesis, 2012.

Bonghi, Ruggiero. *Perché la letteratura italiana non sia popolare in Italia*. Milano: Sugarco, 1993 [1856].

Capasso, Michele. "La critica come compito filosofico. Benjamin lettore di Hölderlin". *Il Pensiero* 60, no. 1 (2021).

Fortini, Franco. "Opus servile". In *Saggi ed epigrammi*, edited by Luca Lenzini. Milano: Mondadori, 2003 [1989].

Gatto, Marco. *Nonostante Gramsci. Marxismo e critica letteraria nell'Italia del Novecento*. Macerata: Quodlibet, 2016.

Gramsci, Antonio. *Quaderni del carcere*, edited by Valentino Gerratana. Torino: Einaudi, 1975.

Gramsci, Antonio. *Prison Notebooks*, edited and translated by Joseph A. Buttigieg. New York: Columbia University Press, 1996.

Jameson, Fredric. *The Political Unconscious: Narrative as a Socially Symbolic Act*. Ithaca: Cornell University Press, 1981.

Luperini, Romano. *Il dialogo e il conflitto. Per un'ermeneutica materialistica*. Roma and Bari: Laterza, 1999.

13

LANGUAGE IN THE AGE OF ITS CAPITALIST TRANSLATABILITY

Sami Khatib

13.1 Gramsci and the Critique of Linguistic Cosmopolitanism

In an article from 1920, Gramsci writes,

> One can easily foresee that when the working class wins its liberty, it will bring to the light of history new complexes of linguistic expressions even if it will not radically change the notion of beauty. The existence of Esperanto, although it does not demonstrate much in itself and has more to do with bourgeois cosmopolitanism than with proletarian internationalism, shows nevertheless, by the fact that the workers are strongly interested in it and manage to waste their time over it, that there is a desire for and a historical push towards the formation of verbal complexes that transcend national limits and in relation to which current national languages will have the same role as dialects now have.[1]

In this passage, Gramsci opposes a genuine proletarian universalism of language to a bourgeois form of linguistic cosmopolitanism, a position that in our times is probably taken by global English. Stressing the desire for a common language that transcends the borders and the imaginary of the nation-state, Gramsci positions proletarian internationalism against the artificial language of Esperanto without dismissing the universalist desire misarticulated in the latter. As a utopian project, Esperanto was created in the early twentieth century by the Polish ophthalmologist Ludwik Lejzer Zamenhof who published *Fundamento de Esperanto* in 1905. Its simplified grammar and vocabulary were formed artificially from the most commonly used words of the Western European languages.

DOI: 10.4324/9781003457039-18

In his *Prison Notebooks*, Gramsci returned to the *questione della lingua*, translatability and Esperanto, coming to terms with the challenge of an artificial language within the wider tendency of abstract formalisation typical of bourgeois-positivist science.

> Philosophical Esperantism is especially rooted in positivist and naturalistic conceptions, 'sociology' perhaps being the principal product of such a mentality. Hence the tendencies towards abstract 'classification', methodologism and formal logic. Logic and general methodology are conceived of as existing in and for themselves, like mathematical formulae, abstracted from concrete thought and from particular concrete sciences (just as one might suppose language to exist in dictionaries and grammar, technique outside work and concrete activity etc.).[2]

Gramsci's critique of Esperanto does not fall into the non-dialectical trap of non-mediated, external oppositions. Instead of pitting concreteness against abstractness or particularism against universalism, he proposes a different non-binary form of what Hegel and Marx would have called concrete universality – a proletarian internationalism developed from the non-formalist translatability of cultures and languages.

Without taking the entirety of Gramsci's oeuvre into consideration, it seems that such a critique of "Philosophical Esperantism" is surprisingly close to Benjamin's early theory of translation and language (1916–1921) and his later remarks on Esperanto in the context of his last text, the "Theses on the Concept of History" (1940). Departing from Gramsci and Benjamin, one could argue that Esperanto and Esperantism are symptoms of societies in which the social bond is mediated by the commodity form and abstract relations. As we will later discuss with Marx, the commodity form is not limited to political economy proper but also affects language and linguistic relations.

13.2   Benjamin and the Translatability of the Untranslatable

In his essay on "The Task of the Translator" from 1921, Benjamin highlights the original sense of translation: translation is not a secondary supplement of literary works but a primary, original feature, demonstrating a linguistic domain irreducible to the intentions, expectations, and needs of writers and readers.

> Translation is a form. . . . Translatability is an essential quality of certain works, which is not to say that it is essential for the works themselves that they be translated; it means, rather, that a specific significance inherent in the original manifests itself in its translatability (SW 1, 254).[3]

Instead of understanding translatability as an anthropocentric relation, formed by its pragmatic use, Benjamin dislocates translatability in the medium of its own linguistic communicability. Translation does not work through formalisation of similarities, equations, and approximations between target-language and source-language. For language is not conceived as an *organon* or envelope of communication, content, meaning, or information; rather, language is understood as mediacy – a pure means of its own communicability as medium.

Already in his early essay on "Language as Such and on the Language of Man" (1916), Benjamin introduced the idea of an a-teleological pure means in linguistic terms. What the later essay calls "pure language", the earlier one introduced as "language as such" or "name-language" (SW 1, 66) – a non-human (i.e. "divine") language indifferent to human communicative ends. That is to say, the "mental being" of humans is not communicated *through* but *in* language as the pure medium of language as such. "All language communicates itself" (SW 1, 63). Name-language, or "language as such", speaks itself in all languages and thereby guarantees the translatability of every language into another.

Language as such (or, what the later essay on "The Task of the Translator" calls "pure language") is not a meta-language, a language of all languages. Rather, it denotes the dimension of language deprived of all its semiotic-denotative function. The task of the translator is "to release in his own language that pure language which is exiled among alien tongues, to liberate the language imprisoned in a work in his re-creation of that work. For the sake of the pure language, he breaks through decayed barriers of his own language." (SW 1, 286) The translation of one language into another is possible by virtue of this non-formalisable medium of pure language, which might be understood as pure relationality. Pure language is not an abstraction from existing "natural" languages but a layer of language embedded in every language. As Werner Hamacher put it:

> The language of translation is not a language among others, but rather a language between others, an intermediary language [*Zwischensprache*] that expresses nothing other than the relation of languages, but that expresses this relation, in turn, not as given but as becoming. Translation expresses that which is not yet there; to this extent, it is historical – oriented toward a historical distance – but, to this extent, it is also not a simple phenomenon, but rather the phenomenon of something still and perhaps indefinitely buried, withheld, and aphenomenal: language as a whole and as such.[4]

In other words, translatability expresses the relation between languages, linguistic relationality as such. This relationality is in becoming; it is not a stable relation between self-identical languages. For translatability has a historical trajectory and messianic direction: in translation "languages continue to grow in this way until the messianic end of their history" (SW 1, 257). In this sense, the translator's task can be described as partaking in the trajectory of *Sprachgeschichtlichkeit*, "linguistic historicality"[5] as agent. The work of the translator contributes to the "motif of integrating many tongues into one true language" (SW 1, 259) while working on the afterlives of literary works in translation. Translatability is thus also a medial form of linguistic afterlife beyond linguistic relations of individual translators, writers, and readers. Human language is decentred in a non-intentional (we might even say: unconscious) pure language, which is unpacked in each act of intentional translation. In this way, quite counter-intuitively, the translatability of works of literature proves the existence of non-human relations in language.[6]

However, one might object that, particularly in poetry, certain idioms and phrases are simply untranslatable. Benjamin wrote the Translator essay as a preface to his somewhat insufficient attempt to translate Baudelaire's *Tableaux parisiens*. Unpacking a tentative theory of pure language, Benjamin's essay takes this impossibility upside down: each work's *singular untranslatability* is the condition of possibility of its *universal translatability*. What is singular and untranslatable becomes the gateway of universal translatability, once the various linguistic modes of meaning are understood as medial configurations of linguistic being. The latter is not an ontological substance or conceptual abstraction but the relationality of all languages in their differentiality. Benjamin writes "both the original and the translation" become "recognizable as fragments of a greater language, just as fragments are part of a vessel" (SW 1, 260). Vessel and fragment, however, do not relate to each other as part and whole. As Paul de Man's commentary pointed out, Benjamin "is not saying that the fragments constitute a totality, he says the fragments are fragments, and that they remain essentially fragmentary".[7] As original fragment, each language expresses a singular difference – each language presents a differential without stable totality (holistic unity, *one* language), and, conversely, each language is a set of transforming differential relations. Pure language *is* the moving integral of all differential relations *in* and *between* languages. Pure language is linguistic mediacy as such, that is to say, it connects difference, multiplicity, and singularity without an abstract totality of "One". Pure language, thereby, is always in becoming and growing *in* and *as* history, until its "messianic end".

13.3 Messianic Universality and Universal History

Such a messianic theory of translatability, grounded in the a-teleological trajectory of literary works' afterlives, sounds far from Gramsci. Peter Ives, however, points out some parallels in Benjamin's and Gramsci's otherwise divergent theories of translatability.

> For Gramsci, like Benjamin, translation is not just the transmission from one language to another, or making accessible a text to people who do not happen to speak the language in which it was written. . . . Both argue that not

every work is translatable and that translation also depends on the languages and cultures from which and into which the translation is to be made. But Gramsci's concern is less with the quality of what is to be translated than with the two (or more) cultures involved . . . Translation is not solely a matter of communicability.[8]

Rephrasing Ives, we could argue that communicability is not solely a matter of communication either, unless communication is thought beyond its instrumental usage as vessel or envelope of extra-lingual content. This parallel between Benjamin and Gramsci becomes more apparent once we read the problem of communicability as a symptom of language in the age of its capitalist translatability. Benjamin's later remarks on Esperanto can serve here as an entry point.

In the sketches of the "Theses on the Concept of History" (1940), Benjamin drafted a series of notes, criticising the utopian promise of Esperanto and contrasting it with a truly universal language.

> The messianic world is the world of universal and integral actuality. Only in the messianic realm does a universal history exist. Not as written history, but as festively enacted history. This festival is purified of all celebration. There are no festive songs. Its language is liberated prose-prose which has burst the fetters of script [Schrift]. (. . . Universal history in the present-day sense is never more than a kind of Esperanto. (It expresses the hope of the human race no more effectively than the name of that universal language).
>
> *(SW 4, 404)*

> The multiplicity of histories resembles the multiplicity of languages. Universal history in the present-day sense can never be more than a kind of Esperanto. The idea of universal history is a messianic idea. The messianic world is the world of universal and integral actuality. Only in the messianic realm does a universal history exist. Not as written history, but as festively enacted history. This festival is purified of all celebration. There are no festive songs. Its language is liberated prose-prose which has burst the fetters of script [Schrift] and is understood by all people (as the language of birds is understood by Sunday's children).
>
> *(SW 4, 405–6)*

While criticising Esperanto as fictitious universality, Benjamin also makes a positive reference to universality as messianic universal history. The nineteenth-century concept of universal history, however, is an oppressive one; it conceived of history as successive progression from lower stages to higher ones and placed the phantasmagoria of Christian Europeans as main protagonists in its centre. In contrast, the messianic idea of universal history maintains an a-teleological point of (messianic) reference without linear progression or preestablished agent. Instead of contributing to the bourgeois fantasy of cultural history as an accumulation of appropriated cultural treasures, the messianic version of universal history is linked to history as a site of negativity – the history of the expropriated, the downtrodden, and the "tradition of the oppressed".[9]

For Benjamin, true (messianic) universality is not an empty concept, deduced from idealistic abstractions or metaphysical teleologies written by the victors of history. In line with his earlier essays on language and the task of the translator, he conceives universality as universal relationality, materially rooted in linguistic mediacy. This mediacy expresses itself in linguistic historicality. Hence, universality is not an end goal but a relational material texture: historical-linguistic relationality is messianic universal history in becoming. While in European medial and early modern times, such linguistic historicality actually had a linguistic medium, at least in scripture (i.e. Latin), in modern industrial capitalism universal history and universal language cannot anymore be posited as "One". In capitalist modernity, universality is relegated to the really existing abstractions of the commodity form. In contrast, the universality of language can only be addressed in the multiplicity of languages and their ever-shifting relationality, which Benjamin earlier called "pure language". In this sense, the invention of Esperanto can be regarded as a symptom of a specifically modern lack of one universal language.

> The idea of a universal history stands and falls with the idea of a universal language. As long as the latter had a basis – whether in theology, as in the Middle Ages, or in logic, as more recently in Leibniz – universal history was not wholly inconceivable. By contrast, universal history as practiced since the nineteenth century can never have been more than a kind of Esperanto. (SW 4, 406)

Without going into the details of these dense and somewhat cryptic notes, let me concentrate on the term "world of universal and integral actuality" (*Welt allseitiger und integraler Aktualität*). Only in such a world language and history can form a truly universal link, proving the ground for universal history. Of course, it is possible to take this reference for pan-linguistic theology, a monotheist phonocentrism of God inaccessible to humans (a divine language "which has burst the fetters of script"). However, it is worth noting that this formulation, "the world of universal and integral actuality", is a self-quotation: it first appeared in Benjamin's essay on surrealism from 1929, where he links it to political action and the immediacy of a bodily image space (*Bildraum*).[10]

In the *Surrealism* essay, Benjamin, with reference to Aragon, calls for the expulsion of the "moral metaphor from politics" in order "to discover within the space of political action the one hundred percent image space. This image space, however, can no longer be measured out by contemplation" (SW 2.1, 217). This stance against representation and moralism aims at setting free political action from instrumental and deterministic ideologies. Political action is no longer the bearer of something else – a higher morale, a programme, or an embodiment of history's progress towards socialism – but an opening that presents itself as an immediate image, an image space where moralism becomes inoperative and metaphorical meaning is extinguished.

It is in this sense that the entrance into this image space cannot be found intentionally; rather it only suddenly opens up in threshold experiences, unintentional jokes, Freudian slips, and other unexpected deviations from conventional political action and intentional speech. "For in the joke, too, in invective, in misunderstanding, in all cases where an action puts forth its own image and exists [überall, wo ein Handeln selber das Bild aus sich herausstellt und ist], absorbing and consuming it, where nearness looks with its own eyes, the long-sought image space is opened, the world of universal and integral actuality" (SW 2.1, 217). The image space unintentionally emerges in collective political action as an immediate presentation of the latter without formal political representation. Where nearness looks with its own eyes, where ultimate proximity and auratic distance enter a stage of mutual indifference, the image space becomes real. This reality is not stable, it is fully charged with dialectical tensions; nevertheless, it contains a higher degree of actuality – an actuality that is more than what reality can contain.

This detour via the essay on Surrealism demonstrates the political stakes of Benjamin's later reference to messianic universality in which language and history truly form a universal texture beyond conventional formalism of language and progressivist teleologies of politics. In the later note from the "Theses on the Concept of History", Benjamin explicitly criticises the nineteenth-century idea of universal history as one of the pillars of historicism. Against the latter, he credits Marx's *Capital* for having "liquidated" the epic moment of historicism (SW 4, 406).

13.4   Abstract Universality and Commodity-Language

Regardless of whether such a critique is on point, Benjamin's reference to Marx allows for an inverse reading of the problem of universal language and universal history by taking them as symptoms of the really existing abstract universalism of global capitalism. Marx, writes Benjamin, "realized that the history of capital could be constructed only within the broad, steel framework of a theory" (SW 4, 406). Indeed, this theory, that is, Marx's critique of political economy, contains a crucial hint concerning the problem of universal language. For Benjamin, it is only in a messianic world where universal *history* based on a truly universal *language* exists. Hence, his rejection of a false universal language ("Esperanto") can be read as an implicit criticism of the formal language of capitalist commodity exchange, that is, money.

In *Capital* (1867–1872), Marx writes, "If commodities could, speak, they would say this: our use-value may interest men, but it does not belong to us as objects. What does belong to us as objects, however, is our value. Our own intercourse as commodities proves it".[11] Marx's prosopopoeia of commodity-language, *Warensprache*,[12] is not to be mistaken for a metaphor, external to what is signified by it. Commodities actually do speak to one another via the prosopopoeic "mouthpieces" of commodity owners. The question, however, is what kind of language this is. If every commodity speaks [*spricht*] and promises [*verspricht*] another commodity, what is the secret of this language, which lends it its seemingly trans-national, trans-cultural, and trans-historical communicability? Although it originated in Europe, capitalism, as Marx predicted in the 1840s, logically leads to the establishment of the world market. This world market necessitates a global language to exchange commodities.

Already in 1930, Benjamin's friend Bertolt Brecht notes,

> Only those who blind themselves to the enormous power of the revolutionary process that drags everything in this world into the circulation of commodities, without exception and without delay, can assume that works of art in any genre could be excluded. For the deeper sense of this process consists in leaving nothing without relation to something, but rather in linking everything, just as all people are linked to each other (in the form of commodities). It is the process of communication itself.[13]

The global expansion of commodity relations weaves an all-encompassing web of social relationality that Brecht, here, calls the process of communication itself. Indeed, circulation, exchange, commerce (*Verkehr*), and communication are functions that the two modes of capital's existence, money and commodity, perform. These functions are social in the precise sense that they mediate – that is, repress and express – social relations in capitalism. The social relations of production are repressed insofar as they are treated as addenda of exchange value, that is, commodity-language and the "communication" of commodities. Marx understands that commodities relate to one another "merely as exchange-values".[14] As exchange-values, commodities express a social relation, that is value, which, in turn, finds its substance in abstract labour. The latter necessitates labour power and all the relations of the working process, historical level of productivity, reproduction of labour and class relations. It is in this indirect, repressed way that the speech acts of commodity-language connect and communicate distinct and separated bearers of labour power on a global market scale. The communication of commodity-language thus *coheres* the social bond as an act of *separation*: labour power as commodity is sold, bought, and expended privately and in competition.

To be sure, commodity-language designates neither *langue*, a language like German, French, or Italian, nor a certain jargon employed by economics; rather, it points to a global structure that expresses capitalist value before and ahead of culturally situated speech acts in national language or vernacular dialects. In contrast to pre-modern communities, capitalist society thrives on an arbitrary mode of the production of meaning (cultural difference) and value (objective validity) by introducing a new kind of social relation, indifferent to *specific* materialities or semantic content. Contrary to the myth of Eurocentric modernity, however, besides this new social relation (which in capitalism *is* the prevailing one), other (pre- and non-modern) social relations do not cease to exist. As Vivek Chibber argues, "the universalizing drive of capital should not be assumed to homogenize power relations, or the social landscape more generally".[15] In fact, "[c]apitalism is perfectly compatible with a highly diverse set of political and cultural formations".[16] According to Marx, capitalism is the violent implementation ("primitive accumulation"), production and reproduction of a specific social form – the commodity form – which consists in a differential social relation. The latter needs heterogeneity as a resource to produce the homogenising effects of commodity exchange and market relations. That is to say, the capitalist accumulation regime relies on the *combination* and *transformation* of *existing* social relations in order to establish its own specific relation, that is, the asymmetric dialectics of capital and labour. In this sense, as Chibber puts it, "capitalism is not only consistent with great heterogeneity and hierarchy, but systematically generates them".[17] Capitalism's abstract universality consists in a relational framework of enforced relations, which puts different cultural and social power relations into relation and thereby makes them countable, commensurable, and exchangeable.

13.5   From the Critique of Language to the Language of Critique

Once language is artificially (i.e. conventionally) framed as a presumably "neutral" medium, it can be abstracted, universalised, and cut off from traces of class position, culture, and place. Such a formalised language is not far away from what Marx called commodity-language, an abstract medium of universal mediation, expressed in the money-form, capable of mediating and calculating a flat sequence of money-mediated past (financial debt), present (investment and credit), and future (surplus value as capital). As such commodity-language constitutes an abstract notion of universal history as the history of capital.[18] Understood in this way, commodity-language comes structurally close to the linguistic structure Esperanto that Benjamin criticised in his earlier mentioned notes to the "Theses on the Concept of History".

If one follows the argument of such a parallel reading of language and history, an "Esperantian" universal history would be the history of an infinite chain of exchangeable events, made accessible for, congruent with, and translatable to the capitalist world market. Just as in historicist universal history, the singularity of histories is levelled down to positivistic cause and effect relations, so in Esperanto, every grammatical, semantic, and syntactic singularity is levelled down to a commensurable general. The transformation of the concrete singular (living language) into the representative of an abstract universal (Esperanto), by which every singularity is made the particular moment of a general, is infinite: it consists in the infinite task of levelling and formalising the vanishing point of which lies in the infinite collection of all linguistic meaning without each language's singular mode of signification.

> Esperanto thus consists in a regularization and extreme grammatical simplification of the structure of historical languages, which leaves intact the fundamental conception of language as a system of signs transmitting meanings. . . . Esperanto is a language of infinite meaning that can never find fulfilment.[19]

A language whose only goal is the simplest possible transmission of meaning remains trapped in an endless movement of pragmatic cross-references without a (messianic or redemptive) direction. Against this background, Benjamin's criticism is aimed not only at the actually existing language of Esperanto but at every "kind of Esperanto" – at all language conception and language practice that is based on uniform communication of linguistic content (meaning). For any language system that assumes the mere sign character of language and subordinates the signifying (symbol as mere sign) to the signified (meaning) treats linguistic expression as an exchange of commensurable signifiers. "To base a discourse on signifieds, however, means to make it translatable. 'Translations' are the discursive 'market, to which the most distant merchants come with their commodities'".[20] The proximity to the value form of capitalist commodity exchange is by no means coincidental. If one relates Benjamin's critique of artificial universal languages to the capitalist commodity form, the notion of formalistic arbitrariness by which language is reduced to a mere sign system can be understood as a correlate of the political economic commodity-language of capitalism.

The world language of capital, the language of commodities, may be an artificial language; in its universal validity, however, it is not mere ideology but an engine that builds social reality.

***

From such a perspective, it is not surprising that Gramsci's critique of bourgeois theories of language is not limited to its contemporary context and particularly the Italian *questione della lingua* in the wake of the establishment of the Italian nation-state. As Peter Ives contends,

> Gramsci displaces the debate about whether language belongs to the base or the superstructure, whether it is purely determined by material conditions or in fact determines those conditions. For Gramsci, language is material, albeit historically material.[21]

For Gramsci "the structure of language, as evident in grammar, documents a society and illustrates aspects of its history as well as existing power relations".[22] Such an understanding of language can be mobilised against both the artificial formalisation of language (as in Esperanto) and the abstract exchange relations of capitalist commodity-language. For language is never a neutral medium, a nomenclature of an external world, a generic human capacity as anthropological constant, or merely an ideological tool of the ruling class. Reading Gramsci's politics of language with Benjamin and Marx, we might add: if language is translatable only in and through the history of its afterlives, the history of translatability is also the history of class struggle. It is this history that the capitalist translatability of language seeks to repress.

Notes

1 Antonio Gramsci, *The Antonio Gramsci Reader: Selected Writings, 1916–1935* (New York: Schocken Books, 1988), 72.
2 Antonio Gramsci, *Further Selections from the Prison Notebooks* (London: Lawrence and Wishart, 1995; London: ElecBook, 1999), 447 (Q11 §45).
3 References to the works of Benjamin are indicated in the text (SW, number of volume, and page). They follow the edition Walter Benjamin, *Selected Writings*, ed. Michael W. Jennings, Howard Eiland, et al. (Cambridge, MA: The Belknap Press of Harvard University Press, 1996–2003).
4 Werner Hamacher, "Intensive Languages", in *MLN* 127 (2012): 485–541, here 539.
5 Hamacher, "Intensive Languages", 490.
6 If, as Benjamin claims, "Translation is a form", one might ask whether "certain relational concepts retain their meaning, and possibly their foremost significance, if they are not from the outset used exclusively with reference to humans. . . . For this thought is valid here: If translation is a form, translatability must be an essential feature of certain works" (Benjamin, SW 1, 254).
7 Paul de Man, " 'Conclusions' on Walter Benjamin's 'The Task of the Translator', Messenger Lecture, Cornell University, March 4, 1983", in *50 Years of Yale French Studies*, ed. Charles A. Porter and Alyson Waters (New Haven, CT: Yale University, 2000), Part 2, 10–35, here 32.
8 Peter Ives, *Gramsci's Politics of Language: Engaging the Bakhtin Circle and the Frankfurt School* (Toronto: University of Toronto Press, 2004), 108.
9 I elaborated this reading of Benjamin in my essay "Where the Past Was, There History Shall Be: Benjamin, Marx, and the 'Tradition of the Oppressed'", *Anthropology & Materialism: A Journal of Social Research* 1 (2017), https://journals.openedition.org/am/789.

10 See Benjamin, SW 2.1, 217. A detailed interpretation of this essay and its phrase "the world of universal and integral actuality" can be found in my essay "'To Win the Energies of Intoxication for the Revolution': Body Politics, Community, and Profane Illumination", *Anthropology & Materialism: A Journal of Social Research* 2 (2014), https://journals.openedition.org/am/348.

11 Karl Marx, *Capital: A Critique of Political Economy* (London: Penguin, 1990), vol. 1, 176–177.

12 Karl Marx, "Das Kapital. Kritik der politischen Ökonomie", in *Marx-Engels-Werke (MEW)* (Berlin: Dietz, 1962), Erster Band, vol. 23, 66.

13 Bertolt Brecht, "The *Three Penny* Lawsuit", in *Brecht on Film and Radio* (London: Bloomsbury, 2000), 169.

14 Marx, *Capital*, vol. 1, 177.

15 Vivek Chibber, *Postcolonial Theory and the Specter of Capital* (London: Verso, 2013), 285.

16 Chibber, *Postcolonial Theory and the Specter of Capital*, 285.

17 Chibber, *Postcolonial Theory and the Specter of Capital*, 285.

18 See Werner Hamacher, "Guilt History: Benjamin's Sketch 'Capitalism as Religion'", trans. Kirk Wetters, *Diacritics* 32, no. 3–4 (2002): 81–106.

19 Giorgio Agamben, *Potentialities: Collected Essays in Philosophy*, trans. Daniel Heller-Roazen (Stanford: Stanford University Press, 1999), 55.

20 Friedrich Kittler, *Discourse Networks 1800/1900* (Stanford: Stanford University Press, 1990), 71. Trans. modified, see quote in the quote: Goethe's letter to Joseph Stanislaus Zauper, 7 September 1821, in Johann W. Goethe, "Goethes Briefe", in *Goethes Werke, IV. Abt. Vol. 35.: Juli 1821–März 1822* (Weimar: Böhlau, 1906), 75.

21 Ives, *Gramsci's Politics of Language*, 34.

22 Ives, *Gramsci's Politics of Language*, 34.

Bibliography

Agamben, Giorgio. *Potentialities: Collected Essays in Philosophy*, translated by Daniel Heller-Roazen. Stanford: Stanford University Press, 1999.

Benjamin, Walter. *Selected Writings*, edited by Michael W. Jennings, Howard Eiland, et al. Cambridge, MA: The Belknap Press of Harvard University Press, 1996–2003.

Brecht, Bertolt. "The Three Penny Lawsuit". In *Brecht on Film and Radio*, translated by Marc Silberman. London: Bloomsbury, 2000.

Chibber, Vivek. *Postcolonial Theory and the Specter of Capital*. London: Verso, 2013.

de Man, Paul. "Conclusions' on Walter Benjamin's 'The Task of the Translator', Messenger Lecture, Cornell University, March 4, 1983". In *50 Years of Yale French Studies*, edited by Charles A. Porter, and Alyson Waters, Part 2, 10–35. New Haven, CT: Yale University Press, 2000.

Goethe, Johann Wolfgang. "Goethes Briefe". In *Goethes Werke*. IV. Abt. vol. 35.: Juli 1821–März 1822. Weimar: Böhlau, 1906.

Gramsci, Antonio. *The Antonio Gramsci Reader: Selected Writings, 1916–1935*, edited by David Forgacs. New York: Schocken Books, 1988.

Gramsci, Antonio. *Further Selections from the Prison Notebooks*, edited and translated by Derek Boothman. London: Lawrence and Wishart, 1995; London: ElecBook, 1999.

Hamacher, Werner. "Guilt History: Benjamin's Sketch 'Capitalism as Religion'", translated by Kirk Wetters. *Diacritics* 32, no. 3–4 (2002): 81–106.

Hamacher, Werner. "Intensive Languages". *MLN* 127 (2012): 485–541.

Ives, Peter. *Gramsci's Politics of Language: Engaging the Bakhtin Circle and the Frankfurt School*. Toronto: University of Toronto Press, 2004.

Khatib, Sami. "'To Win the Energies of Intoxication for the Revolution': Body Politics, Community, and Profane Illumination". *Anthropology & Materialism: A Journal of Social Research*, Issue "The Persistence of Myth", 2 (2014). https://journals.openedition.org/am/348.

Khatib, Sami. "Where the Past Was, There History Shall Be: Benjamin, Marx, and the 'Tradition of the Oppressed'". *Anthropology & Materialism: A Journal of Social Research*. Special issue on Walter Benjamin: "Discontinuous Infinities", edited by Jan Sieber, and Sebastian Truskolaski, 1 (2017). https://journals.openedition.org/am/789.

Kittler, Friedrich. *Discourse Networks 1800/1900*, translated by David E. Wellbery. Stanford: Stanford University Press, 1990.

Marx, Karl. "Das Kapital. Kritik der politischen Ökonomie". In *Marx-Engels-Werke (MEW)*, Erster Band, vol. 23. Berlin: Dietz, 1962.

Marx, Karl. *Capital: A Critique of Political Economy*, translated by Ben Fowkes, vol. 1. London: Penguin, 1990.

14

A NON-REAL FIRE

Gramsci and Benjamin, Interpreters of Futurism

Daniele Balicco

> Every verse I write is a fire,
> Not a real fire,
> It is what I write,
> Not real though it is with intent.
> Aldo Palazzeschi
> In every young person – the pyric dust of Marinetti
> Vladimir Mayakovsky

Walter Benjamin met Filippo Tommaso Marinetti in person only once, in Capri, in September 1924. After the five o'clock tea, in front of a small audience, the founder of Italian Futurism read one of his poetic texts together with Ruggero Vasari and Enrico Prampolini. The ingredients of the performance are not difficult to imagine: a text written as if the page were attacked by typographic explosion and a reading aimed at exaggerating movement and noise. We do not know precisely which text Marinetti dramatised on that occasion. Benjamin speaks of a boring content, where the celebration of the modern era as violent progress passes through the description of gunfire, pursuits, clattering of trains, and horse snorts. Yet, the aesthetic power of the reading enchants him.[1] After all, right here in Capri, he is laboriously writing, for five months, the first draft of his unsuccessful habilitation thesis. And it is not certain that the synesthetic exasperation of Marinetti's poetry did not appear to him, at that time, as a known allegorical gesture: in other words, as the expressive result of that same stubborn artistic will that unites ages of crisis and that, in his eyes, punctuates the fossilised ruins of the German Baroque drama with the violent disharmony of Weimar Expressionism. Moreover, the presence of an unexpected seventeenth-century atmosphere

DOI: 10.4324/9781003457039-19

in Futurist aesthetic experiments – think of the importance that Marinetti himself attributes to analogy, already in the *Technical Manifesto of Futurist Literature* of 1912 – had been noted, albeit with disapproval, in the famous critique that Benedetto Croce launched in 1918 from the pages of *Critica* against Futurism; interpreting it as "something foreign to art".[2]

A few years earlier, Antonio Gramsci had met Filippo Tommaso Marinetti in person in Turin: precisely on 2 April 1922. The occasion was the *International Exhibition of Futurist Art*, set up in the Winter Club premises. He had sought Marinetti himself, proposing to guide, along with Umberto Calosso, a group of workers and students from the Institute of Proletarian Culture – the Italian section of the international Proletkul't in Moscow – of which Gramsci was one of the founders. By 1922, Marinetti had already abandoned any political aspirations. The Futurist party had been dissolved two years earlier, and his tumultuous relations with Mussolini had not yet completely pacified. It is curious, however, that Gramsci has no qualms about involving Marinetti as a guide for the workers at the exhibition, despite being, just three years earlier, among the protagonists of the repeated violence unleashed by *Arditi* and fascists against the territorial structures of Italian socialism. What is the reason for this unusual willingness? And what does it tell us about Gramsci's critical sensibility? In the following pages, we will first reconstruct Gramsci's judgement on Futurist art and its specific political nature. Then, we will compare it with Walter Benjamin's famous thesis, written about a decade after his encounter with Marinetti in Capri, in which Futurist art becomes the emblem of fascism; and, above all, of its dangerous ability to aestheticise politics.

14.1 Distribution of the Sensible

Gramsci's first article on Futurism dates back to 1913.[3] Written for the *Corriere Universitario* of Turin and signed with the pseudonym Alfagamma, it is a brief text defending the experimental efforts of some of the most significant poets of the Italian avant-garde movement, such as Palazzeschi, Govoni, and Buzzi. Gramsci presents them as "the best that contemporary poetic literature can offer to history". An undoubtedly clear, enthusiastic, and aggressively anti-idealistic judgement, confirmed a few lines later when interpreting the synesthetic decomposition of Marinetti's *Adrianople Siege Orchestra* as a magnificent example of the "new trend in very contemporary art, from the music to the painting of the Cubists", aimed to attack the elementary forms of perception through a process of breaking down planes of reality:

> The test of Adrianople Siege-Orchestra is a form of linguistic expression that finds its perfect counterpart in the pictorial form of Ardengo Soffici or Pablo Picasso; it is also a decomposition into planes of the image; it does not present

itself to the imagination in the blurred adverbs or adjectives . . ., but as a successive or parallel or intersecting series of noun-planes, with well-defined limits.[4]

As seen, Gramsci interprets Futurism from the outset as an Italian variant of a common search in European art of those years, a search that is altering, in every artistic field, the traditional forms of aesthetic composition. Without presupposing this new distribution of the sensible, Futurist poetry and painting cannot be understood. It doesn't matter that bourgeois intellectuals like Croce, against whom this art rebels programmatically, don't understand it; more importantly, for Gramsci, is that it is not understood by socialist culture. Because Futurism should be observed as a symptom of a profound cultural transformation. In its gestures of formal disarticulation, as in its technical manifestos, the new sensitivity of industrialised modern life is finding its voice; a life increasingly artificial, simultaneous, distracted, technological, and urban; a life of individual bodies and masses – and therefore potentially egalitarian – that is now beginning to rebel against social hierarchies and the psychic obsolescence of old liberal Europe. Just reading a few passages from Boccioni's *Technical Manifesto of Futurist Sculpture* (1912) – certainly the most complex intellectual figure of the entire movement – is enough to understand how this new distribution of the sensible already prefigures a new political order, well beyond the fragile institutional barriers that the Italian liberal state will try in vain to defend in the immediate postwar period:

> Painting has been rejuvenated, deepened, and expanded through landscape and environment simultaneously acting on the human figure and objects, reaching our Futurist interpenetration of planes. Thus, sculpture will find a new source of emotion, and therefore of style, by extending its plasticity to what our barbaric rudeness has made us consider as divided, impalpable, therefore inexpressible in plastic terms. . . . Sculpture must bring objects to life, making their extension in space sensitive, systematic, and plastic, as no one can doubt that an object ends where another begins, and there is nothing that does not surround our body: bottle, car, house, tree, street, which does not cut and section it with an arabesque of curves and straight lines.[5]

Boccioni lists several aesthetic forms peculiar to the "Futurist reconstruction of the universe": simultaneity, the interpenetration of planes, the impossibility of distinguishing discontinuous physical space, the breaking of boundaries, the capacity of each finite thing to be traversed by its surroundings and the forces radiating from them. These few interpretive elements are sufficient to understand the underlying tendency of the Futurist political unconscious: a programmed sabotage of the institutional forms of bourgeois rationality and its distinctive power: the ability to separate public from private, individual from society, state from market, psyche from body. At this time, the futurist project's call for rupture is expressed only at the symbolic, aesthetic, psychic, and formal levels, while its political expression remains somewhat confused. Before the outbreak of the Great War, the Futurists included anarchists, socialists, republicans, pacifists, warmongers, and ultranationalists. Gramsci would never take seriously Marinetti's vain attempts to transform himself, after the end of World War I, into an organised political force. He himself, in 1918, would record, in the weekly *Il Grido del Popolo*, the founding of the Futurist Party, whose political manifesto can only appear "futurist" in a backward country like Italy, where the European liberal tradition has never had culturally conscious representatives, except for Cavour, who understood what this tradition required of public administration and government:

> This program was written by Filippo Tommaso Marinetti on behalf of the new Futurist political party. Stripped of verbal amplifications, language inaccuracies, some slight contradictions, it is nothing but the liberal program that Cavour's grandchildren forgot they should have realized for Italy's better destinies. But Cavour's grandchildren have forgotten the teachings and doctrines of their ancestor. The liberal program seems so extraordinary and crazy that the Futurists make it their own, convinced of being highly original and ultra-futuristic. It is the most atrocious mockery of the ruling classes. Cavour cannot find in Italy other disciples and advocates than F.T. Marinetti and his band of howling monkeys.[6]

After the founding of the party in 1918, Marinetti will try in vain to realise the Futurist aesthetic rebellion politically. First, he will ally himself with the Veterans and the Ardites, participating, albeit discontinuously, in the Fiume experience. He will even write two essays on political theory (Futurist Democracy in 1919 and Beyond Communism in 1920) and then run in the 1919 elections on the "Fasci di combattimento" lists with Mussolini. His strategy is to exert cultural hegemony "on the activism of the rebellious nationalist petty bourgeoisie, but also trying to establish some links with the minorities of the anarchist and Bolshevik left, in order to draw them into the perspective of the 'Italian revolution', in the name of the common hatred against the established order". However, as we well know, the Italian revolution for which Marinetti was so clumsily making himself the spokesman would take other paths: in May 1920, he himself would break his alliance with Mussolini's party, which had by then abandoned its initial anti-monarchist, anti-clerical, and workers' stance that had characterised the early years of his movement.

During these same years, Gramsci developed a deep aversion to Marinetti's political dilettantism. Moreover, the October Revolution and the direct experience

of the Factory Councils at Fiat in Turin persuaded him that the gesture of radical
rupture, anticipated by the Futurist aesthetic at the turn of the century, was finally
finding its political translation: workers' democracy. However, this new form of
radical democracy will not be achieved through a gradual takeover of the old state
institutions, as socialists still believe. In fact, Gramsci is aware that the liberal
state is providing institutional cover for fascist violence. In the face of this, the
gradualism of the socialists is a naive illusion. Gramsci's position is different: in
the face of the collapse of the bourgeois state, it is necessary to organise a violent
rupture, the steering nucleus of which can only be prepared within the factory
councils. It is precisely in defence of this strategy that he will separate from the
Socialists on 21 January 1921, to found, together with Amedeo Bordiga, Umberto
Terracini, Angelo Tasca and Palmiro Togliatti, the Italian Communist Party.

It may be interesting to note that only a few weeks before the Livorno split,
Gramsci wrote an article once again about Marinetti. On 5 January 1921, he
published in *Ordine Nuovo* an account of an anecdote that had happened the
previous summer in Moscow, during the work of the Second Congress of the
Third International. The article is titled "Marinetti the Revolutionary?", and
reports first of all the astonishment with which Giacinto Serrati reacted to the
words spoken in perfect Italian by the Soviet commissar for education Anatolij
Lunačarskij, who said, "In Italy there is a revolutionary intellectual, and he is
Filippo Tommaso Marinetti":

> The philistines of the workers' movement are extremely scandalized; it is
> certain now that to the insults of 'Bergsonians, voluntarists, pragmatists, spir-
> itualists', will be added the most bloody insult of 'Futurists! Marinettians!'
> Since such a fate awaits us, let us try to elevate ourselves to the self-awareness
> of this new intellectual position.[7]

Lunačarskij's judgement on Marinetti – on which even Lenin seems to have
agreed – serves Gramsci to attack head-on the progressive gradualism of Italian socialists. Their indignation in the face of Futurist aesthetic violence is the
evidence of a deep cultural myopia expressed in an abstract, aspirational political culture, all institutional and now imprisoned in tactics. It is worth quoting
almost in full this brief article because it clearly testifies both to Gramsci's critical finesse, interpreting Futurist aesthetic experimentation as a symptom of a
new distribution of the sensible, and to his political insight that will soon lead
him to recognise in the political use of violence the legitimisation strategy with
which fascism will present itself to Italian industrial and landowning capital as
the only organised subject capable of imposing a new command on labour:

> The field of the struggle for the creation of a new civilization is instead abso-
> lutely mysterious, absolutely characterized by the unforeseeable and the

unthought-of. . . . What remains to be done? Nothing else but to destroy the present form of civilization. . . . The Futurists have carried out this task in the field of bourgeois culture: they have destroyed, destroyed, destroyed, without worrying about whether the new creations produced by their activity were overall a superior work to what was destroyed: they have had trust in themselves, in the fervor of young energies, they have had the clear and precise conception that our era, the era of large industry, the large working-class city, intense and tumultuous life, must have new forms of art, philosophy, costume, language: they have had this distinctly revolutionary, absolutely Marxist conception when socialists were not even remotely concerned with such an issue, when socialists certainly did not have an equally precise conception in the field of politics and economics, when socialists would have been scared (and it is evident from the current fear of many of them) at the thought that it was necessary to break the machine of bourgeois power in the state and in the factory. The Futurists, in their field, in the field of culture, are revolutionaries.[8]

Gramsci is very clear: it is up to the labour movement to continue, in political struggle, the radical break that the Futurists anticipated in art. However, there is an important caveat that socialist realism will do its best to ignore: according to Gramsci, once society is transformed, art will necessarily begin to change. This metamorphosis, just like that of butterflies, will follow autonomous rules. For this reason, it cannot be imposed, prescribed, or tied to any political or philosophical theory. Gramsci interprets art as an unconscious shorthand of the future; therefore, there is no point in politically imposing a prescriptive poetics; on the contrary, this idea – which will be characteristic of later socialist realism – is harmful because it sabotages the possibility of knowing, in figure, an anticipation of the future.

14.2 Aura and Passive Revolution

In 1922, Lev Trotsky wrote almost simultaneously to Gramsci and Mayakovski. During the Civil War, the Red Army commander was working on the essay *Literature and Revolution*[9] and needed some clarification on the European history of Futurism and Marinetti's current political positions. The fact that Trotsky made a similar request to Gramsci is not surprising, since Italian Futurism had an immediate and significant impact on Russian avant-garde culture. Marinetti's first Manifesto, for example, was translated by VeCer magazine only two weeks after its publication in France on 8 March 1909. Relations between the Italian and Russian Futurists were continuous, marked by a fierce struggle for the primacy of the movement – Russian or Italian? This conflict led to a situation where, during his first trip to Moscow in 1914, no Russian futurist wanted to meet Marinetti in person, except Malevič. However, what really separated the two movements during the 1910s was their position on the war: adored by the Italians – with a few exceptions, such as Aldo Palazzeschi; rejected by the Russians, with one significant exception: Vladimir Mayakovski.

Gramsci responded to Trotsky's requests in a letter dated 5 September 1922, while he had been in Moscow since June. The situation in Italy was deteriorating; Mussolini's "March on Rome" was almost a month away, and Gramsci, among the Italian delegates, was the only one – as Trotsky himself would acknowledge in 1932 – who clearly understood that a violent dictatorship was about to begin in Italy. Because of these circumstances (not to mention that Gramsci was writing while hospitalised in the Moscow sanatorium Serebrjanyjbor), the tone of the letter is sombre, often sarcastic:

> After the war, the Futurist movement in Italy completely lost its characteristic features. Marinetti dedicates very little to the movement. He got married and prefers to devote his energies to his wife. The Futurist movement currently includes monarchists, communists, republicans, and fascists. . . . The most important exponents of pre-war Futurism have become fascists, except for Giovanni Papini, who became a Catholic and wrote a History of Christ. During the war, the Futurists were the most steadfast advocates of 'war to the bitter end' and imperialism.[10]

The meaning of the Futurist aesthetic rupture is now viewed differently. Gramsci assesses Futurist political action as a narcissistic game of exalted ex-soldiers, moved by a childlike bellicism. In the face of the exacerbation of social conflict and, above all, the liberal cover-up of Fascist violence, the ideological pamphlets that Marinetti wrote during these years ("if one can define in general the fantasies of this man, who is sometimes witty and always remarkable"[11]) appear for what they are: little more than amusing jokes. In the letter, Gramsci also recalls Marinetti's participation as a guide at the Futurist exhibition in Turin, shortly before Gramsci's departure to Moscow, and his satisfaction "at being convinced that the workers were much more sensitive to the themes of Futurism than the bourgeoisie".[12]

Gramsci will continue to reflect on futurism in later years. In the *Prison Notebooks*, the history of this movement of warrior painters and poets is read by analysing the link between avant-garde intellectual groups, the apoliticality of the masses, and the triumph of fascism as a passive revolution. In the years of fascism, when workers must "fight with arms to defend their freedom",[13] futurist aesthetic revolt indeed becomes irrelevant. In the years of the violent defeat of the workers' movement, it becomes necessary for Gramsci to imagine a new form of creativity, a new distribution of the sensible capable of projecting itself into the long time of history. Gramsci imagines a new kind of political intelligence integrated into popular life, capable of interrogating the common sense of the subalterns to lead it to a political understanding of the present. Against triumphant fascist rule, no vanguard now makes sense. For Gramsci, it is now necessary to begin a long, underground, arduous, and invisible struggle for hegemony. Seen through these new theoretical lenses, the Futurists now appear – but we are already in the 1930s – as "a group of schoolchildren who escaped from a Jesuit boarding school"[14] or, even worse, as a case of intellectual "seicentismo",[15] whose aesthetic acrobatics attract the curiosity of the working classes because they are exaggerated and amusing, just like the acrobatics of a clown. In the *Prison Notebooks*, Gramsci thus rethinks Futurism, situating it in the secular history of cosmopolitan Italian intellectuality and its substantial inability to enter into an authentic – and thus transformative – political relationship with the popular life of the masses.

In 1935, while Gramsci is on parole at the Cusumano clinic in Formia, Walter Benjamin has returned from San Remo to Paris. He has been in exile for more than two years, in economically precarious conditions. Only in the last few months has Horkheimer managed to secure him a stable monthly funding from the funds of the Frankfurt Institute of Sociology. In Paris, Benjamin can finally resume his work on the *Arcades Project*. In April, he managed to meet Friedrich Pollock, who asked him to write a synthesis of the project. The quick drafting of this *exposé*, which will become the famous *Paris, Capital of the Nineteenth Century*, is an opportunity for Benjamin to reflect on the epistemological premises of the research that will give rise to his most famous essay *The Work of Art in the Age of Mechanical Reproduction*.[16]

In its five different drafts, the text discusses a philosophy of the history of perception as an effect of the interaction with the technological transformation of media communication. Benjamin's thesis is radical: the contemporary arts system must be reconfigured from the invention of cinema, the industrial art par excellence, which can only exist in the technical reproducibility and simultaneity of its mass perception. Cinema and photography have also deactivated the aura of traditional works of art – that is, their being unique, unrepeatable objects confined to a closed, cultic space/time – thus corroding, perhaps forever, the relationship of subjects to tradition and the symbolic forms of hierarchy.

But what does this have to do with Futurism? Benjamin, through his analysis of the impact of new film technology on mass sensoriality, is trying to trace a cultural trend polarised in two opposite directions. The first is what he defines by the term *politicization of art*. In the face of the contemporary perceptual earthquake, art can become politicised by consciously assuming the liberating potential inherent in the mass production of this new ubiquitous sensor. The challenge is to transform the tendentially apolitical nature of the masses into political consciousness by establishing a basic principle of equality ("every man today can claim the right to be filmed") that leads to the recognition of each subject's subordinate position within the capitalist production process. For Benjamin, a possible model for this practice of conscious distraction is Brecht's theatrical experimentation, where the author becomes simultaneously a polytechnic producer and a mass educator. The opposite trend is instead defined with the term *aestheticization of politics*. In the first version of the essay, the diagnosis sounds precisely like this:

> The movements in the course of which the masses . . . come to the forefront of the historical stage have necessitated profound transformations in both fields – the aesthetic and the political. These transformations . . . are the battleground of present political struggles. They acquire their particular character through the widely spread attempt to organize those mass movements without considering the subversion of the social bases, of which they are the expression and condition, in the realm of production and property relations. This widely spread attempt is that undertaken by fascism. The secret of this attempt lies in giving mass movements an expression instead of organizing them. Or, put differently: fascism seeks to give these mass movements an immediate form instead of leading them to their mediated form through the subversion of production and property relations. This immediate form in which mass movements manifest themselves, deprived of their own purpose, seemingly aimless but in truth in the service of a few, is fascism. Fascism, consequently, leads to the aestheticisation of politics.[17]

According to Benjamin, fascism succeeds in reversing the direction of the internal liberating thrust of technical reproducibility by restoring a modern cultic dimension. Which, in fact, shortly thereafter will require a mass tribal sacrifice: war. The restoration of the aura and its cult – as an illusion of the possibility that an omniscient subjective viewpoint ("the duce") on reality still exists – serves the dictatorship to provide mass movements with an expressive style, a mental order, a recognisable social position, and a political purpose. In this way, fascism produces an immense aesthetic deception to simulate a revolution, masking the preservation of property relations. Moreover, the transformative force of the new technological sensoriality is imprisoned within the boundaries of the nation. And it is no coincidence, in fact, that it is precisely fascism that invests heavily in the new technology of sound films, which enclose the potentially universal openness of technical reproducibility within a national linguistic dimension. The problem is that the combination of these moves – the restoration of the aura as the cult of the duce and the cult of the nation – leads by internal logic to only one possible outlet: war. And precisely on this issue, namely the aestheticisation of war, Benjamin analyses Marinetti's delirious manifesto/poem in favour of the fascist conquest of Ethiopia.

In 1929, Fascism consecrated Filippo Tommaso as an Italian academic. His conflict with Mussolini was now resolved, although the regime, in its substantial aesthetic liberality, gave rather cold treatment to artists close to Futurism, almost always preferring, on celebratory occasions as well as in tenders for public art, the more traditional *Novecentismo* current. Academic and now harmless, Marinetti celebrated the Ethiopian War in a short 1933 paper anticipating the publication of the *Il poema africano della divisione 28 ottobre*. Benjamin quotes this writing at length at the conclusion of his essay on the technical reproducibility of art. More generally, it should be noted that Futurist themes return undercurrent throughout much of this celebrated essay by Benjamin. Indeed, he analyses the effects of technical reproducibility through the key concepts of Futurist aesthetics: simultaneity, shock production, tactilism, the destruction of tradition, and the absolute emphasis on technology as a force with which to "reconstruct and mechanise the universe". However, on these issues, Benjamin adopts a perspective similar to his interpretation of Surrealism: the aesthetic experiments common to the early twentieth-century avant-gardes must be understood as a handcrafted attempt to produce the perceptual training that only cinema will be able to impose – industrially – on the lives of the masses. What, on the other hand, distinguishes Futurism from other European avant-gardes is undoubtedly the idolatry of war. Benjamin does not interpret this aspect of Futurist poetics in an obvious way, considering it simply as ideology. For the strange modernist nationalism to which Futurism gives voice conceals in the aestheticisation of war an epochal question.

> [For the dialectical thinker], the aesthetics of the present war unfolds as follows: if the natural use of productive forces is prevented by property arrangements, then the increase in technical means, production rates, and energy sources pushes towards an unnatural use. It finds it in war, which, with its destruction, provides evidence that society was not mature enough to make technology its organ, and technology was not developed enough to master elementary social forces.[18]

The Futurist idolatry of war should be read as a tragic symptom, being the pathological consequence of a historical development that reverses into barbarism due to internal contradictions. According to Benjamin, because of fascism, the technological development of productive forces fails to transform property relations. Industrial production, unable to be socially organised, inevitably creates mass unemployment and imbalances in the world market that only war can resolve. As he clearly writes, though only in the first version of the essay, the society imprisoned by fascism, "instead of using the potential provided by technology to produce goods, it will use it for the destruction of men".[19]

And so, Marinetti, in Benjamin's reading, is transformed into a delusional herald of historical catastrophe. Just as in Kafka's novels, which Benjamin analyses in these years, the forces ravaging the world remain unknowable in

Marinetti's writings. But the unsolved enigma does not become a warning of the danger looming over everyone. On the contrary, it turns into a guilty celebration of senseless slaughter. The aestheticisation of politics thus seduces the infantile delirium of omnipotence of fascism, which cannot consciously organise the technological power it has unleashed; and which, for this reason, turns the trajectory of its own annihilation into aesthetic enjoyment:

> "Fiat ars – pereat mundus" says fascism, and, as Marinetti proclaims, it expects from war the artistic satisfaction of sensory perception transformed into technique. This is clearly the task of art for art's sake. Humanity, which once, with Homer, was a spectacle for the Olympic gods, has become a spectacle for itself. Its self-alienation has reached such a degree that it experiences its own annihilation as a first-rate aesthetic pleasure. This is how things stand regarding the aestheticization of politics pursued by fascism. Communism responds to it with the politicization of art.[20]

Paradoxically, what unites Benjamin and Marinetti is an aesthetic interpretation of technology, as if it were still only a neutral machinery whose liberating or oppressive potential depends solely on the political use that can be made of it. That there is an internal question about the kind of rationality employed in the development of reproducibility machines, and that this specific upstream rationality constrains the use that can be made of them, is a theoretical legacy of Marx's thought that Benjamin does not fully embrace.

However, one question remains open. Marinetti and Futurism were undoubtedly more than just a sounding board for the delirium of a totalitarian regime. Not surprisingly, Gramsci himself was fascinated by them for a long time. Benjamin's diagnosis, however, applies regardless of the history of Futurism: as we can easily observe, the aestheticisation of politics, with its associated dangers, still works perfectly well today. In contrast, the politicisation of art has disappeared from our cultural horizon.

Notes

1 On this first meeting between Benjamin and Marinetti, see Howard Eiland and Michael W. Jennings, *Walter Benjamin: A Critical Life* (Harvard: Harvard University Press, 2014), 194–195; Sergio Lambiase, "Futuristi a Capri", in *Capri. 1905–1940. Frammenti postumi*, ed. Lea Vergine (Milano: Il Saggiatore, 2018), 240–252.
2 Benedetto Croce, "Il futurismo come cosa estranea all'arte", *La Critica* 16 (1918): 383–384.
3 Antonio Gramsci, *Per la verità*, ed. Renzo Martinelli (Roma: Editori Riuniti, 1974), 6.
4 Gramsci, *Per la verità*, 6.
5 Umberto Boccioni, "Manifesto tecnico della scultura futurista", in *Manifesti del futurismo*, ed. Viviana Birolli (Milano: Abscondita, 2008), 52.

6 Antonio Gramsci, "Cavour e Marinetti", in *Sul fascismo* (Roma: Editori Internazionali Riuniti, 2012), 46.
7 Antonio Gramsci, "Democrazia operaia", in *L'Ordine nuovo. 1919–1920* (Torino: Einaudi, 1955), 10–13.
8 Gramsci, "Democrazia operaia", 21.
9 Lev Trockij, *Letteratura e rivoluzione* (Torino: Einaudi, 1973), 141.
10 Trockij, *Letteratura e rivoluzione*, 141.
11 Trockij, *Letteratura e rivoluzione*, 141.
12 Trockij, *Letteratura e rivoluzione*, 141.
13 Trockij, *Letteratura e rivoluzione*, 143.
14 Antonio Gramsci, *Quaderni del carcere*, ed. Valentino Giarratana (Torino: Einaudi, 1975), I, 115.
15 Gramsci, *Quaderni del Carcere*, III, 1739.
16 Walter Benjamin, "Parigi, la capitale del XIX secolo [Exposé del 1935]", in *Opere Complete* (Torino: Einaudi, 2000), IX, 5–18.
17 Benjamin, "Parigi, la capitale del XIX secolo", 30–31.
18 Benjamin, "Parigi, la capitale del XIX secolo", 106.
19 Benjamin, "Parigi, la capitale del XIX secolo", 33.
20 Benjamin, "Parigi, la capitale del XIX secolo", 175.

Bibliography

Albanese, Giulia, David, Bidussa, and Jacopo, Perrazzoli. *Siamo stati fascisti. Il laboratorio dell'anti-democrazia. Italia 1900–1922.* Milano: Feltrinelli, 2020.
Asor Rosa, Alberto. "Il futurismo nel dibattito intellettuale italiano dalle origini al 1920". In *Futurismo, cultura e politica*, edited by Renzo De Felice, 49–66. Torino: Fondazione Giovanni Agnelli, 1986.
Benjamin, Walter. "Parigi, la capitale del XIX secolo [Exposé del 1935]". In *Opere Complete*, vol. 9, 5–18. Einaudi: Torino, 2000.
Benjamin, Walter. *L'opera d'arte nell'epoca della sua riproducibilità tecnica. Edizione integrale comprensiva delle cinque stesure*, edited by Fabrizio Desideri, and Marina Montanelli. Roma: Donzelli, 2012.
Boccioni, Umberto. "Manifesto tecnico della scultura futurista". In *Manifesti del futurismo*, edited by Viviana Birolli. Milano: Abscondita, 2008 [1912].
Crispolti, Enrico. "La politica culturale del fascismo, le avanguardie e il problema del futurismo". In *Futurismo, cultura e politica*, edited by Renzo De Felice, 247–280. Torino: Fondazione Giovanni Agnelli, 1986.
Croce, Benedetto. "Il futurismo come cosa estranea all'arte". *La Critica*, 16 (1918): 383–384.
Dantini, Michele. *Arte e politica in Italia fra Fascismo e Repubblica*. Roma: Donzelli, 2016.
De Maria, Luciano. *Marinetti e il futurismo*. Milano: Mondadori, 1983.
De Michelis, Cesare. *Il futurismo italiano in Russia*. Bari: De Donato, 1973.
De Michelis, Cesare. "I contatti politico-culturali fra futuristi italiani e Russia". In *Futurismo, cultura e politica*, edited by Renzo De Felice, 351–380. Torino: Fondazione Giovanni Agnelli, 1986.
De Pero, Fortunato. *Ricostruzione e meccanizzare l'Universo*. Milano: Abscondita, 2019 [1915].
Del Puppo Alessandro. *Modernità e nazione. Temi di ideologia visiva nell'arte italiana del primo Novecento*. Macerata: Quodlibet, 2013.
Eiland, Howard, and Jennings, Michael W. *Walter Benjamin: A Critical Life*. Harvard: Harvard University Press, 2014.

Finelli, Roberto. *Filosofia e tecnologia: una via d'uscita dalla mente digitale.* Genova: Rosenberg & Sellier, 2022.

Gentile, Emilio. *"La nostra sfida alle stelle". Futuristi in politica.* Roma and Bari: Laterza, 2009.

Givone, Sergio. "Due opposte interpretazioni del futurismo". In *Hybris e melancholia. Studi sulle poetiche del Novecento,* 98–118. Milano: Mursia, 1984.

Gramsci, Antonio. "Democrazia operaia". In *L'Ordine nuovo. 1919–1920,* 10–13. Torino: Einaudi, 1955.

Gramsci, Antonio. "Marinetti rivoluzionario?". In *Socialismo e fascismo. L'Ordine nuovo 1921–1922,* 20–22. Torino: Einaudi, 1966.

Gramsci, Antonio. *Per la verità,* edited by Renzo Martinelli. Roma: Editori Riuniti, 1974.

Gramsci, Antonio. *Quaderni del carcere,* edited by Valentino Giarratana. Torino: Einaudi, 1975.

Gramsci, Antonio. "Cavour e Marinetti". In *Sul fascismo.* Roma: Editori Internazionali Riuniti, 2012.

Jangfeldt, Bengt. *Majakovskij: A Biography.* Stockholm: Wahlström & Widstrand, 2007.

Kraiski, Giovanni. *Poetiche russe del Novecento.* Roma and Bari: Laterza, 1968.

Lambiase, Sergio. "Futuristi a Capri". In *Capri. 1905–1940. Frammenti postumi,* edited by Lea Vergine. Milano: Il Saggiatore, 2018.

Marinetti, Filippo Tommaso. *Il poema africano della divisione 28 ottobre.* Milano: Mondadori, 1937.

Martin, James. "Intersecting Planes: Futurism, Fascism and Gramsci". In *One Hundred Years of Futurism: Aesthetics, Politics and Performance,* 79–99. Bristol: Intellect Ltd, 2018.

Massari, Roberto, ed. *All'opposizione nel Pci con Trotsky e Gramsci. Bollettino dell'Opposizione comunista italiana (1931–1933).* Bolsena: Massari, 2004.

Mosse, George. "Futurismo e cultura politica in Europa: una prospettiva globale". In *Futurismo, cultura e politica,* edited by Renzo De Felice. Torino: Fondazione Giovanni Agnelli, 1986.

Rancière, Jacques. *La partage du sensible. Esthétique et politique.* Paris: La Fabrique éditions, 2000.

Stephan, Halina. "Il secondo futurismo russo: la dimensione politica". In *Futurismo, cultura e politica,* edited by Renzo De Felice, 381–406. Torino: Fondazione Giovanni Agnelli, 1986.

Trockij, Lev. *Letteratura e rivoluzione.* Torino: Einaudi, 1973.

15

THE CONTOURS OF THE BANAL

Popular Art and Culture, Folklore and Kitsch

Marina Montanelli

This chapter proposes to return to the writings on folklore by Antonio Gramsci; his famous pages that inspired the influential post-World War II debate on Southern Italy and later, between the 1960s and 1970s, the establishment of demology. A second, apparently paradoxical, attempt will be to bring them into dialogue with Walter Benjamin's reflections on popular art, mass art, and Kitsch. The apparent paradox could be summed up as follows: peasant traditions, archaisms, and economic "backwardness" versus the city, industrialisation, and advanced capitalism. It all depends on how we understand the notion of folklore: whether or not we can expand it and renew it according to socio-historical transformations. In other words, from a position outside the ethno-anthropological framework, we will attempt to take *philosophically* seriously, and try to overcome, the main limitation that demology ran into[1]: having ultimately limited its object of study to an anthropology of folkloric heritage, considered all the more "authentic" when as untainted as possible by the standardising grammars of the culture industry. An anachronistic perspective, given that the languages, thoughts, perceptions, and forms of life of the subaltern classes have rearticulated themselves within (and against) these very grammars. I believe this to be an extremely topical issue. Are we not in urgent need of new historical analyses of folklore, not only of the contemporary "rustic plebeians" but also, and above all, of metropolitan and global folklore? To elaborate on any aspects of freedom and resistance, where present, or to criticise and discard it in the case of the most regressive social phenomena that may emerge? Is this not a fundamental task of today's philosophy of praxis, since we live in an age of powerful resurgence of the archaic and of superstitions?

DOI: 10.4324/9781003457039-20

15.1 Gramsci. Folklore: A Very Serious Matter

Let us begin, then, with *Notebook 27*, from the decisive methodological statement that Gramsci makes there, together with the structured and dialectical definition of the phenomenon of "folklore".[2]

> One can say that until now folklore has been studied primarily as a *"picturesque" element*. (Actually, until now only scholarly material has been collected. . . .) Folklore should instead be studied as a "conception of the world and life" implicit to a large extent in determinate (in time and space) strata of society and in opposition (also for the most part implicit, mechanical and objective) to "official" conceptions of the world . . . that have succeeded one another in the historical process. (Hence the strict relationship between folklore and "common sense", which is philosophical folklore). This conception of the world is not elaborated and systematic because, by definition, the people (the sum total of the instrumental and subaltern classes of every form of society . . .) cannot possess conceptions which are elaborated, systematic and politically organized and centralized in their albeit contradictory development. It is, rather, many-sided . . . if, indeed, one should not speak of *a confused agglomerate of fragments of all the conceptions of the world and of life that have succeeded one another in history*.
>
> Philosophy and modern science are also constantly contributing new elements to "modern folklore" in that certain opinions and scientific notions, removed from their context and more or less distorted, constantly fall within the popular domain and are "inserted" into the mosaic of tradition. . . . Certainly, there is a "religion of the people", . . . which is very different from that of the intellectuals . . . and particularly from that organically set up by the ecclesiastical hierarchy. . . . Thus it is true that there is a "morality of the people". . . . Imperatives exist that are much stronger, more tenacious and more effective than those of official "morality". In this sphere, too, *one must distinguish various strata*: the fossilized ones which reflect conditions of past life and are therefore *conservative and reactionary*, and those which consist of a series of innovations, often *creative and progressive*, determined spontaneously by forms and conditions of life which are in the process of developing and which are in contradiction to or simply different from the morality of the governing strata.[3]

In order, the first crucial questions that emerge: the rejection of the romantic or scholarly classificatory (naturalising and colonial) attitudes towards folklore, the dialectical relationship between folklore and the "official" culture of the ruling classes, between folklore and common sense, and science; cultural *stratification*, which also means the multiplicity of the self and the co-presence of heterogeneous historical moments *within* and outside the subject; the theme of progressive folklore. Above all, Gramsci states his basic methodological principle: folklore, in order to be surpassed in an emancipatory sense, needs to be known, not in a fictitiously disinterested manner, but historically; it needs first of all to be incorporated into the world of history. This knowledge therefore needs to move *from within* the folkloric context itself. Gramsci then goes on to speak of the importance of including the study of folklore in the training of school teachers and university professors:

> to know "folklore" means . . . to know what other conceptions of the world and of life are actually active in the intellectual and moral formation of young people, in order to uproot them and replace them with conceptions which are deemed to be superior. From elementary school to . . . Agricultural faculties . . . the teaching of folklore to teachers should reinforce this systematic process even further.[4]

And again he continues,

> It is clear that, in order to achieve the desired end, the spirit of folklore studies should be changed, as well as deepened and extended. Folklore must not be considered an eccentricity, an oddity or a picturesque element, but as *something which is very serious and is to be taken seriously*. Only in this way will . . . teaching . . . bring about the birth of a new culture . . . so that the separation between modern culture and popular culture of folklore will disappear.[5]

Let us then clarify this point of view, the appropriate "spirit" that research must adopt when dealing with this "very serious" matter, *from within*. We can do so by taking *Notebook 11* (1932–1933) on the relationship between knowing, understanding, and feeling, that is, on the necessary passage from *knowing* to *understanding* and to *feeling* and vice versa.

> The popular element "feels", but does not always know or understand; the intellectual element "knows" but does not always understand and in particular does not always feel. . . . The intellectual's error consists in believing that one can know without understanding and even more without feeling and being impassioned . . .: in other words that the intellectual can be an intellectual . . . if distinct and separate from the people-nation, that is, without feeling the elementary passions of the people, understanding them and therefore explaining and justifying them in the particular historical situation and connecting them . . . to a superior conception of the world, scientifically and coherently elaborated – i.e. knowledge.[6]

202 Marina Montanelli

This *feeling-with* is the methodological approach that allows access to understanding, to *com-prehending* (from Latin *cum-prehendere*, a taking, a grasping together), that offers access to a living rather than a mechanical knowledge, which, alone, can become a "social force", that is, create the "historic bloc" (the question of the difference between the traditional and the organic intellectual is also raised here).[7] What is at stake in the way we interpret the connection between theory and practice is not only the vital quality of knowledge but also the condition of a possible revolutionary transformation, as well as the *manner* in which it takes place. The epistemological premise of such a relationship between *feeling-with* and *com-prehension* lies in the "spontaneous philosophy" that concerns all men and women, expressed by languages, by "common sense", by all doxastic *Weltanschauungen*, up to and including the folklore of determined (in space and time) social groups. Again from *Notebook 11*:

> It must first be shown that all men are "philosophers", by defining the limits and characteristics of the "spontaneous philosophy" . . . contained in: 1. language itself . . .; 2. "common sense" and "good sense"; 3. popular religion and, therefore, also in the entire system of beliefs . . . which are collectively bundled together under the name of "folklore".
>
> In acquiring one's conception of the world one always belongs to a particular grouping. . . . *We are all conformists of some conformism or other, always man-in-the-mass or collective man. . . . When one's conception of the world is not critical and coherent but disjointed and episodic*, one belongs simultaneously to a multiplicity of mass human groups. *The personality is strangely composite: it contains Stone Age elements and principles of a more advanced science, prejudices from all past phases of history at the local level and intuitions of a future philosophy which will be that of a human race united the world over.*[8]

Every language, including dialects and jargons, every set of dogmas and beliefs, contains not one, but several conceptions of the world, historically sedimented, juxtaposed in a seemingly inextricable web between *synchronicity* and the *non-synchronous*.[9] The individual is a *fictio*, we are always spoken and thought first, we are always unconsciously confirmed by the group, by groups. The complexity of *social formations* corresponds to the complexity of *discursive formations*[10]: totalities structured according to various levels of articulation combined in different ways. The ideological terrain is therefore diversified, crossed by a variety of currents. A chaotic plurality that poses more sophisticated problems than the petty false consciousness opposed to a class subject claimed to be homogeneous and pure. What is at play, as we have said, is the combination of several historical periods. Any linear conception of development, based on stages, falters. A lesson that, as we know, has been absorbed and developed by postcolonial studies.[11] The modern is like frosted glass; its *scabrous* limits are at once its premises. It is then up to critique to unravel the plot: any *counter-hegemonic construction* cannot consist in a mere imposition of another world view; above all, it should consist in a *coherent* and *conscious* dis-articulation and re-articulation of ideas, opinions, of common sense; a *disassembling and reassembling* that will allow the transition to "good sense", from "spontaneous philosophy" to "the upper level of philosophy".[12] Critique triggers "a process of differentiation and change" in the "relative weight" of the elements of the old ideologies: what was once "secondary" or "incidental" can become "the nucleus of a new ideological and theoretical complex" – as in the very case of the progressive core of a folkloristic set of beliefs.[13] The philosophy of praxis is first of all the practice of critique, because ideologies are "material forces" and not merely a deterministic reflection of the economic base;[14] "they 'organise' human masses, and create the terrain on which men move" and potentially "acquire consciousness of their position, struggle".[15] This process of clarification, therefore, does not suppress multiplicity, but combs through it and rearranges it according to a congruent and unified historical logic. It is therefore an essential act in the construction of the historic bloc. (Counter) hegemony is in fact an "intellectual and moral unity", beyond the "economic and political aims", it also involves the "passage from the structure to the sphere of the complex superstructures";[16] a unity that is not homogenous in any abstract manner (by means of the dominion of one class over the other alone), but rather in the manner of a *constellation*: a plural combination of social forces, an *expansive system of alliances* – through the conquest of "consensus" by those who "lead" the bloc – an articulation and *translation* of different interests albeit within a convergence in the struggle against capitalism and the bourgeois State.[17]

15.2 Dialectics of the Enlightenment: What Critique of Progressive Reason?

For Gramsci folklore is a culture, however incoherent, and it is a system: it has a vision of the world (common sense), a language (dialects and jargons), a morality and a religion (simplification of Catholic doctrine, in the case of Italy, mixed with superstition and magical beliefs), a (melodramatic, "operatic") taste.[18] At the same time, it is not properly a culture, because it is a contradictory, apparently isolated, hotchpotch of ideas and opinions, which as such are incommunicable. In fact, as mentioned earlier, folklore is not a static conglomerate, separate from society and the more "advanced" cultures. On the contrary, it is always in motion, constantly incorporating new elements into its *ritual schema*: it also assimilates slivers of "modern" thought, however decontextualised and "more or less distorted". For Gramsci, this means, firstly, that folklore cannot be understood independently of the dynamics of capitalist, bourgeois and Church rule; secondly, that it can (and must) have both a diagnostic and prognostic function for revolutionary thought and praxis: by offering crucial insights into the conditions of the subaltern classes, it can both clarify the tendencies of hegemonic projects and provide pointers for counter-hegemonic ones. After all, the relationship between critique, "common sense, and the upper level of philosophy is assured by 'politics', just as it is politics that assures the relationship between the Catholicism of the intellectuals and that of the simple" (and of every gnoseological relationship, against the pseudoneutrality of knowledge), except that stance and aim go in opposite directions: "The philosophy of praxis does not tend to leave the 'simple' in their primitive philosophy of common sense, but rather to lead them to a higher conception of life".[19] It is a perspective not of evangelisation and obedience but of political subjectivation and emancipation of the self and of society as a whole.

The first step towards soliciting such an ambitious and difficult process of liberation involves the militant scholar disengaging from all forms of "romantic idolisation" of popular culture. In this regard, Ernesto de Martino's and Alberto Maria Cirese's readings of Gramsci are fundamental. The *feeling-with* that makes *comprehension* possible is in no way a cult of the "picturesque" or the "primitive" as expressions of a "mysterious 'creative power' of the people".[20] An exaltation, according to this different gradation, embraced by a broad ideological spectrum: from liberal erudition to fascist and national-socialist mythologies. This romantic idolisation was not alien to the cultural policy of the Italian Communist Party (PCI) after the Second World War, and in some cases to Neo-Realism. The priority is to avoid any new, turbid assimilations of the archaic; but also to clear the ground of any "orientalist" impulses, which, by cataloguing the "finds" of subaltern cultures as exotic collectibles, always end up naturalising and infantilising them, confirming the power that oppresses them and excludes them from the historic world.[21]

For Gramsci, folklore is above all an "ideological servitude", the cultural manifestation of an economic and social subjugation.[22] The science of folklore is therefore to be understood as a high "political-scientific knowledge" of the links between "cultural divides" and "socio-economic power divides"[23] – everything but the overcoming of "modern science" in favour of new forms of "witchcraft".[24] Neither purely culturalist analysis nor economism *à la* Nikolaj Bucharin, therefore. There can be no revolutionary transformation without a profound transformation of the superstructures. As de Martino wrote, defending himself from both Crocean criticism (Giuseppe Giarrizzo) and criticism from the PCI (Mario Alicata), "In order to transform a society, it is necessary to have a precise knowledge of the forms of resistance that oppose the process of transformation".[25] Folklore included. If approached *seriously*, it emerges in all its ambivalence: its antagonistic drive can be as reactionary as it can be progressive. The *reawakening* of the matter it is made of, if it is to be developed and even organised politically, is therefore both a necessity and a risk.

This position, a third way between idolisation and the denial typical of a crude rationalism, certainly draws upon a progressive folklore: *from within* the phenomenon, to return to the beginnings, it involves evaluating the elements in which the opportunity for a critique, for breaking marginalisation, is powerful; those elements that "culturally express" the struggles of the subalterns to emancipate themselves from their condition. So, there exists "a folklore of the Resistance", of "land and factory occupations", of "strikes".[26] Cirese would further develop the issue by distinguishing between folklore "*as* protest", that is, folklore in general as the result of bourgeois culture's discrimination, and "*protest* folklore", the genuinely progressive strata of folklore, which bring into play "the acquisition of an awareness of folklore as one's heritage, in which and with which one has been alive, but within which one has also been condemned and confined".[27] This represents the passage from "class instinct" – with reference to Lenin and his definition of the "spontaneous element" as the "*embryonic form*" of consciousness – to class consciousness.[28]

In other words, the study of folklore implies an essential *dialectic of Enlightenment*: most importantly, a *critique of progressive reason* that will allow not only a *disarticulation* and understanding of the *polarities of modernity* – "culture" and "barbarism", "civilisation" and "regression"[29] – but also the self-emendation of that very reason from crude economism and scientism. An end to blind antimagicism, to dull anti-spiritualism, which actually breed superstition and folklore, but a full exploration of these phenomena as truly modern phenomena, in order to construct, on the basis of the critical decomposition of their elements, a new culture, society, and human being. This dialectic of enlightenment therefore advocates an *enhanced humanism* capable of integrating in the realm of history, of thinking, of politics everything that has traditionally been dismissed as "unhistorical", "primitive", and "unpolitical".[30] Integration, not as a charitable reintroduction of the "culture of the marginalised" "into the circle of a relativistic pluralism that . . . leaves intact . . . the structural causes of discrimination",[31] but as a name for new elaborations, new unities, new orders: truly counter-hegemonic ones. Progressive folklore as such should not be opposed to (or replace) the dominant culture but should rather act as a *bridge* between the old and the new. From the dissolution of its previous configurations, the possibility arises to connect what has been examined and preserved to the "process of political and social emancipation",[32] to combine it with the most advanced elements of modern thought to produce new signifying chains, the seeds of the new culture.

Moreover, when Gramsci considers the problem of mass taste and the role of art in this regard, he expresses characteristics and criteria that belong entirely to the Enlightenment (no doubt also under the influence of Soviet experimentation); but not in the sense of a "persecutory" and "odious" Enlightenment, of abstract universalism.[33] First of all, the function of art should be "social" (political, as Benjamin would call it in opposition to the ritual function), that is, it should "create", and "elevate" the taste of the masses. Secondly, the principles of rationalism and functionalism (they too amended, "enhanced") need to respond critically to the new "aesthetics of individualism" such as seen in decorativism (see *art nouveau*) and any type of artistic and literary "baroque".[34] The melodramatic style, which the people love, because it is emotional and empathetic, must give way to a "sober prose". The problem of content is *organically* linked to that of the form: a new art and a new culture should abandon "pompousness, the oratorical style, any stylistic hypocrisy", which, when they infect the subaltern classes, become an even more artificial "walking on stilts", a "faking a redundant style" in imitation of the "nineteenth-century opera libretto" to the detriment of common speech.[35] Almost Brechtianly: essentiality, sobriety, and construction, to overcome the very distinction between elevated and popular culture.

15.3   Benjamin. To the Very Heart of Things Abolished

The thesis of this essay is that Gramsci's enlightenment is much closer to Benjamin's than to that of the Frankfurt School: both seek a very similar *dialectical force internal to damaged life*. Both are philosophers of *praxis*, because for the Marxist Benjamin "Politics attains primacy over history", over knowledge.[36] A Nietzschean *use* of history for the purposes of present practice or, with the 11th thesis on Feuerbach, not so much (or not only) a different interpretation of the world, but its transformation. The knowing subject is the collective and historical "struggling, oppressed class", no longer the Kantian transcendental. We need to only think of one of Benjamin's most innovative concepts, that of *Jetzt der Erkennbarkeit*, which in the last phase of his production is defined as an absolutely gnoseological-practical concept: as a synonym for a revolutionary *chance*.[37] On the contrary, the results of Adorno's *negative* dialectic are well known: the belief that freedom, "in this age of universal social repression" lives "in the crushed, abused individual's features alone".[38] The rejection of the Lukácsian *eschatology* of the class struggle[39] determines in this case the impossibility of distinguishing collective subjects of resistance: the minute head that rises up is that of the theoretical subject, (individual) gnosiology forces out praxis. The same can be said of the relationship between the modern and the archaic, *Aufklärung* and *Mythos*: while Benjamin immerses himself in myth looking at its dissolution, Adorno envisages an endless oscillation between the two extremes. For the former, historical specification remains fundamental; the latter (with Horkheimer) ends up ontologising the link between myth and history: already Ulysses can then embody bourgeois rationality, herald the abstract principle of the "equivalent", of exchange.[40] Such a dehistoricisation inevitably leaves in oblivion the *other* of exploitation in its various forms – in the case of capitalist exploitation, *living labour* – and allows the social totality to rage in the form of dominion. In the analysis of the cultural industry, therefore, the critique of myth, accompanied by the critique of fetishism, is unable to disengage itself from the totalitarian dimension of the "administered world".

Benjamin, after reading Adorno's essay on *Jazz* and responding to his harsh criticism of *The Work of Art in the Age of Its Technological Reproducibility* sums up the differences between their approaches in the relevant image of "two . . . headlamps trained upon the same object from opposite directions".[41] Benjamin thinks in terms of polarities, this is his dialectical method: as if from *inside* an electromagnetic field, he captures the shifts in the centre of gravity that each time determine the weight and role of the poles, their relationship. This enables him to avoid becoming stuck in the direct confrontation between totality and the individual. The new structural formations of matter brought to light by the camera, the distracted mass reception, reveal to him a different spectrum of sensation and perception, akin to that of the oneiric or of psychosis, which can equally be the object of regressive and fascist manipulation or a margin for *progressive* action, pointing the way to a new collective innervation of the human senses, that is, to the aesthetic-anthropological liberation that is the indispensable condition of any true political revolution.[42] An "infantile" reconstruction of reality through mimicry can certainly operate in film editing, as Adorno states, but so can the playful-constructive act that deactivates false appearances, that in fact returns to playing with reality, modifying it starting from a critique of social relations.[43] Sensitive, intellectual, and political growth, then, as opposed to the illusory and ambiguous representations produced by capitalism and fascism for the use and consumption of the masses, which must remain no more than that.

Here we find Benjamin's enlightenment, it too "enhanced"; he crosses terrains of dreams and "madness", in the footsteps of the surrealists, in search of an "image space" as the eminent space of political-revolutionary action, but unlike them, he does so with the "whetted axe of reason".[44] He shuns at once economicist determinism (one of his polemical targets is Bukharin) and the aesthetic and mythological enchantments in which surrealism remains ultimately wrapped. *Cunning of reason*,[45] but with no forms of pan-rationalism or teleological marches of mediation, spirit, progress; cunning of reason, together with a *tenderness* for reified empiricism of Goethian memory.[46] The objective is a "historical awakening"[47] that can nonetheless arise – at penalty of the reaffirmation of an *Aufklärung* at once "persecutory" and ineffective – only *between* the oneiric dynamics themselves. The authentic intelligence of the dream. It is then about Freud (in opposition to the reactionary risk of Jung's archetypal psychoanalysis), although the dream is to be understood as a historical and collective phenomenon.[48] For Benjamin too, the centrality of superstructures as material forces that shape social plots is in question – and a non-mechanistic relationship between superstructures and economic base, but of the "expressive" complex kind, according to a dynamic of continuous and articulated actions and retroactions;[49] also an anticipation of Althusser's notion of overdetermination.[50]

The Arcades Project, the remarkable, unfinished endeavour that occupied Benjamin for the last 13 years of his life sought to plumb the phantasmagoria and imagery of nineteenth-century collectivity in order to understand the original configurations of advanced capitalism. Together with large-scale industry, they marked the very beginnings of mass culture, of the standardisation of aesthetics, of Kitsch. Of those elements that, contrary to what much of the Italian demology of the 1960s was to believe, Gramsci did not consider as "corrupting" any sort of "purity"; instead, he regarded the study of folklore, of the serial novel, and of other modern expressions of popular culture, aspects of the same problem. The act is the same: the salvation of the *refuse* of "true" intellectuality.[51] Hence, a rewriting of history in an "expanded" form, according to a new and effective *organic totality* (in Benjamin – this is his peculiar monadology) capable of taking into account the temporal heterogeneity and the superstructural and structural levels at work in every social formation; naturally, a class history. Among his notes for *The Paris of the Second Empire in Baudelaire*, an essay conceived as a chapter of the *Arcades* before becoming a project for a book on Baudelaire, Benjamin notes, "Sundering truth from falsehood is the goal of the materialist method, not its point of departure. In other words, its point of departure is the object riddled with error, with *doxa*".[52] Again, among the earliest notes for the *Arcades*, he wrote, "We construct here an alarm clock that rouses the kitsch of the previous century to 'assembly'".[53] Kitsch as a category emerged in the last quarter of the nineteenth century: in and around the Munich markets, it initially referred to inferior artistic products sold cheaply, crude reproductions for tourists, new objects passed off as antiques, their stylistic flaws disguised by a decorative and sentimental extravagance – a perversion of Romanticism.[54] A *Weltanschauung* of the ascendant bourgeoisie, Kitsch is one of the fundamental atmospheric conditions of modernity: the new dominant social subject and the levelling out of industrialisation are accompanied by the spread of a culture of clichés, of conformism, naivety, and amateurism, of a "dictatorship of the heart"[55] – Gramsci's melodramatic. It is undoubtedly an aesthetic category, but also, from the outset, an anthropological and political one – kitsch taste belongs to the *Kitsch-Mensch*.[56] Kitsch, Benjamin writes in the first hermetic text dedicated to the surrealists, "is the last *mask* of the banal" – a counterweight to the Marxian mask of the abstract subject of law, guardian and representative of commodities – which, from this juncture of the century, is worn to rediscover "the energies of an outlived world of things"[57] that has evaporated between the meshes of the viscous mixture of fetishism, aestheticism, and consumerism.[58] An evaporation that is also a relocation – the outcome of the dialectic between hegemonic and subaltern levels – of popular art and culture, and folklore within the unifying framework of the Kitsch category. Transfusions and displacements that speak of the elaboration by society of the transition to the modes of production (and reproduction) of advanced capitalism, of the reception of an overwhelming technological growth;

the more these are unconscious from the point of view of the critique of relations of exploitation, the more they become a source of inequality and destruction.[59]

Kitsch is "the very last, the topmost face" of "the totemic tree" of objects lost in "the thicket of primal history [*Urgeschichte*]". It is the side of things "worn through by habit and patched with cheap maxims" – an exorcism to survive the catastrophe of tradition – as well as the side, as surrealism teaches, where the oneiric enigmas of the collective unconscious are set.[60] It is the very side that presents itself to critical thinking as a *crossroads*: the banal is adjacent to the good.[61] The banal contains the dream of the liberating drive, the banal can turn into fascism. *Kitsch offers a great deal to think about.* Benjamin's third way opens up again. Though he embraces Constructivism, Adolf Loos and Le Corbusier, the radical critique of *Art Nouveau* decorativism, the glass architecture of Paul Scheerbart, the functionalism of the Bauhaus, the engineer-like figures of Paul Klee, the Brechtian *Verfremdungseffekt*, sobriety versus emotional identification,[62] his position, like Gramsci's, is not the result of a crude rationalist negation. On the contrary, it involves finding how to "blaze a way into the heart of things abolished", that is "to decipher the contours of the banal".[63] It is the knowledge, which the Surrealists missed, that returns to the plot of the historical, social, and economic origins of *dream images* as *dialectical images*. Only in this way can the fetishistic context open up to emancipation. Only in this way can an "other" human being be formed, who will be able to plough through the cultural apocalypse with the "barbaric" attitude of those who are not afraid to start anew guided by the constructive principle, breaking away both from nostalgia for worlds of the past and from "new", artificial ideological hubbubs that have no bearing on the era – Benjamin's example: "the revival of astrology and the wisdom of yoga, Christian Science and chiromancy, vegetarianism and gnosis, scholasticism and spiritualism".[64]

This approach is driven by the intuition that the original configurations of advanced capitalism are the original configurations of capitalism's becoming an anthropogenic machine. The relevance of Kitsch lies in taking us to the centre of this anthropogenesis. In a note on folk art most likely written around 1929, Benjamin writes, "Art teaches us to look into objects [*in die Dinge hineinsehen*]. Folk art and kitsch allow us to look outward from within objects [*aus den Dingen heraus zu sehen*]".[65] The world of things itself in Kitsch returns to "advance on the human being": "it yields to his uncertain grasp", whereas "what we used to call art begins at a distance of two meters from the body".[66] And again: "Folk art and kitsch ought for once to be regarded as a single great movement that passes certain themes from hand to hand, like batons, behind the back of what is known as great art. They both depend on great art at the level of detail but apply what they have taken in their own way and in the service of their own 'goals', their *Kunstwollen*".[67] The *Kunstwollen* of folk art and Kitsch, unlike that of great art and of the avant-garde, does not refer to art itself (something which, according to Adorno, is dialectically far more fertile), but fulfils the much more archaic, compelling, purpose of attracting women and men by making the idea emerge in them that that same space and that given moment in which the aesthetic experience takes place have already existed once in their lives. It is the reassuring feeling of being wrapped in one's "favourite old coat". This particular ability to *re-actualise* "is the deepest temptation awakened by the refrain of a folk song" and the "basic feature of all folk art", of Kitsch, and of folklore.[68] What is at work, in other words, is the reassurance of what has already been, of a time outside history, of an *intrauterine heterotopia*. "The *déjà vu* is changed from the pathological exception that it is in civilized life to a magical ability at whose disposal folk art (no less than kitsch) places itself", it digs out from the unconscious "the primitive, with all its implements and pictures", the "infinite arsenal" (not archetypal, but always historical) of "the masks of our fate".[69] This is where the essay on technological reproducibility becomes fundamental once again. The note to paragraph XI of the version in which the synchronic polarity immanent to every work of art is mentioned. Polarity – located by Benjamin in "mimesis as the primal phenomenon of all artistic activity" – between *semblance*, linked to the cult and the ritual function of art, and *play*, linked to the exhibition value, to experimentation, and to the political function of art.[70] The *comfort zone* that Kitsch, folk art, and folklore in general create is in the order of semblance. The general economy of the text also leads us to understand that this polarity is constitutive not only of artistic production but of the human being in the broadest sense. Ritual and play, then, as two sister and antithetical responses to the human need for guidance and protection, as two different ways of constituting the world, of conceiving the relationship with nature, with technology and with history. In the former, technology is an *instrument* for dominating nature, perceived as alien and threatening, and time is the destinal and mythical time of eternal return; in the latter, it is a *medium* of emancipation, for improving nature, and time is the historical time of ludic, differential, constructive repetition. In the face of the radical changes of modernity, with the new phenomena of "crisis of presence", to quote De Martino again,[71] Kitsch re-updates the production of aesthetic semblances: compared to great art, replications of extremely simplified patterns that tug to the heartstrings, that appeal to the phantasmatic sphere of the unconscious. They are *modern exorcisms* to dominate the foreign, aimed at assuring one's "being-there" in the world (and often also the continuity of exploitation). *Masks*, precisely, behind whose appearance of the latest novelty, dwell the most ancient needs of the human being.

Mass culture is an industrial fact from which there is no return; from here, according to Benjamin, we must move towards the politicisation of art, a radical transformative process capable of reuniting aesthetic pleasure (which inevitably passes through consumption) and critique.[72] It is not only a cognitive question but also a sensitive one: only by adopting this assumption will we be able to compete with the aestheticisation of politics. It is therefore above all a serious exploration of popular art forms, of new forms of folklore that can allow the deactivation of regressive options, but also of the very dualism between utopia (or avant-garde) and reaction. In the hope of a new season of barbaric, revolutionary enlightenment.

Notes

1 On this and from within the discipline, see Fabio Dei, "Popolo, popolare, populismo", *International Gramsci Journal* 2, no. 3 (2017): 208–238.

2 We recall that part of the *Observations on Folklore* (1935) is from *Notebook* 1 (Q1; 1929–1930), §§ 86, 89, Gramsci's first commentary on G. Crocioni, *Problemi fondamentali del Folklore* (1928; *Fundamental Problems of Folklore*), whose theses he most likely derived from Raffaele Ciampini's review of Crocioni, with whom he critically interjected. Costanza Orlandi returned to the comparative analysis of the two texts in the *Prison Notebooks*; see Costanza Orlandi, "Folclore e modernità nella riflessione gramsciana", in *Domande dal presente. Studi su Gramsci*, ed. Lea Durante and Guido Liguori (Roma: Carocci, 2012), 127–139.

3 Antonio Gramsci, *The Gramsci Reader: Selected Writings 1916–1935*, ed. David Forgacs, with a new Introduction by Eric J. Hobsbawm (New York: New York University Press, 2000), 360–361 (Q27 [1935]). Our italics. For "religion" and "morality of the people", Gramsci answers the questions posed by Ciampini in his review.

4 Antonio Gramsci, *Quaderni del carcere*, ed. Valentino Gerratana (Torino: Einaudi, 1975), 2314 (Q27) (our translation).

5 Gramsci, *The Gramsci Reader*, 362 (Q27); our italics.

6 Antonio Gramsci, *Selections from the Prison Notebooks*, ed. Quintin Hoare and Geoffrey Nowell Smith (New York: International Publishers, 1992), 418; see also Gramsci, *The Gramsci Reader*, 349–350.

7 Gramsci, *Selections From the Prison Notebooks*, 323–324; also in Gramsci, *The Gramsci Reader*, 325–326; our italics.

8 Gramsci, *Selections From the Prison Notebooks*, 418; also in Gramsci, *The Gramsci Reader*, 350.

9 The reference is of course to Ernst Bloch, "Nonsynchronism and Its Obligation to Its Dialectics", *New German Critique* 11 (1977): 22–38.

10 On this, see, respectively, Louis Althusser, "The Object of Capital", in *Reading Capital*, trans. Ben Brewster and David Fernbach (New York: Verso, 2009), 77–220, and Stuart Hall, "Gramsci's Relevance for the Study of Race and Ethnicity", *Journal of Communication Inquiry* 10 (1986): 5–27, in part. 22.

11 See Dipesh Chakrabarty, *Provincializing Europe: Postcolonial Thought and Historical Difference* (Princeton, NJ: Princeton University Press, 2000); Ranajit Guha, *History at the Limit of World-History* (New York: Columbia University Press, 2002).

12 Gramsci, *Selections From the Prison Notebooks*, 331; also in Gramsci, *The Gramsci Reader*, 332 (Q11).

13 Gramsci, *Selections From the Prison Notebooks*, 195 (Q8 [1931–1932]); see also Gramsci, *Selections From the Prison Notebooks*, 324–326 (Q11).

14 Gramsci, *Selections From the Prison Notebooks*, 165; also in Gramsci, *The Gramsci Reader*, 215 (Q13 [1932–1934]). On this, see likewise Gramsci, *Selections from the Prison Notebooks*, 330–331 (Q11).

15 Gramsci, *Selections From the Prison Notebooks*, 377; also in Gramsci, *The Gramsci Reader*, 199 (Q7 [1930–1932]).

16 Gramsci, *Selections From the Prison Notebooks*, 181; also in Gramsci, *The Gramsci Reader*, 205 (Q13).

17 Stuart Hall also spoke of a constellation with regard to the notion of hegemony: Stuart Hall, "Gramsci's Relevance for the Study of Race and Ethnicity": 15. Here, the term is emphasised, as is also Benjamin's fundamental concept.

18 See Gramsci, *The Gramsci Reader*, 373–374; and also Gramsci, *Quaderni del carcere*, 1738 (Q14 [1932–1935]).

19 Gramsci, *Selections From the Prison Notebooks*, 331–332; also in Gramsci, *The Gramsci Reader*, 332–333 (Q11).

20 Ernesto De Martino, "Gramsci e il folklore", *Il calendario del popolo* 8 (April 1952): 1109. See also Ernesto De Martino, "Due inediti su Gramsci. *Postille a Gramsci* e *Gramsci e il folklore*", *La Ricerca Folklorica* 25 (April 1992): 73–79, and Ernesto De Martino, "Gramsci e il folklore nella cultura italiana", *Il de Martino* 5–6 (1996): 87–90; Alberto Maria Cirese, "Gramsci e il folklore come concezione tradizionale del mondo delle classi subalterne", *Problemi* 49 (1977): 155–167.

21 We take up the suggestion of the Orientalist flaw in Western knowledge highlighted by De Martino – with reference to Edward Said, *Orientalism* (New York: Pantheon Books, 1978) – from Marco Gatto, "Oltre il paradigma leviano. Subalternità e mediazione da Ernesto de Martino a Rocco Scotellaro", *Filologia Antica e Moderna 1* 31, no. 51 (2021): 151–180.

22 Ernesto De Martino, "Gramsci e il folklore nella cultura italiana", *Il de Martino* 5–6 (1996): 88.

23 Cirese, "Gramsci e il folklore come concezione tradizionale del mondo delle classi subalterne", 162.

24 Gramsci, *Selections From the Prison Notebooks*, 196–197 (Q3 [1930]).

25 Ernesto De Martino, "Per un dibattito sul folklore", *Lucania* 2 (1954): 76.

26 De Martino, "Gramsci e il folklore nella cultura italiana", 89.

27 Alberto Maria Cirese, *Intellettuali, folklore, istinto di classe. Note su Verga, Deledda, Scotellaro, Gramsci* (Torino: Einaudi, 1976), 116–117.

28 Cirese, *Intellettuali, folklore, istinto di classe*, 113–115. See also Vladimir Il'ič Lenin, "What Is to Be Done? Burning Questions of Our Movement", in *Collected Works* (Moscow: Foreign Languages Publishing House, 1961), vol. 5, 374–375.

29 In Italy, Renato Solmi was the first to suggest, in his *Introduction* to the first Italian edition of *Minima Moralia*, an affinity between de Martino's folkloric research and Theodor Adorno and Max Horkheimer's understanding of the "dialectic of enlightenment": Renato Solmi, *Introduzione a "Minima moralia" di Theodor W. Adorno* (Macerata: Quodlibet, 2015).

30 See again De Martino, "Gramsci e il folklore nella cultura italiana"; De Martino, "Due inediti su Gramsci"; De Martino, "Gramsci e il folklore".

31 Cirese, *Intellettuali, folklore, istinto di classe*, 117.

32 Ernesto De Martino, "Il folklore progressivo", *L'Unità*, 26 June 1951, 3.

33 Gramsci, *Quaderni del carcere*, 1727 (Q14).

34 Gramsci, *Quaderni del carcere*, 1724–1725 (Q14).

35 Gramsci, *Quaderni del carcere*, 1737–1739 (Q14).

36 Walter Benjamin, *The Arcades Project* (Cambridge, MA and London: The Belknap Press of Harvard University Press, 1999), 388–389.

37 Walter Benjamin, "On the Concept of History", in *Selected Writings: Volume 4, 1938–1940*, ed. Howard Eiland and Michael W. Jennings (Cambridge, MA and London: The Belknap Press of Harvard University Press, 2006), 394, 396.

38 Theodor Wiesegrund Adorno, *Negative Dialectics* (London and New York: Routledge, 2004), 265.

39 In the aftermath of the Stalinist catastrophe; see Theodor Wiesengrund Adorno, et al., "Wissenschaft und Krise. Differenz zwischen Idealismus und Materialismus. Diskussionen über Themen zu einer Vorlesung Max Horkheimers", in Max Horkheimer, *Gesammelte Schriften*, ed. Gunzelin Schmid Noerr (Frankfurt am Main: Fischer, 1985), vol. 12, 364.

40 Theodor Wiesengrund Adorno and Max Horkheimer, *Dialectic of Enlightenment: Philosophical Fragments*, ed. Gunzelin Schmid Noerr (Stanford: Stanford University Press, 2002), 39–40; trans. mod. On this, see Hans-Jürgen Krahl, "The Political Contradictions in Adorno's Critical Theory", *Telos* 21 (1974): 164–167.

41 Theodor Wiesengrund Adorno and Walter Benjamin, *The Complete Correspondence 1928–1940*, ed. Henri Lonitz and trans. Nicholas Walker (Cambridge: Polity Press, 1999), 144.

42 See Walter Benjamin, "The Work of Art in the Age of Its Technological Reproducibility", in *Selected Writings: Volume 3, 1935–1938*, ed. Howard Eiland and Michael W. Jennings (Cambridge, MA and London: The Belknap Press of Harvard University Press, 2002), 101–133. On the new collective innervation, see also Walter Benjamin, "Surrealism: The Last Snapshot of the European Intelligentsia", in *Selected Writings: Volume 2, part 1, 1927–1930*, ed. Michael W. Jennings, Howard Eiland and Gary Smith (Cambridge, MA and London: The Belknap Press of Harvard University Press, 1999), 207–218, in part. 217–218.

43 Adorno and Benjamin, *The Complete Correspondance 1928–1940*, 127–134, in part. 131; Benjamin, "The Work of Art in the Age of Its Technological Reproducibility", in part. 106–108.

44 Benjamin, *The Arcades Project*, 456. For the concept of "image space" [*Bildraum*], see Benjamin, "Surrealism: The Last Snapshot of the European Intelligentsia", 217.

45 Benjamin, *The Arcades Project*, 13.

46 On the fundamental Benjamin–Goethe relationship, see at least Ursula Marx and Alexandra Richter, "Johann Wolfgang Goethe: Philosophische Alchimie", in *Entwendungen. Walter Benjamin und seine Quellen*, ed. Jessica Nitsche and Nadine Werner (Paderborn: Wilhelm Fink, 2019), 97–124.

47 Benjamin, *The Arcades Project*, 13.

48 Benjamin, *The Arcades Project*, 907. On Benjamin's project of critique of Jungian categories, see Marina Montanelli, "Baudelaire Laboratory: Brief History of a Project by Walter Benjamin", *Aisthesis* 13, no. 2 (2020): 17–29.

49 Benjamin, *The Arcades Project*, 392, 460, 484.

50 Louis Althusser, "Contradiction and Overdetermination: Notes for an Investigation", in *For Marx* (London and New York: Verso, 2005).

51 In the draft "History of Italian Intellectuals" (see Antonio Gramsci, *Quaderni del carcere*, ed. Valentino Gerratana (Torino: Einaudi, 1975), vol. 4, Q8), Gramsci included both the "Popular literature of serial novels" and "Folklore and Common Sense" in the summary; see Gramsci, *Quaderni del carcere*, Q8. On this, see also Cirese, "Gramsci e il folklore come concezione tradizionale del mondo delle classi subalterne", 155–167.

52 Walter Benjamin, "The Paris of the Second Empire in Baudelaire", in *Selected Writings: Volume 4, 1938–1940*, ed. Howard Eiland and Michael W. Jennings (Cambridge, MA and London: The Belknap Press of Harvard University Press, 2006), 63.

53 Benjamin, *The Arcades Project*, 883, 205.

54 For the history of the concept, see at least Ute Dettmar and Thomas Küpper, eds., *Kitsch. Texte und Theorien* (Stuttgart: Reclam, 2007).

55 Milan Kundera, *The Unbearable Lightness of Being* (New York: Harper & Row, 1984).

56 Hermann Broch, "Notes on the Problem of Kitsch", in *Kitsch: The World of Bad Taste*, ed. Gillo Dorfles (New York: Universe Books, 1968), 49–76.
57 Walter Benjamin, "Dream Kitsch. Gloss on Surrealism", in *Selected Writings: Volume 2, Part 1, 1927–1930*, ed. Michael W. Jennings, Howard Eiland and Gary Smith (Cambridge, MA and London: The Belknap Press of Harvard University Press, 1999 [1927]), 4.
58 Abraham Moles, *Le kitsch: L'art du bonheur* (Paris: Mame, 1971).
59 On this point, see the epilogue to all versions of the essay on *The Work of Art*.
60 Benjamin, "Dream Kitsch", 4, 3.
61 Benjamin, "Dream Kitsch", 4. On "currents of thought at the crossroads", see also Benjamin, *The Arcades Project*, 857.
62 See Walter Benjamin, "Experience and Poverty", in *Selected Writings: Volume 2, Part 2, 1931–1934*, ed. Michael W. Jennings, Howard Eiland, and Gary Smith (Cambridge, MA and London: The Belknap Press of Harvard University Press, 2005 [1933]), 733–734.
63 Benjamin, "Dream Kitsch", 4.
64 Benjamin, "Experience and Poverty", 733, 732.
65 Walter Benjamin, "Some Remarks on Folk Art", in *Selected Writings: Volume 2, Part 1, 1927–1930*, eds. Michael W. Jennings, Howard Eiland, and Gary Smith (Cambridge, MA and London: The Belknap Press of Harvard University Press, 1999 [1929]), 279.
66 Benjamin, "Dream Kitsch", 5, 4.
67 Benjamin, "Some Remarks on Folk Art", 278.
68 Benjamin, "Some Remarks on Folk Art", 278.
69 Benjamin, "Some Remarks on Folk Art", 279.
70 Benjamin, "The Work of Art in the Age of Its Technological Reproducibility", 127–128.
71 Ernesto De Martino, *Il mondo magico: prolegomeni a una storia del magismo* (Torino: Bollati Boringhieri, 2007), 222.
72 Benjamin, "The Work of Art in the Age of Its Technological Reproducibility", 116–117, 120–122.

Bibliography

Adorno, Theodor Wiesengrund. *Negative Dialectics*. London and New York: Routledge, 2004 [1966].
Adorno, Theodor Wiesengrund, et al. "Wissenschaft und Krise. Differenz zwischen Idealismus und Materialismus. Diskussionen über Themen zu einer Vorlesung Max Horkheimers". In Max Horkheimer, *Gesammelte Schriften*, edited by Gunzelin Schmid Noerr, vol. 12. Frankfurt am Main: Fischer, 1985 [1932].
Adorno, Theodor Wiesengrund, and Benjamin, Walter. *The Complete Correspondence 1928–1940*, edited by Henry Lonitz, translated by Nicholas Walker. Cambridge: Polity Press, 1999 [1928–1940].
Adorno, Theodor Wiesengrund, and Horkheimer, Max. *Dialectic of Enlightenment: Philosophical Fragments*, edited by Gunzelin Schmid Noerr, translated by Edmund Jephcott. Stanford: Stanford University Press, 2002 [1969].
Althusser, Louis. "Contradiction and Overdetermination: Notes for an Investigation". In *For Marx*, translated by Ben Brewster, 87–128. London: Verso, 2005 [1962].
Althusser, Louis. "The Object of Capital". In *Reading Capital*, translated by Ben Brewster, and David Fernbach, 77–220. London and New York: Verso, 2009 [1965].
Benjamin, Walter. "Dream Kitsch: Gloss on Surrealism". In *Selected Writings: Volume 2, Part 1, 1927–1930*, edited by Michael W. Jennings, Howard Eiland, and Gary Smith,

3–5. Cambridge, MA and London: The Belknap Press of Harvard University Press, 1999 [1927].

Benjamin, Walter. *The Arcades Project*, translated by Howard Eiland, and Kevin McLaughlin. Cambridge, MA and London: The Belknap Press of Harvard University Press, 1999 [1927–1940].

Benjamin, Walter. "Some Remarks on Folk Art". In *Selected Writings: Volume 2, Part 1, 1927–1930*, edited by Michael W. Jennings, Howard Eiland, and Gary Smith, 278–280. Cambridge, MA and London: The Belknap Press of Harvard University Press, 1999 [1929].

Benjamin, Walter. "Surrealism: The Last Snapshot of the European Intelligentsia". In *Selected Writings: Volume 2, Part 1, 1927–1930*, edited by Michael W. Jennings, Howard Eiland, and Gary Smith, 207–218. Cambridge, MA and London: The Belknap Press of Harvard University Press, 1999 [1929].

Benjamin, Walter. "The Work of Art in the Age of Its Technological Reproducibility". In *Selected Writings: Volume 3, 1935–1938*, edited by Howard Eiland, and Michael W. Jennings, 101–133. Cambridge, MA and London: The Belknap Press of Harvard University Press, 2002 [1936].

Benjamin, Walter. "Experience and Poverty". In *Selected Writings: Volume 2, Part 2, 1931–1934*, edited by Michael W. Jennings, Howard Eiland, and Gary Smith, 731–736. Cambridge, MA and London: The Belknap Press of Harvard University Press, 2005 [1933].

Benjamin, Walter. "The Paris of the Second Empire in Baudelaire". In *Selected Writings: Volume 4, 1938–1940*, edited by Howard Eiland, and Michael W. Jennings, 3–92. Cambridge, MA and London: The Belknap Press of Harvard University Press, 2006 [1938].

Benjamin, Walter. "On the Concept of History". In *Selected Writings: Volume 4, 1938–1940*, edited by Howard Eiland, and Michael W. Jennings, 389–400. Cambridge, MA and London: The Belknap Press of Harvard University Press, 2006 [1940].

Bloch, Ernst. "Nonsynchronism and Its Obligation to Its Dialectics". *New German Critique* 11 (1977 [1932]): 22–38.

Broch, Hermann. "Notes on the Problem of Kitsch". In *Kitsch: The World of Bad Taste*, edited by Gillo Dorfles, 49–76. New York: Universe Books, 1968 [1950].

Chakrabarty, Dipesh. *Provincializing Europe: Postcolonial Thought and Historical Difference*. Princeton, NJ: Princeton University Press, 2000.

Cirese, Alberto Maria. *Intellettuali, folklore, istinto di classe. Note su Verga, Deledda, Scotellaro, Gramsci*. Torino: Einaudi, 1976.

Cirese, Alberto Maria. "Gramsci e il folklore Come concezione tradizionale del mondo delle classi subalterne". *Problemi* 49 (1977): 155–167.

Dei, Fabio. "Popolo, popolare, populismo". *International Gramsci Journal* 2, no. 3 (2017): 208–238.

De Martino, Ernesto. "Il folklore progressivo". *L'Unità* (26 June 1951): 3.

De Martino, Ernesto. "Gramsci e il folklore". *Il calendario del popolo* 8 (April 1952): 1109.

De Martino, Ernesto. "Per un dibattito sul folklore". *Lucania* 2 (1954): 76–78.

De Martino, Ernesto. "Due inediti su Gramsci. *Postille a Gramsci* e *Gramsci e il folklore*". *La Ricerca Folklorica* 25 (April 1992 [1951]): 73–79.

De Martino, Ernesto. "Gramsci e il folklore nella cultura italiana [1951]". *Il de Martino* 5–6 (1996): 87–90.

De Martino, Ernesto. *Il mondo magico: prolegomeni a una storia del magismo*. Torino: Bollati Boringhieri, 2007 [1948].

Dettmar, Ute, and Küpper, Thomas, eds. *Kitsch. Texte und Theorien*. Stuttgart: Reclam, 2007.

Gatto, Marco. "Oltre il paradigma leviano. Subalternità e mediazione da Ernesto de Martino a Rocco Scotellaro". *Filologia Antica e Moderna I* 31, no. 51 (2021): 151–182.

Gramsci, Antonio. *Quaderni del carcere*, edited by Valentino Gerratana, vol. 4. Torino: Einaudi, 1975.

Gramsci, Antonio. *Selections from the Prison Notebooks*, edited and translated by Quintin Hoare, and Geoffrey Nowell Smith. New York: International Publishers, 1992.

Gramsci, Antonio. *The Gramsci Reader: Selected Writings 1916–1935*, edited by David Forgacs, with a new Introduction by Eric J. Hobsbawm. New York: New York University Press, 2000.

Guha, Ranajit. *History at the Limit of World-History*. New York: Columbia University Press, 2002.

Hall, Stuart. "Gramsci's Relevance for the Study of Race and Ethnicity". *Journal of Communication Inquiry* 10 (1986): 5–27.

Krahl, Hans-Jürgen. "The Political Contradictions in Adorno's Critical Theory". *Telos* 21 (1974 [1969]): 164–167.

Kundera, Milan. *The Unbearable Lightness of Being*, translated by Michael H. Heim. New York: Harper & Row, 1984.

Lenin, Vladimir Il'ič. "What Is To Be Done? Burning Questions of Our Movement". In *Collected Works*, translated by Joe Fineberg, and George Hanna, vol. 5, 347–530. Moscow: Foreign Languages Publishing House, 1961 [1902].

Marx, Ursula, and Richter, Alexandra. "Johann Wolfgang Goethe: Philosophische Alchimie". In *Entwendungen: Walter Benjamin und seine Quellen*, edited by Jessica Nitsche, and Nadine, 97–124. Paderborn: Wilhelm Fink, 2019.

Moles, Abraham. *Le kitsch: L'art du bonheur*. Paris: Mame, 1971.

Montanelli, Marina. "Baudelaire Laboratory: Brief History of a Project by Walter Benjamin". *Aisthesis* 13, no. 2 (2020): 17–29.

Orlandi, Costanza. "Folclore e modernità nella riflessione gramsciana". In *Domande dal presente. Studi su Gramsci*, edited by Lea Durante, and Guido Liguori, 127–139. Roma: Carocci, 2012.

Said, Edward W. *Orientalism*. New York: Pantheon Books, 1978.

Solmi, Renato. *Introduzione a "Minima moralia" di Theodor W. Adorno*. Macerata: Quodlibet, 2015 [1954].

INDEX